Counseling for Social Justice
Second Edition

Edited by Courtland C. Lee

To Lacey / Best Wishes,

American Counseling Association
5999 Stevenson Avenue
Alexandria, VA 22304
www.counseling.org

Counseling for Social Justice
Second Edition

10   9   8   7   6   5   4   3   2

American Counseling Association
5999 Stevenson Avenue
Alexandria, VA 22304

Director of Publications
Carolyn C. Baker

Production Manager
Bonny E. Gaston

Cover design by Carlos Soto

Library of Congress Cataloging-in-Publication Data

Counseling for social justice / edited by Courtland C. Lee. — 2nd ed.
    p. cm.
Includes bibliographical references and index.
ISBN-13: 978-1-55620-264-3 (alk. paper)
ISBN-10: 1-55620-264-4 (alk. paper)
1. Social justice. 2. Counseling. 3. Social action. I. Lee, Courtland C.

HM671.C68 2006
361'.06—dc22

2006018858

Dedication

To all those who have struggled, are struggling,
or will struggle to make the world a better place

Contents

Part I: Promoting Social Justice and Challenging Oppression

Preface

Much like its predecessor, *Social Action: A Mandate for Counselors,* this book concerns social justice and its role in the counseling profession. In the counseling context, social justice encompasses the professional, ethical, and moral responsibility that counselors have to address the significant social, cultural, and economic inequalities that may negatively affect the psychosocial development of various groups of people. Social justice relates to counselors' sense of social responsibility. It involves counselors taking stands on social issues and working to eradicate systems and ideologies that perpetuate discrimination and disregard human rights.

The tradition of confronting social inequalities and promoting social justice within the counseling profession is reflected in a body of literature on the role of the counselor as change agent. *Counseling for Social Justice* provides professional counselors with guidance for becoming agents of social change and champions of social justice who intervene not only in the lives of their clients, but in the world around them as well. It emphasizes the need to direct one's counseling skills toward the significant contemporary social, cultural, and economic issues that often negatively affect the lives of clients. It also provides a critical analysis of actions needed to advance social justice in counseling practice.

Counseling for Social Justice is divided into an introduction and two parts. "Introduction: Counselors as Agents of Social Justice," by Courtland C. Lee and Carlos P. Hipolito-Delgado, introduces the notion of social justice and its historical and contemporary context in the profession of counseling.

Part I presents ideas for promoting social justice among client groups that have historically been marginalized or oppressed in some fashion. This section offers specific direction for adopting counseling roles that advance social justice for these client groups. Allison A. Cox and Courtland C. Lee begin with "Challenging Educational Inequities: School Counselors as Agents of Social Justice." The authors discuss the dynamics of the achievement gap in U.S. education and its impact on students in poverty and those of color. They also discuss important ways the roles of school counselors can be transformed to promote access, equity, and social justice, and hence begin to close the pervasive achievement gap.

In chapter 2, "Advancing Social Justice by Challenging Socioeconomic Disadvantage," Kathleen L. Armstrong examines trends in poverty in the United States and the effects socioeconomic disadvantage can have on individual well-being. She then explores strategies for working with economically disadvantaged clients, and addresses how counselors can and must challenge systems that negatively affect poor clients.

Pamela S. Lassiter and Bob Barret, in chapter 3, "Gay and Lesbian Social Justice: Strategies for Social Advocacy," briefly review some of the issues that gay men and lesbians experience relating to language, visibility, and the role of the mental health profession. They next explore the recruitment and choice myths about homosexuality, and conclude with a discussion of the ways counselors may become involved in promoting social justice for sexual minorities.

In chapter 4, "Combating Ageism: Advocacy for Older Persons," Jane E. Myers explores demographic changes in the United States with a focus on the aging of our population and within-group factors that predispose some older persons to significant personal and social risks. She then describes counselors' responses to the graying of America and the consequences of these responses for the needs of older persons. Ageism, an unreasonable prejudice against persons based on chronological age, is discussed in relation to its personal impact on older individuals. The author concludes with recommended strategies and actions for counselors and with suggestions for counselor advocacy and empowerment relative to aging and the needs of older individuals.

The issues relating to social justice for people with disabilities are examined in chapter 5, "Counselor Advocacy for Access: Addressing the Challenges of Disability." Ellen S. Fabian describes the historical and contemporary context of disability and rehabilitation in the United States and examines how counselor roles and functions need to change in response to the changing social and political context of disability.

Judy A. Lewis, in chapter 6, "Challenging Sexism: Promoting the Rights of Women in Contemporary Society," explores issues of women's oppression and the nature of sexism in a global perspective. She then considers the nature of empowerment for women and how counselors can advocate for the rights of women on individual and systemic levels.

Similarly, in chapter 7, "Promoting Healthy Male Development: A Social Justice Perspective," Mark S. Kiselica and Mark S. Woodford describe challenges to healthy male development and suggest advocacy and systems-change strategies that build upon male strengths and foster the optimal development of boys and men. The chapter begins with an overview of social justice counseling and its value as an approach to promoting healthy male development. A discussion of how sexist attitudes about women hurt boys and men in their interpersonal relationships follows. The authors then suggest how counselors can work with the profeminist and male advocacy organizations to change systems so that they foster psychologically healthy male development. Finally, myths about the emotional lives of males are described and critiqued, and suggestions for challenging misguided assumptions about boys and men are offered.

Cheryl Holcomb-McCoy and Natasha A. Mitchell conclude part 1 of the book with a discussion of social justice in a racial/ethnic context in chapter 8, "Promoting Racial/Ethnic Equality Through Empowerment-Based Counseling." The authors begin with a historical overview of oppression experienced by ethnic minorities in the United States. They next examine the legacy of this oppression for ethnic minority groups with respect to economic and educational inequities. Following a discussion of the socioemotional impact of injustice and inequity, the authors conclude with empowerment and advocacy-focused counseling interventions for ethnic minority client groups.

Part II of the book examines professional issues that must be considered when social justice becomes an integral part of counseling practice. William A. Borgen begins this section with chapter 9, "Counseling and Social Justice: An International Perspective." He first looks at the origins of social justice in North American counseling traditions, then provides an international context for social justice in counseling by exploring the activities of the International Association for Counselling (IAC). Through specific examples of IAC activities throughout the world, he underscores important social justice issues for counselors to address on a global scale.

In chapter 10, "Social Justice and Counseling Ethics," Barbara Richter Herlihy and Zarus E. P. Watson discuss their belief that a social justice perspective on counseling requires a paradigm shift in how counselors think about ethics. In this chapter they suggest an alternative approach to ethical decision making that they believe enhances ethical counseling practice and promotes social justice.

Larry C. Loesch in chapter 11, "Fair Access to and Use of Assessment in Counseling," poses the question, how can professional counselors manifest a belief in social justice in the assessment component of their work? In answering this question and providing a social justice framework for assessment, he distinguishes between socially responsive and socially responsible assessment.

In chapter 12, "Conducting Research That Makes a Difference," William E. Sedlacek offers guidance for conducting research with a social justice emphasis. Using his own experience as a social science investigator, the author discusses research that will have systemic impact and promote access, equity, and social justice.

Fred Bemak and Rita Chi-Ying Chung discuss counselor training that fosters commitment to social justice in chapter 13, "Training Counselors in Social Justice." They describe the development, philosophy, implementation, and evaluation of a counselor education program designed to train counselors to become client advocates devoted to social justice.

Courtland C. Lee completes the book with "Conclusion: A Counselor's Call to Action." Within the context of the critical issues raised in the preceding chapters, he focuses on the counselor as an individual and what personal actions he or she must engage in to become an effective force for social justice. The thrust of the call to action is that counseling for social justice is more than a professional obligation; it is about living one's life in a manner that is dedicated to promoting access and equity.

Acknowledgments

I am indebted to a number of individuals for their assistance with the development of *Counseling for Social Justice*. First and foremost are the contributors to this book. Thank you for the time and thought you put into preparing your chapters. Your scholarly efforts and commitment to social justice are greatly appreciated. It was an honor and a privilege to work with you.

I am also grateful to Dr. Garry Walz for his enthusiasm for and sponsorship of this project. He has been tireless in his efforts to advance knowledge, and I thank him for his belief in this book and its importance to the profession.

Thank you also to the American Counseling Association Foundation (ACAF) for its support of this project. I am honored that the members of the ACAF board of directors see this book as an important way to advance the foundation's mission of enhancing excellence in human development through strengthening the counseling profession.

I also express my appreciation to Carolyn C. Baker, director of publications for the American Counseling Association (ACA), for her participation in this effort. Carolyn's support has been most helpful. It is always a pleasure to work with her.

I would also like to express my heartfelt appreciation to all those who read *Social Action: A Mandate for Counselors* and urged me to update that work. Thank you for your efforts to advance social justice and your support of the ideas presented in that book. This book became a reality in large measure because of your encouragement and commitment.

Finally, I thank my wife, Vivian, for her love and support. Her personal courage and unbridled determination to make the world a better place are a true inspiration to me.

Introduction: Counselors as Agents of Social Justice

Courtland C. Lee and Carlos P. Hipolito-Delgado

Injustice anywhere is a threat to justice everywhere.
—Martin Luther King, Jr., 1963

Improving society by challenging systemic inequities has always been a major objective of the counseling profession. Social justice, therefore, offers a conceptual basis for social action on the part of counselors. This introduction provides counselors with a context for becoming agents of social justice who intervene not only in the lives of their clients, but in the world around them as well.

As a new wave of social conservatism emerges in the early years of the 21st century, it is imperative that counselors remain committed to social justice and the quest for equity. The increasing economic divisions between the social classes, the high incarceration rate for Black and Latino males, the achievement gap in education, and the struggle of same-sex couples for equal rights are prime examples of pressing issues that are representative of social inequities. Additionally, many of the gains of the civil rights era—such as affirmative action and a woman's right to choose—are now under intense attack. These are just a sample of social and political issues that underscore inequities in American society. Although many gains have been achieved over the past several decades, the struggle for social justice must be ongoing. We strongly assert that counselors have both a professional and personal stake in actively participating in this struggle. Through active participation in social justice initiatives counselors have the opportunity to ameliorate many societal ills and in the process promote a more socially just society for themselves and for the people with whom they work.

Defining Social Justice and Its Meaning for Counselors

Social justice is a construct at once easy to define yet extremely difficult to explain. A review of the literature (Bell, 1997; Hartnett, 2001; Miller, 1999; Rawls, 1971) suggests that, broadly defined, social justice involves promoting access and equity to ensure full participation of all people in the life of a society, particularly for those who have been systematically excluded on the basis of race or ethnicity, gender, age, physical or mental disability, education, sexual orientation, socioeconomic status, or other characteristics of background or group membership. Social justice is based on a belief that all people have a right to equitable treatment, support for their human rights, and fair allocation of societal resources.

Social justice places a focus on issues of oppression, privilege, and social inequities. For counselors, socially just practice entails professional conduct that opposes all forms of discrimination and oppression. Counseling practices rooted in social justice seek to challenge inherent inequities in social systems. Counselors must consider social justice and the professional actions they take to promote access and equity within the context of their own self-awareness as both people and professionals.

In order to be effective as a helper, a counselor must possess three levels of awareness:

> *Level 1: Awareness of self.* A counselor must understand the important dynamics of his or her personality and how they contribute to the counseling process (Gladding, 2004; Kottler, 2003; Nugent & Jones, 2005).

> *Level 2: Interpersonal awareness.* A counselor must be able to enter a client's reality in a nonjudgmental manner (Rogers, 1951). He or she must possess both an appreciation of a client's perception of the world and the psychosocial context for that worldview. The essence of counseling lies at this level; it is the art of helping another person to resolve problems or make decisions.

> *Level 3: Systemic awareness.* A counselor must be able to perceive accurately the environmental influences on client development and possess the skills to intercede at that level to challenge systemic barriers that block optimal psychosocial development (Dinsmore, Chapman,

& McCollum, 2000; Katz, 1985; Lee, 1998; Lee, Armstrong, & Brydges, 1996; Lewis, Lewis, Daniels, & D'Andrea, 1998).

It is the third level of counselor awareness that forms the basis of social action. Within the context of counseling for social justice, social action refers to two important, interrelated concepts. The first involves the ability to intervene not only in the lives of clients to help with problem resolution or decision making, but in the social context that affects clients' lives as well. Social action is based on the premise that the environment is the key factor in determining behavior. Problematic behavior can often be traced to negative environmental effects on cognitive and affective functioning. Client issues, therefore, are often merely reactions to or symptoms of deep-seated problems in the social environments in which people must interact.

Second, from a preventive perspective, social action encompasses the professional and moral responsibility that counselors have to address the significant social, cultural, and economic challenges that may negatively affect psychosocial development. This second aspect relates to counselors' sense of social responsibility. It involves counselors taking stands on social issues and working to eradicate systems and ideologies that perpetuate discrimination and oppression. A sense of social responsibility gives counselors an important role to play in fostering and supporting a society that is more enlightened, just, and humane (Lee & Sirch, 1994; McWhirter, 1997).

Counseling, Social Justice, and Social Action:
A Conceptual Overview

In order to fully understand the role of social justice and subsequent social action in counseling, one must consider several concepts: empowerment, advocacy, and the counselor as an agent of social change. Social responsibility is predicated on comprehensive knowledge of these interrelated notions.

Empowerment

The past several decades have seen an increased awareness of the importance of empowerment to counseling theory and practice. This concept, which has its origins in social work, community psychology, feminist therapy, multicultural counseling, and education, forms a framework for social action in counseling

(McWhirter, 1994, 1997). McWhirter (1994) offered the following definition of empowerment:

> the process by which people, organizations, or groups who are powerless or marginalized (a) become aware of the power dynamics at work in their life context, (b) develop the skills and capacity for gaining reasonable control over their lives, (c) which they exercise, (d) without infringing on the rights of others, and (e) which coincides with actively supporting the empowerment of others in their community. (p. 12)

This definition suggests that empowerment is a complex process that encompasses self-reflection and action, awareness of environmental power dynamics that may influence psychosocial development, and development of skills to enhance communities (McWhirter, 1997).

With its focus on environmental awareness and community action as well as individual insight, the concept of empowerment provides an important foundation for social action. The process of empowerment puts the onus on both client and counselor to look beyond intervention at a strictly individual level.

Advocacy

Advocacy refers to the process or act of arguing or pleading for a cause or proposal, either of one's own or on behalf of someone else. The concept of advocacy helps to frame the social action context of counseling for social justice. As advocates, counselors channel their energy and skill into helping clients challenge institutional and social barriers that impede academic, career, or personal-social development. When necessary, counselors need to be willing to act on behalf of marginalized or disenfranchised clients and to actively challenge longstanding traditions, preconceived notions, or regressive policies and procedures that may stifle human development. Acting as advocates, through efforts both with and for clients, counselors help their clients become empowered so that they can challenge systemic barriers and seize new educational, career, or personal-social opportunities (Lee, 1998; J. A. Lewis, Arnold, House, & Toporek, 2003; J. A. Lewis & Bradley, 2000).

There are three important aspects of assuming an advocate role. First, counselors who act as advocates view helping from a systemic perspective. Second, advocates attempt systemic change in partnership with clients who often lack the knowledge or skill base to effect such change alone. Third, advocates must have an understanding of important systems-change principles, along with the skill to translate them into action (Lee, 1998; J. A. Lewis et al., 2003; Toporek, 2000).

The Counselor as an Agent of Social Change

The concepts of empowerment and advocacy provide the basis for the counselor's role as a social change agent. Any counselor with a belief in the possibility of a better world should dedicate himself or herself to social justice and develop a sense of social responsibility. This philosophy entails a commitment to the idea of social change and the counselor's role as catalyst for such change.

A counselor who is an agent of social change possesses the awareness, knowledge, and skill to intervene not only at an individual level, but at a systemic level as well. Either in partnership with or on behalf of clients, a social change agent challenges cultural, social, historical, or economic barriers that stifle optimal human development. Such a professional should have two important goals in the counseling process: (a) to help clients understand the etiology of a problem by recognizing the influence of the social context on human development; and (b) to empower clients by assisting them in developing and implementing strategies to eliminate or reduce all forms of systemic discrimination or oppression. The chapters in this book offer a multifaceted analysis of such action on the part of counselors.

Translating Social Justice Into Social Action:
A Counseling Tradition

Although often viewed as a relatively conservative and somewhat passive profession, counseling has established a tradition of translating social justice into social action. McWhirter (1997) suggested that social action is implicit in the work of Frank Parsons and Carl Rogers. Both of these giants in the profession advocated that counselors respond to the injustice of the status quo, work to change social policy, and intervene at both the individual and societal levels.

In May 1971, a special issue of *Personnel and Guidance Journal* entitled "Counseling and the Social Revolution" was published. This seminal issue, edited by Michael D. Lewis, Judith A. Lewis, and Edward P. Dworkin, was published near the end of the great social revolution begun in the 1960s, which saw massive protest against a war considered to be unjust and against various forms of social discrimination. The goal of this special issue was to put the realities of the social revolution before the counseling profession and to suggest that counselors need not only to understand but also to participate in the social change process. The articles in this issue addressed how the counselor should face social issues such as racism, sexism, destruction of the environment, and ending warfare. There were also articles about counselor self-evaluation and training with respect to social action.

This special issue was followed by a number of articles in professional counseling journals that exhorted counselors to social action. Some of these articles accused the profession of being reactionary and serving oppressive social systems that harmed client groups (Banks & Martens, 1973). Others called on counselors to become social change agents (D. R. Cook, 1972; Gunnings & Simpkins, 1972; Herbert, 1971; Kincaid & Kincaid, 1971; Schlossberg, 1977; Smith, 1971; Tucker, 1973; Warnath, 1973).

The 1980s saw a wave of conservatism sweep the United States, which severely challenged the relevance to professionals of social justice, social action, and social responsibility. Despite this, however, the counseling profession continued to build on a tradition of confronting social issues. This tradition is reflected in the literature on counselor training, research, and service delivery of that era (Buhrke, 1988; J. A. Cook, 1983; Corvin & Wiggins, 1989; Crabbs, 1989; Downing, 1982; Eldridge, 1983; Lee, 1989; Ponzo, 1981; Sander, 1982; Wilcoxon, 1989). Significantly, in 1987 the American Association for Counseling and Development (as it was then known) published a position paper on human rights (AACD, 1987). The paper was a clarion call to professional counselors to advocate for social change through personal, professional, and political activity.

The decade of the 1980s also witnessed the rise of multicultural counseling as a major discipline in the profession. Multicultural concepts in counseling fostered a new sense of social responsibility and activism within the profession (Lee, 1997). While counseling culturally diverse clients, counselors were often forced to consider the negative effects of racism, sexism, classism, homophobia, and other forms of oppression on psychosocial development (E. P. Cook, 1993; Priest, 1991; Schreier, 1995; Solomon, 1992). This contributed to increased professional awareness that the etiology of problems often lies not in clients, but rather in intolerant or restrictive environments. Counselors who worked with culturally diverse client groups therefore were called on to become agents of systemic change, channeling energy and skill into helping clients from marginalized or powerless groups break down institutional and social barriers to optimal development (De la Cancela & Sotomayor, 1993; Evans & Wall, 1991; Lee, 1991; Ponterotto & Pedersen, 1993).

As the profession entered the 21st century the amount of counseling literature addressing issues of social justice and social action increased. A recent search of the literature yielded more than 200 journal articles, dissertations, and book chapters that address in some fashion these issues in counseling. Many of these publications call for a shift from the assumption of value neutrality, advocate additional training and skill development for social action, outline various forms and levels of social action, and call for more early interventions to prevent the development of bias.

In supporting the importance of social justice and counselors taking part in social action, authors have begun to challenge the notion of value neutrality in the field of counseling. Value neutrality assumes that the act of counseling operates in a vacuum that is free of sociopolitical considerations. The assumption of value neutrality serves to support the status quo of inequity in society (McClure & Russo, 1996; Seem & Hernandez, 1998). By neglecting societal inequities, counselors fail to detect environmental conditions that affect individual clients (McClure & Russo, 1996; Moeschberger & Ordonez, 2003; Seem & Hernandez, 1998). This eventually leads to a "blame the victim" mentality, in which the client's problems are seen as originating internally (McClure & Russo, 1996; Seem & Hernandez, 1998). Consequently, the client is prescribed interventions that call on him or her to adapt to unjust or inequitable social systems, leaving larger societal issues unaddressed. Because under the assumption of value neutrality the counseling profession perpetuates an inequitable society, it has been called upon to move to a stance that supports social action (McClure & Russo, 1996).

An argument has surfaced in recent years that counselors need specific skills to participate in social advocacy (Kiselica & Robinson, 2001; Moeschberger & Ordonez, 2003). To promote these skills, authors have called for social advocacy training in counselor education programs (Dworkin & Yi, 2003; McClure & Russo, 1996; Toporek, 2000). Dworkin and Yi (2003) called for counselors to be trained in public policy, whereas McClure and Russo (1996) called for a more interdisciplinary approach to training counselors in a social justice context. This approach would include training in sociology, psychology, history, and education as a way to promote social consciousness.

In encouraging counselors to participate in social action, authors have outlined the various forms and levels of social advocacy. These range from those requiring very little active involvement, such as letter writing campaigns and monetary donations to groups involved in social justice initiatives, to those that require a substantial level of involvement, such as journal writing, lobbying for federal legislation, and program development (Kiselica, 2004; Moeschberger & Ordonez, 2003; Pope et al., 2004; Toporek, 2000).

Importantly, social action can have an individual perspective, focusing on one client at a time, or a larger systemic perspective that requires the counselor to be active in advocacy with and on behalf of a community or organization (Kiselica, 2004; Kiselica & Robinson, 2001; Toporek, 2000). Social action with and on behalf of a community or organization can take the form of working with constituents at a grassroots level or of lobbying political representatives (Dworkin & Yi, 2003; Moeschberger & Ordonez, 2003; Kiselica & Robinson, 2001; Toporek, 2000).

Lastly, the most recent wave of literature has called for preventive social action interventions of an educative nature. The purpose of such interventions is to ensure that people learn about issues of social inequities so that they do not adopt roles or practices that perpetrate oppressive acts or policies. For example, these interventions are aimed at promoting social justice through education that challenges stereotypes related to gender socialization or sexuality (Forbes, 2003; Pope et al., 2004; Seem & Hernandez, 1998).

A major development in the acceptance of the importance of social justice in professional counseling was the chartering of the Counselors for Social Justice (CSJ) division of the American Counseling Association in 2001. CSJ listed as part of its mission a commitment to "challenge oppressive systems of power and privilege . . . [by] disseminating social justice scholarship . . . [and] maintaining an active support network online and in person for engaging in social justice activities" (CSJ, 2005).

One of the goals of CSJ was the creation of advocacy competencies for counseling professionals. The counseling profession's commitment to a social justice and social action orientation was further solidified in 2003 when the ACA Governing Council adopted the CSJ *Advocacy Competencies*. These competencies span levels of advocacy from the micro level of client or student intervention to the macro level of intervention in the public arena. They also describe social advocacy that requires social action in partnership with the client and on behalf of the client (J. A. Lewis et al., 2003).

The growth of counseling literature that discusses social justice and social action coupled with the acceptance of the advocacy competencies led Ratts, D'Andrea, and Arredondo (2004) to argue that social justice, from a theoretical perspective, is the "fifth force" in the counseling field, following the paradigms of the psychodynamic approach, the cognitive/behavioral approach, humanism, and multiculturalism. Significantly, for Ratts, D'Andrea, and Arredondo, social justice counseling is the next logical evolution of the multicultural counseling movement—moving from understanding the experiences of oppressed groups toward social action with the goal of achieving social equity for these groups.

Translating Social Justice Into Social Action:
The Personal and Professional Risks

Personal and professional risks are inherent when counselors move to translate social justice into social action. Counselors need to be aware that speaking or acting out against social inequities may engender some professional or personal consequences. For example, they may become vulnerable to different forms of harassment in the workplace when they take a stand on a controversial issue. Likewise, they may develop reputations as troublemakers because of their efforts to challenge social inequities. Such a reputation could lead to professional backlash in the form of disciplinary action or limited opportunities for advancement. In addition, choosing to promote social causes may result in being ostracized by professional colleagues.

A counselor who chooses to advocate for social justice also runs the risk of stretching ethical limits. Although it is important and often necessary to adopt nontraditional practices when participating in social action, counselors must remain cognizant of ethical practice. A major risk is losing sight of relationship boundaries with clients. This risk is particularly acute when and if a counselor assumes the role of client advocate. For example, acting on behalf of marginalized or disenfranchised clients in challenging institutional or social inequities may lead a counselor to foster dependent relationships. It is important, therefore, that client advocacy be part of an integrated individual or group counseling intervention that is jointly planned by the counselor and client. Advocacy by a counselor should be part of an intervention whose ultimate goal is to help clients become empowered so that they develop the skills to challenge systemic inequities and seize new educational, career, or personal-social opportunities for themselves.

Counselors choosing to confront social challenges in their work must understand that such a choice transcends the boundary between personal life and professional role. Professional actions taken to advocate for social justice and to promote social action may resonate in one's personal life. Counselors need to consider that various forms of harassment may affect their home and family life. Moreover, they may become so associated with social justice as to jeopardize their relationships with people who do not share such views.

Counselors in academic positions must be aware that many universities and colleges place a greater value on research and publication than on service, although service is part of the tenure process.

Thus, a counselor educator who becomes intensely involved in social action to the detriment of his or her scholarly activities may miss opportunities for promotion and tenure (Kiselica, 2004). One way counselor educators may avoid the possible negative consequences of devoting extensive amounts of time to social action is to incorporate research and assessment into their social advocacy initiatives (Kiselica, 2004). Incorporating assessment into social advocacy will aid in the development of projects that better serve clients and students. Additionally, the publication of successful social action projects will inform the practice of other counselors and improve social conditions for more individuals and communities.

Counselors striving to advance social justice and become agents of social change must consider such risks as part of the process of promoting an enlightened and just society. They must reach a point in their own personal and professional lives where they believe that the benefit to individuals and society from their social action is well worth the risks.

Conclusion

Profound contemporary social issues and their impact on client well-being suggest a need to examine the current philosophy and practice of professional counseling. They offer an opportunity for counselors to reexamine and potentially redefine their commitment to helping. Traditionally, counselors' energy and skill have been focused on helping individuals resolve problems and make decisions. Yet often problems and impediments to effective decision making originate not in individuals, but in an intolerant, restrictive, or oppressive environment. We have attempted to provide a conceptual basis for the role of counselor as agent of social justice. We have also provided a context in which counselors can become engaged in helping to challenge serious social inequities that impede human development.

Professional counselors must be competent agents of social change at both the individual level and in the public arena. Counselors should employ their diverse expertise both to help individuals and to challenge the profound social, cultural, and economic inequities that plague the quality of life of scores of people. Through their own sense of social justice, counselors can help to foster the empowerment of people and to advance an equitable society as well.

References

American Association for Counseling and Development (AACD). (1987). *Human rights position paper.* Alexandria, VA: Author.

Banks, W., & Martens, K. (1973). Counseling: The reactionary profession. *Personnel and Guidance Journal, 51,* 457–462.

Bell, L. A. (1997). Theoretical foundations for social justice education. In M. Adams, L. A. Bell, & P. Griffin (Eds.), *Teaching for diversity and social justice: A sourcebook* (pp. 3–15). New York: Routledge.

Buhrke, R. A. (1988). Lesbian-related issues in counseling supervision. *Women and Therapy, 8,* 195–206.

Cook, D. R. (1972). The change agent counselor: A conceptual context. *The School Counselor, 20,* 9–15.

Cook, E. P. (Ed.). (1993). *Women, relationships, and power: Implications for counseling.* Alexandria, VA: American Counseling Association.

Cook, J. A. (1983). The hydra-headed nature of prejudice: Research perspectives concerning cross-cultural counseling with elementary age children. *Elementary School Guidance and Counseling, 17,* 294–300.

Corvin, S. A., & Wiggins, F. (1989). An antiracism training model for White professionals. *Journal of Multicultural Counseling and Development, 17,* 105–114.

Counselors for Social Justice (CSJ). (2005). *Mission.* Retrieved February 14, 2005, from http:/www.counselorsforsocialjustice. org/mission.html

Crabbs, M. A. (1989). Future perfect: Planning for the next century. *Elementary School Guidance and Counseling, 24,* 160–166.

De la Cancela, V., & Sotomayor, G. M. (1993). Rainbow warriors: Reducing institutional racism in mental health. *Journal of Mental Health Counseling, 15,* 55–71.

Dinsmore, J. A., Chapman, A., & McCollum, V. J. C. (2000, March). *Client advocacy and social justice: Strategies for developing trainee competence*. Paper presented at the annual conference of the American Counseling Association, Washington, DC.

Downing, C. J. (1982). Counseling the culturally different. *Counseling and Values, 26*, 259–263.

Dworkin, S. H., & Yi, H. (2003). LGBT identity, violence, and social justice: The psychological is political. *International Journal for the Advancement of Counseling, 25*(4), 269–279.

Eldridge, W. D. (1983). Affirmative social action and the use of power in clinical counseling. *Counseling and Values, 27*, 66–75.

Evans, N. J., & Wall, V. A. (Eds.). (1991). *Beyond tolerance: Gays, lesbians, and bisexuals on campus*. Alexandria, VA: American Counseling Association.

Forbes, D. (2003). Turn the wheel: Integral school counseling for male adolescents. *Journal of Counseling & Development, 81*, 142–149.

Gladding, S. T. (2004). *Counseling: A comprehensive profession* (5th ed.). Upper Saddle River, NJ: Prentice Hall.

Gunnings, T. S., & Simpkins, G. A. (1972). A systemic approach to counseling disadvantaged youth. *Journal of Non-White Concerns in Personnel and Guidance, 1*, 4–8.

Hartnett, D. (2001). *The history of justice*. Paper presented at the Social Justice Forum, Loyola University, Chicago.

Herbert, R. (1971). Ecology: A shared journey. *The Personnel and Guidance Journal, 49*, 737–739.

Katz, J. H. (1985). The sociopolitical nature of counseling. *The Counseling Psychologist, 13*, 615–624.

Kincaid, M., & Kincaid, J. (1971). Counseling for peace. *Personnel and Guidance Journal, 49*, 727–735.

Kiselica, M. S. (2004). When duty calls: The implications of social justice work for policy, education, and practice in the mental health professions. *The Counseling Psychologist, 32*(6), 838–854.

Kiselica, M. S., & Robinson, M. (2001). Bringing advocacy counseling to life: The history, issues and human dramas of social justice work in counseling. *Journal of Counseling & Development, 79,* 387–397.

Kottler, J. A. (2003). *On being a therapist.* New York: Wiley.

Lee, C. C. (1989). Needed: A career development advocate. *The Career Development Quarterly, 37,* 218–220.

Lee, C. C. (1991). Empowerment in counseling: A multicultural perspective. *Journal of Counseling & Development, 69,* 229–230.

Lee, C. C. (1997). The promise and pitfalls of multicultural counseling. In C. C. Lee (Ed.), *Multicultural issues in counseling: New approaches to diversity* (2nd ed., pp. 3–13). Alexandria, VA: American Counseling Association.

Lee, C. C. (1998). Counselors as agents of social change. In C. C. Lee & G. R. Walz (Eds.), *Social action: A mandate for counselors* (pp. 3–14). Alexandria, VA: American Counseling Association.

Lee, C. C., Armstrong, K. L., & Brydges, J. L. (1996). The challenges of a diverse society: Counseling for mutual respect and understanding. *Counseling and Human Development, 28,* 1–8.

Lee, C. C., & Sirch, M. L. (1994). Counseling in an enlightened society: Values for a new millennium. *Counseling and Values, 38,* 90–97.

Lewis, J. A, Arnold, M. S., House, R., & Toporek, R. (2003). *Advocacy competencies.* Retrieved February 19, 2005, from http://www.counselorsforsocialjustice.org/advocacycompetencies.html

Lewis, J. A., & Bradley, L. (Eds.). (2000). *Advocacy in counseling: Counselors, clients, and community.* Greensboro, NC: ERIC Counseling and Student Services Clearinghouse.

Lewis, J. A., Lewis, M. D., Daniels, J., & D'Andrea, M. J. (1998). *Community counseling: Empowerment strategies in a diverse society.* Pacific Grove, CA: Brooks/Cole.

Lewis, M. D., Lewis, J. A., & Dworkin, E. P. (Eds.). (1971). Counseling and the social revolution [Special issue]. *Personnel and Guidance Journal, 49*(9).

McClure, B. A., & Russo, T. R. (1996). The politics of counseling: Looking back and forward. *Counseling and Values, 40,* 162–175.

McWhirter, E. H. (1994). *Counseling for empowerment.* Alexandria, VA: American Counseling Association.

McWhirter, E. H. (1997). Empowerment, social activism, and counseling. *Counseling and Human Development, 29,* 1–14.

Miller, D. (1999). *Principles of social justice.* Cambridge, MA: Harvard University Press.

Moeschberger, S. L., & Ordonez, A. (2003). Working towards building a culture of peace: A primer for students and new professionals. *International Journal for the Advancement of Counseling, 25,* 317–323.

Nugent, F. A., & Jones, K. D. (2005). *Introduction to the profession of counseling* (4th ed.). New York: Merrill.

Ponterotto, J. G., & Pedersen, P. B. (1993). *Preventing prejudice: A guide for counselors and educators.* Newbury Park, CA: Sage.

Ponzo, Z. (1981). Counseling the elderly: A lifetime process. *Counseling and Values, 26,* 68–80.

Pope, M., Barret, B., Symanski, D. M., Chung, Y. B., Singaravelu, H., McLean, R., & Sanabria, S. (2004). Culturally appropriate career counseling with gay and lesbian clients. *The Career Development Quarterly, 53,* 158–177.

Priest, R. C. (1991). Racism and prejudice as negative impacts on African American clients in therapy. *Journal of Counseling & Development, 70,* 213–215.

Ratts, M., D'Andrea, M., & Arredondo, P. (2004, September 13). Social justice counseling: 'Fifth force' in field. *Counseling Today.*

Rawls, J. A. (1971). *A theory of justice.* Cambridge, MA: Harvard University Press.

Rogers, C. (1951). *Client-centered therapy.* Boston: Houghton Mifflin.

Sander, D. (1982). Age discrimination in employment: Counselor responsibilities. *Counselor Education and Supervision, 21,* 213–217.

Schlossberg, N. K. (1977). Hide and seek with bias. *Personnel and Guidance Journal, 55,* 481–484.

Schreier, B. A. (1995). Moving beyond tolerance: A new paradigm for programming about homophobia/biphobia and heterosexism. *Journal of College Student Development, 36,* 19–26.

Seem, S. R., & Hernandez, T. J. (1998). Considering gender in counseling center practice: Individual and institutional actions. *Journal of College Counseling, 1,* 154–168.

Smith, P. M. (1971). Black activists for liberation, not guidance. *Personnel & Guidance Journal, 49,* 721–726.

Solomon, A. C. (1992). Clinical diagnosis among diverse populations: A multicultural perspective. *Families in Society, 73,* 371–377.

Toporek, R. L. (2000). Developing a common language and framework for understanding advocacy in counseling. In J. Lewis & L. Bradley (Eds.), *Advocacy in counseling: Counselors, clients, and community* (pp. 5–14). Greensboro, NC: ERIC Counseling and Student Services Clearinghouse.

Tucker, S. J. (1973). Action counseling: An accountability procedure for counseling the oppressed. *Journal of Non-White Concerns in Personnel and Guidance, 2,* 35–41.

Warnath, C. F. (1973). The school counselor as institutional agent. *The School Counselor, 20,* 202–208.

Wilcoxon, S. A. (1989). He/she/they/it?: Implied sexism in speech and print. *Journal of Counseling & Development, 68,* 114–116.

Part I
Promoting Social Justice and Challenging Oppression

Chapter 1

Challenging Educational Inequities:
School Counselors as Agents of Social Justice

Allison A. Cox and Courtland C. Lee

The United States is confronted with an ever-widening achievement gap between ethnic minority and low-income students versus their more advantaged White and middle-class peers. The continuation of this pervasive gap represents a major issue of social justice for everyone concerned about the future of American society and the academic and social development of its youth. This gap in school performance is evident in such areas as grades, standardized test scores, course selection, and college completion. It affects students in city, suburban, and rural school districts across the country. For the past decade, closing this achievement gap and accompanying school reform have become the rallying cries of both politicians and educators across the nation. Over the last 40 years, the country has focused on the inequities in education that exist among racial, ethnic, and social groups (Haycock, 2001; U.S. Department of Education, 2004). The focus has become more intense in recent years with the passage of the federal No Child Left Behind Act, or NCLB (2001). This act holds educators more accountable for their teaching practices, places major emphasis on test scores, and significantly redefines what constitutes a successful school system (Haycock, 2001).

Educational data collected over an extended period show alarming results that underscore the nature and extent of the achievement gap. For example, at the end of grade 4, African American, Latino, and poor students of all races are already approximately 2 years behind other students. This gap continues to widen to 3 years behind at the culmination of grade 8, and to 4 years by the time students reach grade 12. In 1999, by the end of high school, only 1 in 50 Latino and 1 in 100 African American

17-year-olds could read to gain information from specialized texts compared to 1 in 12 Whites (Education Trust, 2000).

The problem does not stop there. Comparing students aged 18 to 24 years, about 90% of Whites and 94% of Asians have either completed high school or earned a GED, whereas among African Americans the rate drops to 81%, and among Latinos to 63%. With respect to higher education, African American and Latino students obtain college degrees at only half the rate of their White counterparts. Additionally, economically advantaged students are nearly seven times more likely than those from poor families to earn a bachelor's degree (Haycock, Jerald, & Huang, 2001).

Perhaps the most troubling statistics related to the achievement gap concern educational attainment for U.S. kindergartners. Out of any group of 100 Asian young children, approximately 74 will complete at least some college. For the same size group of White children, the number is 65; for African American children 50; and for Latino children 32. These numbers are cut in more than half for every group except Asians when tracking how many kindergarteners will obtain at least a bachelor's degree (Education Trust, 2000; Haycock, 2001).

Experts continue to ponder the reasons behind the achievement gap in American education. Three significant identified reasons are differential standards and expectations, variation in teacher quality, and unequal allocation of educational resources. First, with respect to standards and expectations, historically there has been no agreement as to what American students should learn at each grade level nor specific expectations set for achievement. Decisions about curriculum and standards have been left to individual school districts and teachers. The result has been educational processes that by and large do not ask much of large numbers of students, in particular those who are poor, of color, or both. Second, large numbers of students of color and those who are poor are consistently taught by underqualified teachers who lack sufficient knowledge in the subjects they are teaching. Finally, the allocation of educational funding has been grossly unequal. In 42 out of 49 states studied by the Education Trust, school districts with the greatest numbers of poor children have less money to spend per student than districts with fewer poor children. The national resource gap between high- and low-poverty districts is $1,139 per student. The same unequal funding tendency exists in school districts with high percentages of ethnic minority students (Haycock, 2001; Haycock et al., 2001; Jerald & Haycock, 2002).

All of this suggests that the U.S. educational system takes students who have less to begin with and systematically gives them less in school.

The achievement gap and its many manifestations make clear that the American educational system is characterized by what Kozol (1991) described as "savage inequalities." From a social justice perspective, the gap in achievement among various groups of students is evidence that many young people are not getting equitable treatment in their quest for education. Many young people, because of either the color of their skin or their socioeconomic status, are having their human rights violated by limited access to a quality education.

The Achievement Gap: The Psychosocial and Economic Impact

Education is power. It is a lifelong process of developing the knowledge and skills to be all that one can be. Education is also a highly prized commodity. In most cultural groups it is considered to be the primary vehicle for improving one's quality of life. Poor people and those from ethnic groups of color in the United States, for example, have always placed a great value on education. Indeed, the social and economic progress that individuals from these groups have made in this country has been in direct proportion to the educational opportunities available to them.

The inherent educational inequities in U.S. schools present formidable challenges to the psychosocial development of many young people. School systems throughout the country seriously stifle achievement, aspiration, and pride among many of their youth. The educational reality for scores of students comprises frustration, underachievement, and ultimately failure.

The achievement gap also has a significant impact on economic development. Education increases a worker's average earnings and productivity, and also reduces the incidence of social problems such as drug abuse, crime, welfare dependency, and lack of access to medical care (Schweke, 2004). Importantly, data indicate that adults with relatively higher levels of education are more likely to participate in the labor force, whereas adults with lower levels of educational attainment are more likely to be unemployed (U.S. Department of Labor, 2002). It is evident that increased investment in education provides future returns to the economy through increases in labor productivity (Schweke, 2004).

It is readily apparent, therefore, that the achievement gap and its inherent educational inequities are major challenges for those who have a stake in fostering the academic, career, and personal-social development of young people. Differences in educational opportunity and academic achievement based on race/ethnicity, socioeconomic status, gender, disability, sexual orientation, or any other characteristic ultimately deny many youth the potential for full and productive participation in society.

The continued existence of educational inequities should be a clarion call to educators to work to promote access, equity, and social justice in U.S. schools. We devote the remainder of this chapter to how professional school counselors can heed the call to advance social justice in education. We examine new and reconfigured roles for school counselors that are designed to move them to the forefront of eliminating the achievement gap and promoting school reform and educational equity.

School Counseling: Redefining the Profession

Within the last decade, school counseling has undergone a transformation. School counselors have been challenged to achieve new professional goals and assume new and more proactive roles (Education Trust, 2000; Erford, House, & Martin, 2003; House & Hayes, 2002; Lambie & Williamson, 2004; Martin, 2002). Professional school counselors are being called upon to become visible leaders in national educational reform movements and central to the mission of schools (ASCA, 1994; Dahir, 2004; House & Martin, 1998). The work of a school counselor in this transformational effort is predicated on the principles of access, equity, and social justice. These principles reflect a commitment to ensuring that all children, regardless of race/ethnicity or socioeconomic status, have the opportunity to achieve to their fullest potential. Within the context of these principles, the goals of school counseling are conceptualized as (a) achieving equity and social justice for students, and (b) increasing student learning and achievement (Education Trust, 2000).

School counselors are being challenged to assume roles that reflect a commitment to these principles and goals. Accordingly, they are being asked to shift from an individual focus to a systemic focus in their work (Education Trust, 2000; Erford et al., 2003; Lee, 2005). Rather than work in isolation with individual students, professional school counselors are being asked to team and collaborate with other educational stakeholders and work at a macro level to bring about systemic change (Bemak, 2000). In addition, they are being called upon to move beyond a strict focus on school counseling activities to more extensive involvement as leaders in both the school and community (Education Trust, 2000). Finally, in an era of greater educational accountability, professional school counselors are being called upon to demonstrate with data that their efforts make a difference in the lives of the students with whom they work (Dahir & Stone, 2003; Hughes & James, 2001).

What follows is an examination of the roles considered critical to professional school counselors as they confront the challenges associated with contemporary education. School counselors must assume these critical and strategic roles in order to become proactive in meeting the needs of all students and in assisting them to achieve to their fullest academic potential. As counselors strive to meet these new expectations, they emerge as agents of social justice committed to eliminating environmental or institutional barriers that impede academic, career, or personal/social success.

Counselor Role 1: Leadership

Professional school counselors must be leaders in their schools and within the larger community. They should be in the forefront of developing new educational initiatives that promote student development. They should also be active participants on leadership teams within their respective schools and school districts. These leadership initiatives should place school counselors in the forefront of shaping new educational policies and procedures at all levels from the board of education to the school building (Education Trust, 2000; House & Sears, 2002; Lee, 2005).

Likewise, school counselors must be politically and socially active leaders in the community at large. They should seek leadership positions within strategic community organizations and institutions that affect the quality of life of young people and their families. As leaders, counselors should position themselves to have direct influence on important community political decisions and policy initiatives that relate to the quality of education for all students and the welfare of their families (Education Trust, 2000; Lee, 2005).

The essence of school leadership is voicing the need for necessary change, presenting data that justify the need for change, challenging negative attitudes and beliefs about students, knowing how to problem solve and advocate for systemic change, and creating a climate that leads to increased achievement for all students. Such a climate is enhanced by leadership on the part of school counselors that results in the initiation of policies and programs to promote success (Education Trust, 2000).

Counselor Role 2: Advocacy

As professional school counselors become agents of social justice, they must assume the role of advocate for students and families. As advocates, school counselors become risk takers as opposed to enablers of the status quo that perpetuates educational inequities. School counselors who are advocates confront old paradigms and power structures while they promote professionalism and the well-being of students (Bemak & Chung, 2005).

As student advocates, counselors can intervene in the educational system in order to eliminate possible institutional barriers and cultural insensitivities that may negatively affect student learning (Lee, 2001). An example of such advocacy is school counselors working to help students who have been systematically excluded from rigorous academic preparation because of their ethnic background or socioeconomic status gain access to such experiences. In addition, as these students gain access to rigorous preparation, advocates work to ensure that supports are in place to foster academic success (House & Martin, 1998). While working to foster such access, advocates also develop working alliances with students to empower students to advocate for themselves (Lee, 2005).

School counselors must also advocate for students' families. This is particularly important when families are systematically excluded from educational participation or when their influence on student learning is discounted. Working both with and for families, counselors can advocate for systemic accommodations to increase family involvement in their children's education. An example of this type of advocacy is ensuring that educators are sensitive to the unique realities and challenges that confront many ethnic minority and poor families as they attempt to provide a nurturing educational environment for their children.

Counselor Role 3: Counseling

Individual and group counseling for social justice in schools should address challenges that impede academic success, promote the development of positive attitudes, foster academic competency, and promote positive self-identity and cultural awareness among all students. Counseling interventions must be framed within the context of ensuring that the achievement gap is effectively closed. This can be achieved by counseling interventions grounded in the concept of empowerment. Given the personal and structural challenges that confront many young people in the school setting, counselors should be able to move beyond traditional counseling practice in order to promote academic, career, and personal-social development. They should have the skills to engage in programmed intervention that facilitates a process through which young people become empowered to proactively address challenges that impede their overall educational success (Lee, 2005).

Counselor Role 4: Collaboration

Professional school counselors must collaborate with key educational stakeholders to promote student development (Bemak, 2000; Bryan & Holcomb-McCoy, 2004; Lee, 2005). They should collaborate, for example, with families to empower them as proactive forces in their children's educational success. Educators have long recognized the influence of home and family life on academic achievement (Christianson & Sheridan, 2001; U.S. Department of Education, 1997). School counselors, therefore, should take action to facilitate family-school partnerships that promote students' academic and career success. Such partnerships should be based on important considerations about diversity in family life. Counselors must be sensitive to the economic and social realities of families and meet them where they are with respect to such things as language proficiency and cultural customs (Bemak & Cornely, 2002).

In addition, school counselors must collaborate with community stakeholders to advance the educational interests of students. Counselors should form alliances within the business, religious, and political sectors of the community to promote education. They should be able to broker alliances that result in the channeling of community resources into school programming to support both counseling and teaching initiatives. An example of this might be collaborating with community stakeholders and actively supporting their efforts to develop supplemental academic support programs (e.g., tutoring programs) in neighborhood religious institutions, community centers, and other areas of social activity.

School counselors should also collaborate with educational stakeholders within the school setting. In particular, they should assist teachers and administrators to increase their educational effectiveness given the social and structural challenges confronting the educational system. School counselors should facilitate faculty development initiatives that focus on increasing awareness of systemic factors impinging upon student development or that introduce innovative methods for promoting the success of students who are in challenging social or economic environments.

Counselor Role 5: Effective Use of Data

The effective use of data can be a driving force for promoting social justice. School counselors must use data to point out systemic inequities, advocate for systemic change, and create urgency for change. Therefore, school counselors must become competent in accessing, analyzing, interpreting, and presenting educational and social data (Dahir & Stone, 2003; Education Trust, 2000). It is crucial that counselors use data to make decisions about the focus of their work. If the achievement data for a given school suggest that there are gaps based on race/ethnicity, socioeconomic status, or any other characteristic, then the counselor's efforts must be focused on addressing the issues affecting those students who are most in need. In order to underscore the scope of inequities, therefore, counselors must be skilled at disaggregating data by variables such as race/ethnicity, gender, socioeconomic status, course enrollment patterns, and teacher assignment (Education Trust, 2000).

In addition, counselors should possess the ability to collect and effectively present data as a major strategy for influencing policy and programming initiatives aimed at closing gaps in achievement (Dahir & Stone, 2003). School counselors who are committed to challenging educational inequities must be skilled at using data effectively to communicate to key educational stakeholders the pervasive nature of the achievement gap. The use of data is a powerful way to persuade such stakeholders of the urgent need for change in policies and practices.

Concomitantly, with the advent of NCLB, all educators share accountability for student achievement. The use of data is a proactive way to contribute to the accountability, advocacy, and advancement of school counseling (Dahir & Stone, 2003). School counselors must respond to accountability mandates such as NCLB and demonstrate through data the effectiveness of their contributions to the mission of a school (Eschenauer & Chen-Hayes, 2005). Be it with tabulation methods, time analyses, rating scales, questionnaires, case studies, interviews, or expert or peer reviews, school counselors can use data to answer fundamental educational questions such as, "How are students better off as a result of the school counseling program?" or "How has student achievement increased as result of the school counseling program?"

The Challenge of Professional School Counseling Redefined

The pervasive failure and wasted potential of many young people that characterize the U.S. educational landscape underscore the importance and urgency of these roles for professional school counselors. Adopting these roles entails a rejection of many longstanding traditions in school counseling, requires a transcendence of the traditional boundaries of school counseling practice, and challenges professional school counselors to think outside the box and take risks in their efforts to address educational inequities. In assuming these roles, school counselors must believe that all children can achieve to high standards. They must be willing to commit themselves to the principles of access, equity, and social justice and to translating these principles into action. They must also embrace the concept of empowerment and approach their work with students and other educational stakeholders from this affirming perspective. In addition, they must be willing to collaborate in innovative ways with all educational stakeholders and exert leadership within the school and community to promote academic success and advance social justice in American education.

Conclusion

The future of the United States depends on every young person being assured a quality education and having an equal opportunity for academic success. It is therefore incumbent upon everyone who is committed to social justice to work to eradicate the inequities in the educational system that perpetuate gaps in achievement. Professional school counselors should be counted among the leaders of this crucial effort. Every school counselor should dedicate himself or herself to the cause of increasing student learning and achievement and advancing social justice and equity for all young people. The commitment and effort of every school counselor should guarantee that, truly, no child is left behind.

References

American School Counselor Association (ASCA). (1994). *The school counselor's role in educational reform*. Alexandria, VA: Author.

Bemak, F. (2000). Transforming the role of the counselor to provide leadership in educational reform through collaboration. *Professional School Counseling, 3*, 323–333.

Bemak, F., & Chung, R. (2005). Advocacy as a critical role for urban school counselors: Working toward equity and social justice. *Professional School Counseling, 8*, 196–202.

Bemak, F., & Cornely, L. (2002). The SAFI model as a critical link between marginalized families and schools: A literature review and strategies for school counselors. *Journal of Counseling & Development, 80,* 322–329.

Bryan, J., & Holcomb-McCoy, C. (2004). School counselors' perceptions of their involvement in school-family-community partnerships. *Professional School Counseling, 7,* 162–171.

Christianson, S. L., & Sheridan, S. M. (2001). *Schools and families: Creating essential connections for learning.* New York: Guilford Press.

Dahir, C. A. (2004). Supporting a nation of learners: The role of school counseling in educational reform. *Journal of Counseling & Development, 82,* 344–353.

Dahir, C. A., & Stone, C. B. (2003). Accountability: A M.E.A.S.U.R.E. of the impact school counselors have on student achievement. *Professional School Counseling, 6,* 214–221.

Education Trust. (2000). *National initiative for transforming school counseling summer academy for counselor educators proceedings.* Washington, DC: Author.

Erford, B. T., House, R., & Martin, P. (2003). Transforming the school counseling profession. In B. T. Erford (Ed.), *Transforming the school counseling profession* (pp. 1–20). Upper Saddle River, NJ: Merrill Prentice Hall.

Eschenauer, R., & Chen-Hayes, S. F. (2005). The transformative individual school counseling model: An accountability model for urban school counselors. *Professional School Counseling, 8,* 244–248.

Haycock, K. (2001, March). Closing the achievement gap. *Educational Leadership,* pp. 6–11.

Haycock, K., Jerald, C., & Huang, S. (2001). Closing the gap: Done in a decade. In *Thinking K–12* (pp. 3–22). Washington, DC: Education Trust.

House, R. M., & Hayes, R. L. (2002). School counselors: Becoming key players in school reform. *Professional School Counseling, 5,* 249–256.

House, R. M., & Martin, P. J. (1998). Advocating for better futures for all students: A new vision for school counselors. *Education, 119,* 284–292.

House R. M., & Sears, S. J. (2002). Preparing school counselors to be leaders and advocates: A critical need in the new millennium. *Theory Into Practice, 41,* 154–162.

Hughes, D. K., & James, S. H. (2001). Using accountability data to protect a school counseling program: One counselor's experience. *Professional School Counseling, 4,* 306–310.

Jerald, C., & Haycock K. (2002). Closing the gap: The Education Trust's recipe for meeting new federal standards on student achievement. *School Administrator, 59,* 16–20.

Kozol, J. (1991). *Savage inequalities: Children in America's schools.* New York: Crown.

Lambie, G. W., & Williamson, L. L. (2004). The challenge to change from guidance counseling to professional school counseling: A historical proposition. *Professional School Counseling, 8,* 124–131.

Lee, C. C. (2001). Culturally responsive counselors and programs: Addressing the needs of all students. *Professional School Counseling, 4,* 257–262.

Lee, C. C. (2005). Urban school counseling: Context, characteristics, and competencies. *Professional School Counseling, 8,* 184–188.

Martin, P. J. (2002). Transforming school counseling: A national perspective. *Theory Into Practice, 41,* 148–154.

No Child Left Behind Act, Reauthorization of the Elementary and Secondary Education Act, H.R. 1. (2001).

Schweke, W. (2004). *Smart money: Education and economic development.* Washington, DC: Economic Policy Institute.

U.S. Department of Education. (1997). *Achieving the goals: Goal 8: Parent involvement and participation.*Washington, DC: U.S. Government Printing Office.

U.S. Department of Education. (2004). *Closing the achievement gap in America's public schools.* Retrieved February 17, 2005, from http://www.ed.gov/nclb/overview/welcome/closing/index.html

U.S. Department of Labor. (2002). *Current population survey.* Washington, DC: U. S. Government Printing Office.

Chapter 2

Advancing Social Justice by Challenging Socioeconomic Disadvantage

Kathleen L. Armstrong

A 55-year-old man with schizophrenia was able to work for many years before becoming disabled. Once he qualified for Social Security Disability Insurance (SSDI), his monthly check reflected his having paid into the Social Security system. Because of his relatively high income, he was ineligible for Medicaid health coverage. His out-of-pocket medical medication expenses are substantial; he therefore realizes a monthly net income less than if he had never worked a day in his life.

A 30-year-old woman left her abusive husband, taking her two small children with her. She is currently living in a domestic violence shelter, but can stay there no more than 1 month. She has no income of her own, no family in the area, and limited education and job skills. She has no idea what she can do short of moving back home with her abusive husband.

A 15-year-old high school student is in a counseling group for at-risk adolescents. He mentions that he enjoys learning about computers but has limited access to them in his classrooms. His single mother works long hours and cannot regularly take him to the local library where he can use public computers. There is no computer in his home. His grades are fair, and he expresses an interest in pursuing a college education.

These three scenarios are based on real-life encounters I have had with clients. In each situation, lack of money exerted a powerful influence over the individual's life and future. In our society, more money means more choices; less money, fewer choices. Economic help is available to society's poor through government assistance and social programs, and medical and mental health services are available through a variety of agencies. However, accessing these benefits can be confusing, cumbersome, demeaning, and frustrating for clients. It sometimes appears to clients that the "system" is really a series of tests to pass, which will winnow out anyone not smart enough or persistent enough to pursue help. In this chapter, I examine the trends in poverty in the United States and what effects poverty may have on individual well-being. I then explore strategies for working with clients who are economically disadvantaged. Lastly, I address how counselors can and must challenge systems that negatively affect poor clients.

Poverty in the United States

As illustrated in the latest statistics from the U.S. Census Bureau (2004), poverty rates in the United States continue to rise. Poverty, as defined by the U.S. Census, means having had a 2003 total annual income (before taxes) of less than $9,393 for an individual, of less than $12,015 for a couple, or of less than $22,245 for a family of five. These measurements are called *poverty thresholds*. When a household's income falls below the pertinent threshold, each member of the household is considered to be living in poverty (U.S. Census Bureau, 2004).

The rate of poverty in the United States increased between 2000 and 2003 (U.S. Census Bureau, 2004). As of 2003, 12.5% of the population was living in poverty, up from 12.1% in 2002 (U.S. Census Bureau, 2004). In real numbers, this translates to 35.9 million people living in poverty in 2003. For children, in particular, poverty rates rose between 2002 and 2003, from 16.7% in 2002 to 17.6% in 2003 (U.S. Census Bureau, 2004).

The demographics of poverty in the United States are also noteworthy. Ethnic minorities are disproportionately represented in poverty statistics. Non-Hispanic Whites comprise 44.3% of those in poverty but 67.6% of the population (U.S. Census Bureau, 2004). Therefore, there are disparities for other ethnic groups between their percentage of the population and the percentage in poverty. African Americans showed a poverty rate of 24.4% for 2003 but made up only 13% of the population; Hispanics showed a poverty rate of 22.5% but made up 13.6% of the total population; and Asian Americans showed a poverty rate of 11.8% but were only 4.4% of the total population (U.S. Census Bureau, 2004).

As illustrated in poverty statistics, children and women are at higher risk than men of being in poverty. In 2003, children under age 18 comprised 35.9% of those in poverty (real number = 12.9 million children) but only 25.4% of the total U.S. population (U.S. Census Bureau, 2004). Households run by females with no husband present had an extremely high poverty rate of 52.9% in 2003; this is compared to a rate of 9.6% for households headed by a married couple (U.S. Census Bureau, 2004). Furthermore, the gap between male and female wage earnings increased in 2003, with females earning only 76% of the average wage for males in 2002–2003. The median income for males in this time period was $40,668, whereas the median income for comparably employed women was $30,724 (U.S. Census Bureau, 2004).

Therefore, being an ethnic minority, being female, or being a child puts one at greater than average risk of living in poverty. Poverty is on the rise in the population as a whole and also in almost all of these subgroups (U.S. Census Bureau, 2004). The disparity between the haves and the have nots continues to grow. Keep in mind, however, that in addition to the millions of people living below the poverty thresholds, millions more live just above these thresholds and face all or most of the same challenges created by poverty.

Correlates of Poverty

Many health and mental health conditions are correlated to poverty. As Chen, Matthews, and Boyce (2002) stated, "Individuals lower in SES [socioeconomic status] experience higher rates of morbidity and mortality in almost every disease category than individuals higher in SES" (p. 295). Many factors appear to influence health concerns, including poor living conditions, malnutrition, and restricted access to or use of medical care (Chen et al., 2002; Holleman, Bray, Davis, & Holleman, 2004).

Everson, Maty, Lynch, and Kaplan (2002) found evidence that low socioeconomic status was related to several major health concerns. Higher rates of smoking and alcohol consumption and less exercise among the poor may contribute to chronic health conditions. For example, obesity is more prevalent in lower SES patients. Data collected over three decades confirm that higher weight gains were correlated to lower education, which is one measure of SES (Everson et al., 2002).

Perhaps due in part to the increased risk of obesity, low SES is related to the prevalence of type II diabetes. In a study reported by Everson and colleagues (2002), the risk of developing diabetes was found to be 80% higher in the lowest SES participants as compared to the highest SES participants. Because both obesity and diabetes are themselves related to other medical conditions, it is clear that the health risks of poverty are substantial.

Poor children are at particular risk of health deficits and even death. Chen and colleagues (2002) reported that poor children are more likely to die from both chronic conditions (respiratory disorders, cancer, heart problems) and acute health problems (flu, injury, pneumonia). Children in poor families are more likely to live in crowded environments where germs are shared among family members, are more likely to miss days at school due to illness, and are more likely to develop illnesses such as rheumatic fever (Chen et al., 2002).

Mental health concerns are also pronounced among the poor. As reported in the *World Health Report,*

> The poor and the deprived have a higher prevalence of mental and behavioural disorders, including substance use disorders. This higher prevalence may be explainable both by higher causation of disorders among the poor and by the drift of the mentally ill into poverty. . . . For example, the causal mechanism may be more valid for anxiety and depressive disorders, while the drift theory may account more for the higher prevalence of psychotic and substance use disorders among the poor. But the two are not mutually exclusive: individuals may be predisposed to mental disorder because of their social situation and those who develop disorders may face further deprivation as a result of being ill. Such deprivation includes lower levels of educational attainment, unemployment, and, in extreme cases, homelessness. Mental disorders may cause severe and sustained disabilities, including an inability to work. (World Health Organization, 2001, p. 10)

It is therefore possible that being impoverished may itself heighten psychological distress, and further psychological distress may negatively affect earning potential, thereby keeping one in an impoverished lifestyle.

This relationship between economic disadvantage and mental health symptoms has been documented by many investigators (see, e.g., Artazcoz, Benach, Borrell, & Cortes, 2004; Costello, Compton, Keeler, & Angold, 2003). Everson and associates (2002), for example, analyzed data from four large studies on depression involving different regional and even international samples ranging from California to Detroit to Finland. Despite the heterogeneity of participants, comparing data from all studies illustrated a strong inverse association between level of education or level of income and symptoms of depression. In each study, lower income or education was associated with higher levels of depression.

Costello and colleagues (2003) also assessed psychiatric symptoms in children characterized as never poor, persistently poor, and ex-poor. Participants in this study were children between the ages of 9 and 13 who were given psychiatric assessments each year for 8 years. Findings indicated that poor children had consistently higher levels of oppositional-defiant and conduct symptoms than the never poor children. Additionally, when families moved out of poverty, the children's symptoms became as low as those of children of never poor households. Symptoms of depression and anxiety were found to be more prevalent in poor children, but these symptoms were not significantly alleviated by moving out of impoverished circumstances. One mediating factor in lowering behavioral symptoms was that of parental supervision; the authors posited that increased income may have allowed parents to apportion more time to direct supervision of children.

Another relationship that has been investigated is that between poverty and stress. It makes intuitive sense that stress is a salient feature of being poor or impoverished; after all, the real dilemma of poverty is not having enough material resources, which could be expected to result in more numerous stressful situations. In fact, this is exactly what investigators have found.

Gallo and Matthews (2003) reviewed studies in several areas to look at possible relationships among socioeconomic status, mental health symptoms, and medical health outcomes. They discovered that low-SES environments are related to more negative emotional experiences and more negative cognition. Their analysis of these findings is that the common factor in all of the studies is the exposure to stress from being poor. In other words, being poor promotes negative attitudes and emotions through continual stressful experiences. In turn, continually experiencing stressful events depletes all of an individual's reserves—financial, emotional, and interpersonal. Therefore, a pernicious cycle develops in which more stress results in progressively lower levels of functioning in several areas, and this can ultimately lead to physical illness.

Attitudes and Beliefs of the Poor

As noted in the previous section, some researchers have investigated whether impoverished individuals hold particular attitudes or beliefs. Some of these beliefs or attitudes may actually promote the continuation of poverty. This concept may seem like dangerous territory—frightfully close to blaming the victim. As counselors, however, we understand that attitudes and beliefs can powerfully affect clients' life decisions and general well-being. Therefore, in order to understand more fully these clients' worldview, we must be willing to explore this aspect of their experiences of poverty.

Many poor members of our society are routinely discriminated against, judged, and maligned due to their low SES status (Lott, 2002). It therefore seems understandable that these individuals might begin to view the world as an unfriendly, unhelpful, and unsupportive place. Furthermore, these attitudes and beliefs might then begin to color their interactions with others, with an end result of reinforcing their negative view of society.

Gallo and Matthews (2003) commented upon this phenomenon in their synthesis of numerous studies of mental health, physical health, and SES. From this body of literature, one can draw inferences about the attitudes and cognitions of some low-SES individuals. In particular, some low-SES individuals have been found to interpret relatively neutral situations as being negative (Gallo & Matthews, 2003). This may, in fact, be an understandable reaction, considering that low-income individuals face so many daily situations in which they are treated as "less than" (see, e.g., Lott, 2002; Mofidi, Rozier, & King, 2002). Because of the inverse relationships between SES and mental health symptoms of depression, anxiety, and hostility, one can project that a disproportionate percentage of low-income individuals will tend to interpret neutral situations or interactions in a negative manner. These interpretations could cause further stress, leading to more negative cognitions or mental health symptoms.

In addition, attitudes toward breaking out of poverty may be an issue for impoverished clients. Several factors may affect these attitudes, including negative life events, lack of feelings of self-efficacy, and identification with others who are poor. For example, divorced women and elder adults may find themselves in poverty for the first time in their lives (Bottomly, Bissonette, & Snekvik, 2001; Grella, 1990). These individuals may have neither the skills nor any longer the resources to successfully raise their income again.

For those who have been living in poverty, poor feelings of self-efficacy may be an issue. In a study comparing women at two different low-income levels, Robinson, Davis, and Meara (2003) found differences between the two groups. Women who were taking community college courses of their own volition showed many more actions related to self-efficacy and the belief that they could improve their material lifestyles. Women on public assistance, while having the same desires for material resources, indicated much less clarity in terms of what they could do to change their current standard of living.

Interestingly, some people may also have ambivalent feelings about upward mobility. In discussing African Americans' upward mobility, Cole and Omari (2003) pointed out that there are both benefits and liabilities to attaining a middle-class standing. African Americans may feel caught between two worlds—the White middle-class world they work in and the poor African American community they left. The authors pointed out that many middle-class African Americans have poor relatives whom they help support, thereby straining their own finances. In addition, psychological stress may result from moving into a primarily White neighborhood, which can weaken extended family support, and from trying to form a new class identity while caught between two economic and cultural worlds.

Related to the notion of upward mobility are attitudes and beliefs concerning education. Traditionally, education has been conceived of as one of the tickets out of an existence of poverty, of limited choices, of dead-end jobs. The American dream that you can become whatever you want to if you just work hard enough is often, though not always, predicated on the foundation of getting a good education.

Considering that education can be a real avenue for career choices and financial gain, one might expect that all children raised in poverty will hold the possibility of a good education in high regard. This, however, is not so. Not only are there real and persistent inequities in terms of educational resources for poor children (Hochschild, 2003), but there may also be various attitudes toward the value of education and the world of work (Kenny, Blustein, Chaves, Grossman, & Gallagher, 2003).

Kenny and associates (2003) found that school engagement and career aspirations of urban high school students were related both to perceived barriers to education and to level of family and other support. That is, if barriers to further education were present and support for education were lacking, then students were more likely to devalue education and the career options it could bring. However, family and other support had a mitigating effect on overcoming perceived barriers to education and career attainment. These findings are particularly noteworthy for school counselors, as they are in a position to develop programs that will motivate and support these students.

Additionally, young adults' views of work and career have been found to relate to socioeconomic background. Low-SES individuals have described work simply as a means for financial gain. In contrast, high-SES individuals, although acknowledging the need for money, have also expressed receiving personal satisfaction from work and finding personal meaning in their work experience (Blustein et al., 2002). These differences could have great implications for how we plan and implement career interventions.

Barriers to Counseling

Many barriers interfere with poor clients' ability to access counseling (and many other) services. These barriers include lack of money, lack of transportation, lack of time, and the stigma attached to reaching out for help. Each of these barriers is formidable by itself; taken together, they may seem insurmountable to some clients.

Lack of money is obviously always a pressing concern for low-income clients. Therefore, any services which require payment must be justified. Thompson, Bazile, and Akbar (2004) used a focus group format to discover, among other factors, what barriers African Americans perceived in relation to accessing psychotherapy services. They found that African Americans who have consistent trouble paying their basic bills may perceive counseling services as a luxury. Additionally, for those clients who could afford to access only free or low-cost services, there were questions about whether the reduced services were worthwhile; and Medicaid recipients complained of being offered only medication management without counseling or psychotherapy.

Even when clients do desire free or low-cost counseling services, they report other difficulties. Reliable, convenient, and inexpensive transportation is a necessity in order for poor people to access services. Transportation can be a particular problem for rural clients (Myers & Gill, 2004). Even within urban areas, however, having to travel too far for services can be a deterrent. In studying this problem, Beardsley, Wish, Fitzelle, O'Grady, and Arria (2004) found correlations between distance traveled for substance abuse treatment and completion of treatment. Specifically, the researchers found that having to travel more than 1 mile to the treatment center was associated with a 50% reduction in treatment completion. Having to travel more than 4 miles also resulted in significantly fewer treatment appointments.

Finally, poor clients may face embarrassment and stigma when trying to reach out for services. Poor people are often stereotyped in our culture. Lott (2002) declared that "the dominant images of poor people in the United States include negative beliefs about their characteristics, negative expectations about their behavior, and the attribution that their poverty is caused by their own failings" (p. 101). These stereotypes are illustrated in studies that document the attitudes toward the poor held by middle-class college students (Cozzarelli,

Tagler, & Wilkinson, 2003), and particularly by White Americans (Brezina & Winder, 2004; Kim, 2001).

These attitudes may not be as prevalent when services are targeted directly to a low-income population. For example, Bomalaski (1999) found that meaningful therapeutic alliances were the norm between therapists and female homeless clients living in a women's shelter. However, when SES is only one characteristic of a served population, it may become a stumbling block for therapists. Falconnier (2004) found that low-SES clients being treated for depression had either better or worse outcomes depending on therapists' attitudes. Therapists who were able to approach and help process issues of finances, unemployment, and work stress had a greater effect in treatment than those who were not.

It is also important to remember that being stigmatized because of poverty is a factor in other health settings as well. Mofidi and colleagues (2002) interviewed caregivers of Medicaid-insured children to assess their satisfaction with dental providers. Respondents typically complained about being treated differently due to their Medicaid status. Providers were difficult to find, appointments were not flexible, waits within offices were excessive, and reception staff were disrespectful, sometimes even making comments about Medicaid recipients in earshot of other patients. Repeated experiences of this sort could prevent poor clients from even reaching out for supportive services.

Strategies for Counseling and Advocacy With Poor Clients

Thankfully, there are many ways counselors can both counsel and be advocates for poor clients. They can work individually with clients, can work collaboratively within greater helping systems, and can also work to change the existing political and social systems that permit poverty to continue to grow. I address each of these levels of intervention.

Before beginning counseling with impoverished clients, counselors must first examine their own worldviews regarding low-income or impoverished people. The literature described previously (see, e.g., Lott, 2002) has described how many people in the United States both stereotype and distance themselves from poor people. In order to be effective with this client population, we counselors must first examine and admit any biases we have internalized about attributions of poverty, ethnic or racial stereotypes, and the possibilities of achieving the American dream. In order to advocate with and for our clients, we need to believe wholeheartedly in the basic humanity of all people and the need to allow all humans opportunities for growth.

Working Individually With Clients

Based on the literature described earlier, an obvious place to start in a counseling intervention with a poor client is to be willing to admit openly to the socioeconomic disparities that exist in our society and to recognize that these disparities are unjust. As Falconnier (2004) described, clients may build a better working alliance with counselors who are willing and able to talk about the socioeconomic realities in their lives and to value their struggles. As counselors, we need to approach these topics with clients as we would any other multicultural differences—with openness, invitation to discuss, and respect for different experiences.

Another strategy in working individually with clients is to promote empowerment and resiliency. Myers and Gill (2004) pointed out that many poor clients are not aware of the strengths they possess, such as persistence in the face of adversity, ability to be a good caregiver, and extended social support; these qualities should not be overlooked. Rather, strengths can be built upon in counseling by using a holistic, wellness approach in which clients identify areas they wish to change and believe they can change (Myers & Gill, 2004).

These dynamics of empowerment and resiliency echo throughout the literature on working with impoverished clients. Client empowerment is seen as a process nurtured by professionals having a more collaborative than hierarchical relationship with clients (Finfgeld, 2004). Empowerment also entails clients' learning skills they will need to navigate systems and to become self-advocates (Finfgeld, 2004). Resiliency is viewed in the literature as the ability to continue to strive despite chronic adversity. Individuals who are resilient also seem to share certain characteristics, including good social skills and an internal locus of control (Gordon-Rouse, 1998). Therefore, when working with low-SES clients, we can try to emphasize interventions that raise client understanding of systems, encourage them to be active collaborators in treatment, develop or enhance social skills, and develop or enhance internal locus of control.

Working Within Systems on Behalf of Clients

Advocacy with and for poor clients must become an integral part of our service to them. Ezell (2001) has described advocacy as "the abilities of human service practitioners to make a difference, to influence policy, program, and funding decisions that will positively impact their clients" (p. xvii). In order to be effective advocates for clients, we must first understand the systems they inhabit. To do this, we must be willing to learn from and collaborate with professionals in other agencies and programs. These programs may include social service agencies, hospitals and clinics, mental health agencies, schools, colleges, and jails.

In some cases, counselors may need to step outside their traditional sphere of providing counseling. The three client cases at the beginning of the chapter can be used to illustrate collaboration and acting as a case manager. In the first case, a seriously mentally ill client could not afford to pay for needed medications. Working with the local hospital to establish an "indigent" status allowed this client to receive medications at a greatly reduced cost. Another possible strategy would have been to work directly with the pharmaceutical companies, which sometimes have programs to provide medicines at reduced prices to low-income patients. Additionally, some doctors are able to give out samples of medication to cover part of the patient's needs, thereby reducing the cost to poor patients.

In the second case of the woman who left her abuser, several immediate concerns needed to be resolved. This client needed financial assistance, housing, and job training. Through collaborating with social service agencies, counselors helped her to get financial benefits such as Aid to Families With Dependent Children. They explored housing options available through both transitional housing programs and Section 8 housing lists, and investigated job skills training through a local women's career agency. These linkages would have been extremely difficult for this client in crisis to make for herself, especially when she had no experience working with these systems.

The third case involved a low-income high school student who wanted a computer but could not afford one. By spending approximately 45 minutes on the phone, I was able to identify a program that donates rehabilitated computers. The student's school administrator and I were able to get him on the list to receive a free computer. These three examples, I hope, illustrate the need for counselors to gain some understanding of the complex systems our low-income clients interact with each day.

Working to Change Systems

In addition to helping clients navigate systems, counselors must be willing to examine existing systems and point out injustices or inadequacies. Issues to be considered in examining agency systems, for example, can include ineffective programs, inaccessibility of programs to some clients, poor outcomes of programs, lack of coordination, and people or programs that disempower rather than empower (Ezell, 2001). Working to change a system can also include diverse strategies such as talking to supervisors and supervisees about concerns, developing new training programs for staff, eliciting feedback from client groups, and bringing concerns to various governing boards. These types of actions empower counselors in being or becoming social change agents.

On a broader scale, advocacy can also influence educational, community, political, and policy-making systems. Training and supervision of counseling students need to include teaching them about the impact of poverty and the importance of social justice issues. As we train future counselors to be more aware of these dynamics, we can affect all counseling systems. Counseling research can also inform practitioners and educators about special needs of impoverished clients. More research is needed to clarify which interventions are most helpful with this population.

Counselors can also be advocates in their communities. Many community members may be unaware of the inequities that exist so close to home. Counselors can effectively use the media, the Internet, community education, and special trainings and presentations to raise awareness and increase understanding about the community costs of poverty (Ezell, 2001). Poverty can affect any community through homelessness, mental health issues, physical health issues, the need for a living wage, and unemployment issues.

Politically, counselors can be advocates and social change agents on several levels. The most individual level is for us to exercise our right to vote and to vote our conscience in each election. We must become informed about the issues affecting low-income clients at the local, state, and national levels. Second, we must empower our low-income clients to vote. Their voices need to be heard by policymakers. Third, we can become politically active by engaging in peaceful protests, by writing to elected officials and policymakers, and by signing or circulating petitions regarding social injustices.

Creating New Systems

Some innovative systems have been created to try to address many of the issues related to poverty. Holleman and colleagues (2004) described one such system of programs, in which several services are provided to low-income clients through a collaboration among family physicians, family therapists, and psychologists. Individual programs are aimed at increasing effective use of medical services through, for example, building a relationship with a primary-care physician. This particular program is cofacilitated by family physicians and family therapists, because these professionals are best equipped to answer clients' medical questions and also build their social skills. Another program helps clients better understand medication management by having a therapist accompany them to psychiatric appointments, both as an advocate and to help them process information. Another service provides information about family-of-origin issues and helps clients understand how these dynamics can be either helpful or hurtful. As a treatment system, these programs provide a spectrum of services through the collaborative efforts of interdisciplinary teams, to make treatment more convenient, more effective, and more understandable for the low-income client.

Myers and Gill (2004) also described innovative ways to serve poor rural female clients using a wellness model with an emphasis on holistic assessment and intervention. They urged counselors to uncover all of the challenges these clients face and all of the strengths with which they face them. Counselors can then use these strengths as an opportunity to convey respect for clients and to empower clients to collaborate in setting treatment goals. Within this counseling model, counselors are urged to address systems challenges at levels of the individual and the family, and to become social change agents by also addressing policy decisions and by furthering research and advocacy goals.

Conclusion

Poverty is again on the rise in the United States, with women, minorities, and children at special risk of being or becoming impoverished. Poverty has far-reaching consequences for individuals, including physical and mental health problems and challenges to general well-being. Counselors are in a position that allows them not only to work directly with this client population, but also to advocate for them in larger systems. Through advocacy and other efforts, counselors make a commitment to be social change agents and to attempt to eradicate poverty from our society.

References

Artazcoz, L., Benach, J., Borrell, C., & Cortes, I. (2004). Unemployment and mental health: Understanding the interactions among gender, family roles, and social class. *American Journal of Public Health, 94,* 82–88.

Beardsley, K., Wish, E. D., Fitzelle, D. B., O'Grady, K., & Arria, A. M. (2004). Distance traveled to outpatient drug treatment and client retention. *Journal of Substance Abuse Treatment, 25,* 279–285.

Blustein, D. L., Chaves, A. P., Diemer, M. A., Gallagher, L. A., Marshall, K. G., Sirin, S., & Bhati, K. S. (2002). Voices of the forgotten half: The role of social class in the school-to-work transition. *Journal of Counseling Psychology, 49,* 311–323.

Bomalaski, S. H. (1999). Effects of counseling services with homeless women: Social indicators and intrapersonal outcomes. *Dissertation Abstracts International: The Sciences and Engineering, 60*(4-B), 1842.

Bottomly, J. M., Bissonette, A., & Snekvik, V. C. (2001). The lives of homeless older adults: Please, tell them who I am. *Topics in Geriatric Rehabilitation, 16,* 50–64.

Brezina, T., & Winder, K. (2004). Economic disadvantage, status generalization, and negative racial stereotyping by White Americans. *Social Psychology Quarterly, 66,* 402–418.

Chen, E., Matthews, K. A., & Boyce, W. T. (2002). Socioeconomic differences in children's health: How and why do these relationships change with age? *Psychological Bulletin, 128,* 295–329.

Cole, E. R., & Omari, S. R. (2003). Race, class, and the dilemmas of upward mobility for African Americans. *Journal of Social Issues, 59,* 785–802.

Costello, E. J., Compton, S. N., Keeler, G., & Angold, A. (2003). Relationships between poverty and psychopathology. *Journal of the American Medical Asociation, 290,* 2023–2029.

Cozzarelli, C., Tagler, M. J., & Wilkinson, A. V. (2003). Do middle-class students perceive poor women and poor men differently? *Sex Roles, 47,* 519–529.

Everson, S. A., Maty, S. A., Lynch, J. W., & Kaplan, G. A. (2002). Epidemiologic evidence for the relation between socioeconomic status and depression, obesity, and diabetes. *Journal of Psychosomatic Research, 53,* 891–895.

Ezell, M. (2001). *Advocacy in the human services.* Pacific Grove, CA: Brooks/Cole.

Falconnier, L. A. (2004). Socioeconomic status and the treatment of depression: The role of therapist attitudes, the therapeutic relationship, and addressing stressful life circumstances. *Dissertation Abstracts International: Humanities and Social Sciences, 64*(10-A), 3844.

Finfgeld, D. L. (2004). Empowerment of individuals with enduring mental health problems: Results from concept analyses and qualitative investigations. *Advances in Nursing Science, 27*, 44–52.

Gallo, L., & Matthews, K. (2003). Understanding the association between socioeconomic status and physical health: Do negative emotions play a role? *Psychological Bulletin, 129*, 10–51.

Gordon-Rouse, K. A. (1998). Resilience from poverty and stress. *Human Development and Family Life Bulletin, 4.*

Grella, C. E. (1990). Irreconcilable differences: Women defining class after divorce and downward mobility. *Gender and Society, 4*, 41–55.

Hochschild, J. L. (2003). Social class in public schools. *Journal of Social Issues, 59*, 821–840.

Holleman, W. L., Bray, J. H., Davis, L., & Holleman, M. C. (2004). Innovative ways to address the mental health and medical needs of marginalized patients: Collaborations between family physicians, family therapists, and family psychologists. *American Journal of Orthopsychiatry, 74*, 242–252.

Kenny, M. E., Blustein, D. L., Chaves, A., Grossman, J. M., & Gallagher, L. A. (2003). The role of perceived barriers and relational support in the educational and vocational lives of urban high school students. *Journal of Counseling Psychology, 50*, 142–155.

Kim, Y. M. (2001). Whites' explanations of Blacks' socioeconomic underachievement: Individualism, structuralism, and status inconsistency. *Current Research in Social Psychology, 5.*

Lott, B. (2002). Cognitive and behavioral distancing from the poor. *American Psychologist, 57,* 100–110.

Mofidi, M., Rozier, R. G., & King, R. S. (2002). Problems with access to dental care for Medicaid-insured children: What caregivers think. *American Journal of Public Health, 92,* 53–58.

Myers, J. E., & Gill, C. S. (2004). Poor, rural, and female: Understudied, undercounseled, more at risk. *Journal of Mental Health Counseling, 26,* 225–242.

Robinson, B. S., Davis, K. L., & Meara, N. M. (2003). Motivational attributes of occupational possible selves for low-income rural women. *Journal of Counseling Psychology, 50,* 156–164.

Thompson, V. L. S., Bazile, A., & Akbar, M. (2004). African Americans' perceptions of psychotherapy and psychotherapists. *Professional Psychology: Research and Practice, 35,* 19–26.

U.S. Census Bureau. (2004). *Income, poverty, and health insurance coverage in the United States: 2003.* Washington, DC: U.S. Government Printing Office. Retrieved Dec. 15, 2003, from http://www.census.gov/hhes/www/poverty03.html

World Health Organization. (2001). *The World Health Report 2001.* Retrieved January 2, 2004, from http://www.who.int/whr/2001/chapter1/en/index3.html

Chapter 3

Gay and Lesbian Social Justice:
Strategies for Social Advocacy

Pamela S. Lassiter and Bob Barret

Gay and lesbian people are perhaps the most misunderstood minority in our country. Children of other marginalized groups mature with the support of an extended community that includes parents, grandparents, neighbors, and even teachers and religious figures. For gay and lesbian youth, identity development takes place in the absence of family support and in the presence of almost universal stigma. As a result, these youth learn to hide who they are, and many gay and lesbian adults master the art of passing as heterosexual. They date and may even marry persons of the opposite sex. Some hide their sexual orientation even from themselves; others may create fictive lives, changing the pronouns of friends and lovers so that their family members and coworkers will not know they are gay. The loneliness of such an experience is enormous and can be very destructive to healthy personality development.

Recent national events have created social and cultural debates over civil rights for gay and lesbian people. For many sexual minorities, the personal is definitely becoming more and more political. Conversely, the political is having more of a personal impact. The success of domestic partner legislation in New Hampshire, gay marriage in Massachusetts and Oregon, and other initiatives contrasts with the 2004 presidential election, which was reportedly swayed by religiously conservative voters roused by fears of the so-called homosexual agenda. The recent emphasis on "moral values" has empowered many conservatives to push for a federal constitutional amendment banning gay marriage. This personal versus political dynamic is also visible in the 11 other states that recently passed protection-of-marriage acts defining marriage as an exclusively heterosexual right, and in a recent U.S. Senate vote denying employment protection to gays and lesbians under the Federal Non-Discrimination Act. These policy initiatives, combined with greater visibility of gay and lesbian characters on television and in film, seem to be creating both greater societal acceptance and greater opposition and discrimination toward gay men and lesbians.

In this chapter we provide a brief overview of some of the issues that gay men and lesbians face in their experience, including language, visibility, and the role of the mental health profession. We next explore the recruitment and choice myths about homosexuality, and conclude with a discussion of the ways counselors may become involved in working for social justice for sexual minorities, first by increasing awareness, becoming informed, and finding support, then by seeking out and taking advantage of the many opportunities in the community to promote the well-being of gay men and lesbians.

Issues

For many counselors, understanding the gay and lesbian experience is difficult. Few counselors receive formal training that includes sound information about this community. Counselors need to remember that the bewilderment most nongay people experience as they confront the stereotypes of homosexuality is minute compared to that of the man or woman who is trying to understand himself or herself as gay or lesbian. Important issues for both gay and nongay counselors and clients include the terminology used, the increased visibility of gays and lesbians, and the role of the mental health profession as social activists for gay and lesbian clients.

Terminology

The problem of language is a basic consideration:

- The term *homosexual* suggests that this community is just about sex. In fact, sexuality plays the same role in all of our lives regardless of sexual orientation. Gay men and lesbians are no more sexual than nongay people.
- The words *gay* and *lesbian* suggest these are the only two groups within the community of sexual minorities, but bisexual and transgendered people are also represented in the gay community. Although they exist in smaller numbers, the kind of discrimination and oppression they experience is like that of gay men and lesbians.

- The term *gay community* in many ways represents a myth; the community may be deeply divided, and various subgroups may have entirely opposite goals.
- The term *sexual preference*, commonly used by uninformed people, is considered offensive. More correct is *sexual orientation*, because preference suggests a choice that most sexual minorities do not recall making; gay persons, like nongay persons, discover their sexual orientations. Gay men and lesbians come out as a statement of integrity. They are simply being who they are. The only choice they make is how to integrate this part of their being into their lives.
- The term *coming out* implies a single event or action that one performs, when in reality this is a complex process that occurs repeatedly over a lifetime. Because people are assumed to be heterosexual, gays and lesbians have to decide when, where, and with whom they disclose their sexual orientation on an ongoing basis with varying consequences.
- The term *homophobia*, a word that has been used to describe those who support the oppression of gay persons, presents another language problem. Homophobia, or the fear of those whose sexual orientation is different, does add momentum to the efforts to suppress this minority. Recently, Logan (1996) suggested that a more accurate word is *homoprejudice*. Understanding gay and lesbian oppression as a prejudice, rather than as a fear, assists all of us as we consider how to work toward greater inclusivity.
- Deciding on the proper term to describe the person one loves also causes consternation. Is she my partner? That sounds like a business arrangement. Lover? Well, we are more than sex mates. How about significant other? Spouse? Life partner? This choice is often confusing both within and outside the gay community.

Language problems like these interfere with understanding and can make communication difficult. Just what is this gay, lesbian, bisexual, transgendered group of people, and what is it they want? The sheer complexity of these names tells us the community is complex. Trying to understand it is not going to be easy for most. In this chapter, for the sake of clarity, we use the words *gay* and *lesbian* to represent all sexual minorities, and the term *gay community* likewise includes all those whose sexual orientation is different from that of the majority.

Visibility

Until recently, gay men and lesbians pretty much stayed out of sight, denying the nongay community the opportunity to know who they were and how their lives were very like everyone else's. They lived primarily in a subculture that provided social support and protected them from having to be more visible. They had few role models and routinely encountered negative stereotyping in the news and entertainment media. They have been virtually absent even from professional literature.

Happily, that situation is changing rapidly. Gay liberation began in the 1960s when gay men and lesbians in New York City fought back against police who were harassing them. The Stonewall Riots marked the first time the gay community stood up publicly and said, "We have had enough! We will no longer let fear force us into silence against oppression." In the past 30 years, this movement has grown, and the community has become much more visible. Role models now appear in the news and on popular television shows. In the last decade, increasing numbers of gay men and lesbians are becoming parents outside of traditional heterosexual contexts through such means as donor insemination, surrogacy, and adoption (Brodzinsky & Patterson, 2002; James, 2002). An estimated 8 to 10 million children are being parented by gay men and lesbians in the United States (Ariel & McPherson, 2000). There are organizations like PFLAG (Parents and Friends of Lesbians and Gays) that represent the needs of this misunderstood minority. Churches, bowling and softball leagues, outdoor clubs, reading groups, political groups, square dance clubs, and rodeos for gay men and lesbians provide opportunities to learn about the community, to socialize, and to have fun. Combined with greater resources and fueled in part by those who were forced to be public because of their HIV status or because they wanted to become parents (Lassiter, Dew, Newton, Hays, & Yarbrough, 2004), the gay community is emerging with much vitality and energy.

Role of the Mental Health Profession

The mental health profession has played both a positive and a negative role in the increased visibility of sexual minorities. In the 1950s and

1960s, psychological research began to challenge the notion that homosexuality was inherently pathological. In 1973, the American Psychiatric Association removed homosexuality as a mental disorder from its *Diagnostic and Statistical Manual of Mental Disorders (DSM)*; soon after this move, psychologists, counselors, and social workers adopted more affirmative positions toward homosexuals. Nevertheless, research tells us that sexual minorities continue to experience discrimination when they seek mental health services.

Within 5 years of the American Psychiatric Association's depathologizing of homosexuality, researchers were reporting that mental health practitioners continued to have negative attitudes toward gay and lesbian clients (Fassinger, 1991; Martin, 1982). Clients reported that their counselors seemed reluctant to assist them as they explored questions about their sexual orientations. Counselors telling clients "you cannot be gay" or changing the subject when sexual orientation came up was not a rare experience. Even worse, many counselors insisted that clients work to change their sexual orientation. These experiences intensified rather than diminished the shame and guilt that sexual minorities had to overcome in order to create healthy and stable lives and probably did more harm than good.

Even decades later, the situation has not changed much. Garnets, Hancock, Cochran, Goodchilds, and Peplau (1991) reported that 99% of mental health practitioners provide services to gay men or lesbians, yet negative attitudes toward sexual minorities and practices persist. Fassinger (1991) identified studies revealing that mental health professionals are uninformed, work from heterosexist perspectives, and hold on to societal stereotypes about gay and lesbian people. McHenry and Johnson (1993) spelled out ways that nongay counselors may unconsciously collude with their gay and lesbian clients' self-hate. Failing to congratulate the gay client who has decided to live with a partner or not appropriately supporting clients who are distressed when their coming out has resulted in rejection are just two examples. The overwhelming finding is that gay persons rarely find mental health professionals who are informed and affirming about their issues. Our profession has failed to provide accurate information and high-quality services to sexual minorities.

Some of this bias and mistreatment is understandable. Few mental health professionals ever receive training in the unique needs of gay and lesbian clients. Graduate programs and accrediting agencies fail to include this population in their curricula or standards. Even programs at professional meetings are few and may not be well attended. The stigma attached to homosexuality prevents many of those who are curious or who see the need to improve their knowledge from learning about this often invisible group. The same shame and fear that make it difficult for many gay and lesbian persons to approach a clerk in a bookstore with questions about resources are also barriers for nongay persons. In a decade that emphasizes moral values, often as defined by the religious right, counselors' religious beliefs may encourage their own homophobia. Today, however, there are some who appropriately encourage gay-affirmative stances in counseling. Even among psychoanalysts, the change is evident. Frommer (1994), for example, advocated that "an affirmative stance that emotionally communicates to the patient the analyst's belief that homosexuality is a natural developmental end point for some individuals is viewed as the correct application of psychoanalytic technique with homosexual patients" (p. 215).

Myths About Homosexuality

Resistance to the acceptance of homosexuality is widespread. Because of the complexity of understanding this community, oppression may be fueled by those who see homosexuality as a moral issue. These opponents use religious organizations to lobby against gay and lesbian rights. One of their tactics is to perpetuate myths about the so-called gay lifestyle in order to justify oppression. Two principal myths about sexual minorities are most often advanced. In one, hate and fear of homosexuals are encouraged by trumpeting that the gay community "recruits" its members through the sexual abuse of children. In the second, prejudice against this community is supported by encouraging others to believe that homosexuality is a choice.

Although research studies could be assumed to refute such myths, research on homosexuality is not only extremely complex but also generates findings that are far from conclusive. Well-designed empirical studies of this population are complicated by a number of factors. One is that subjects are often difficult to find. Given the invisible nature of many gay and lesbian adults, locating what might be a representative sample is incredibly difficult. Another factor is that most gay persons who participate in research studies are self-selected, and most reports are based on self-administered inventories. Yet another factor is that sample sizes are generally small, and the demographic information that exists about the gay community is woefully incomplete. Even estimates of the population that is gay or lesbian may be in error. Estimates range from 3% to 15% of the population. A recent estimate by the Human Rights Campaign, based on the 2000 Census report, suggests that 5%

of the total U.S. population over 18 years of age is gay, lesbian, bisexual, or transgendered (Smith & Gates, 2001). The actual number, however, may never be known. Given these complications, research studies should be seen as merely an indication of what we may find once the science becomes more exact.

The Myth of Equal Rights

Because sexual minorities can hide their identities (pass as heterosexual), many in the general nongay population believe that gay and lesbian people already have equal rights. They do not and in some ways cannot understand the often subtle discrimination inherent in a world created by and for heterosexuals. The assumed heterosexual nature of our society ignores the fact that gay and lesbian people have equal access to resources only if they deny their identities. Examples include access to health-care benefits for partners and children, the right to file joint tax returns, and coparenting rights for gay families with children as well as many other legal protections given through state- and government-sanctioned marriage. The still commonly used "gay panic defense," a strategy used by defense lawyers to excuse hate crimes perpetrated on gays and lesbians, is more evidence that equality for homosexuals is far from secure. One should not assume that greater tolerance and visibility for gays and lesbians adds up to equal rights and protections. Although it is difficult to become and stay motivated for causes that do not affect us directly, it is imperative that nongay allies advocate regularly for civil rights reform for this minority population.

Gay and lesbian people contribute greatly to society in many roles. They live, work, and participate as citizens in 99% of counties in the United States (Smith & Gates, 2001). They regularly pay local and state property taxes that in large part fund schools, programs, and other resources that are often inaccessible to the gay and lesbian population. They even join gyms and other community activities in which family discounted memberships are not available to them. The many rights and privileges given to heterosexuals remain deceptively elusive for the gay community.

The Myth of Recruitment and Molestation

Gay men and women grow up in heterosexual families with heterosexual parents, brothers, sister, aunts, and uncles. Many report that they know they are different at an early age and eventually find ways to locate other gay people. They frequently describe feeling as if they are the "only ones who are attracted to persons of the same sex" until they discover others who are like them. This discovery can come through news reports, television talk shows, or local gossip about gay bars or events. The incidence of homosexuality among children raised by gay and lesbian parents appears to mirror that of children who grow up in nongay households (Barret & Robinson, 1990; Perrin, 2002). Interestingly, after 20 years of research comparing children from gay families with children from heterosexual families, findings show only one significant difference in outcome: The children of gay or lesbian parents tend to be more open to diversity in all its forms (Perrin, 2002).

The myth that gay men and lesbians seek out unsuspecting children and lure them into destructive sexual relationships that result in a homosexual orientation has never been substantiated and defies common sense. Equating homosexuality with child molestation is a myth that seems to be promoted primarily by conservative religious groups and the political candidates they endorse. In fact, U.S. Senate candidate Jim DeMint from South Carolina won his seat in the 2004 election based in part on a platform that called for the ousting of public school teachers who are gay or lesbian (Sheinin, 2004). The enduring power of this myth is evident in that it exists despite evidence that in more than 90% of the cases in law enforcement statistics, sexual abuse of children is a crime perpetrated by persons who are heterosexual (Voeller & Walters, 1978). Beliefs based on these myths continue to contribute to a lack of resources and healthy models for teens struggling with sexuality issues in our culture at large and in our school systems specifically.

The Myth of Choice

Is the more accurate term *sexual preference* or *sexual orientation?* This question and the appropriate terminology are at the heart of the debate about extending civil rights to gay men and lesbians. Although the research on the cause of homosexuality is not definitive, most experts believe that sexual orientation is fixed at a relatively young age and cannot be changed. Research findings are inconclusive about the genetic bases of sexual orientation. As the science of genetics becomes more exact, however, many predict that homosexuality will in fact be proved to have a biological basis.

Some persons suggest that gay men and lesbians just need the correct kind of counseling in order to become heterosexual. However, respected professional organizations such as the American Psychiatric Association (1993), the American Psychological Association (1997), the National Association of Social Workers (1992), and the American Academy of Pediatrics (1994) have published position papers noting that so-called reparative or conversion therapies that attempt to change sexual orientation from homosexual to heterosexual are ineffective and inappropriate. Although there may indeed be some short-term behavior change, these therapies are ineffective in terms of real success at changing sexual orientation (Edwards, 1996).

Many gay men and lesbians respond to the question of choice by reminding the questioner that the notion of deciding to join a minority that encounters daily discrimination, faces rejection from parents and friends, and creates enormous career conflicts could not be rational (Marcus, 1993). Most nongay persons are unable to recall that they ever "decided" to be heterosexual. The same is true for gay men and lesbians. The choice that exists is how one will merge sexual orientation and sexual behavior into a sexual identity and whether to be "out" or closeted.

The Lesbian and Gay Equal Rights Movement

By understanding the problems and myths, counselors may begin to see that gay men and lesbians need and deserve the kind of social support that advocacy can create. The general absence of laws that protect this minority from discrimination in employment, housing, and public accommodation supports the prevailing negative attitude about homosexuality and institutionalizes prejudice. Unlike other countries such as Belgium, the Netherlands, Switzerland, New Zealand, South Africa, and Canada, the United States is no longer at the forefront of equal rights initiatives for gay and lesbian citizens.

According to a U.S. General Accounting Office report (1997), same-sex couples are denied more than 1,000 federal benefits and protections of marriage. In all states but Vermont, they are denied most of the state rights and responsibilities that come with marriage. Employees in same-sex relationships are not given the right to take care of a seriously ill partner or parent of a partner under current provisions in the federal Family and Medical Leave Act. Same-sex couples are denied Social Security benefits when a life partner dies. U.S. citizens who have same-sex partners are prohibited from petitioning for their partners to immigrate, forcing thousands of couples to live apart or to migrate to one of the 15 countries with more hospitable immigration laws. Under federal tax laws, same-sex couples are taxed on employer-provided insurance benefits for domestic partners whereas married spouses receive those benefits tax free (Bennett, 2002).

Still, in communities across the nation and in all kinds of organizations, gay men and lesbians are becoming more visible and demanding that discrimination end. Jamie Nobozny, for example, successfully sued school administrators and counselors who refused to protect him from antigay violence in the Ashland, Wisconsin, school system ("Lambda wins," 1997). He endured threats, intimidation, beatings, and humiliation from his classmates. He was trapped in bathrooms, kicked, and even urinated on while school officials took no disciplinary action. His and his parents' requests for assistance were ignored with the admonition that such actions were only natural given his open homosexuality. However, the federal jury thought otherwise and awarded him just under $1 million. This successful suit sends a clear message about the consequences of failing to extend civil protection to gay persons. Contrary to some public discourse, the gay rights movement does not seek special rights, but rather equal protection under the law.

Strategies for Social Action

Counselors who seek to become advocates for gay men and lesbians have abundant choices. Activities on behalf of sexual minorities are not just opportunities to participate in the worldwide human rights movement, they also offer a unique chance to assist as this largely invisible minority becomes visible. Those who were active in the civil rights struggles of the 1950s and 1960s or who worked for women's rights in the 1970s were present during a similar time. Today the momentum of the gay and lesbian rights movement is increasing, and those who join in this effort can make a difference that will endure for generations. The power of heterosexual allies to create change in gay and lesbian rights is immeasurable. This truly is one of the cutting edges, both in our nation and in our profession.

A first step toward social action is to become more aware of individual biases and prejudices. The question is not, "Are you homoprejudiced?" Rather, the proper orientation to this issue is, "How can I become more aware of my homoprejudices and limit the ways they influence my behavior?" One starting point is to take a self-inventory to discover where individual prejudices are likely to influence your action. Consider your feelings if others thought you might be lesbian or gay. Ask yourself how you might feel if you were to discover your child or another family member was gay or lesbian. How might you respond if you knew your child's favorite teacher was a lesbian woman or a gay man? Visit a gay bookstore in the city nearest you. Observe your feelings as you mingle with other customers. Check out your reactions to people, books, and other objects there. Discover your areas of discomfort and discuss them with a colleague. Understanding of self is essential for those who seek to join in the gay rights movement.

Another starting point is to take an inventory of heterosexual privileges. As with all prejudices, the majority is often unconscious about their privileges, and most people take heterosexual rights for granted. A class was asked to brainstorm heterosexual privileges, and they came up with a list of more than 30 items, ranging from the right to marry to the right to hold hands in public. Class members used this list to examine their internal reactions if such privileges were granted to gay men and lesbians. Here, they stumbled upon some of their discomforts with equality for gay men and lesbians. Thinking of a same-sex couple being married or publicly displaying affection was uncomfortable for these students. These same discomforts would certainly influence their verbal and nonverbal responses to gay clients. Responding to the complex challenge of seeking out information and increasing their appreciation for the gay experience will help all who initiate social action for this community.

A second step toward social action is to become informed. Educate yourself about the current needs, both political and personal, of the gay and lesbian community. Join a local chapter of PFLAG or a local GLBT political group to learn about specific social action steps you can take now. The bottom line rests with improving counseling services. Far too many gay men and lesbians continue to access counselors who are uninformed about their needs. Isay (1989) and Dworkin and Gutierrez (1992) provided useful starting points for understanding the unique mental health needs of sexual minorities. Workshops, journal readings, informal conversations with professional colleagues, and sound supervision will enhance service delivery and individual counseling skills.

Learning about gay and lesbian persons is not difficult. For those who are involved in clinical work, asking gay clients to become teachers is an easy and respectful method of learning more. Let them know you are not as informed as you want to be, and they will tell you a lot about resources in your community. You can also enhance your understanding of sexual minorities through reading. Marcus (1992, 1993) has written two books that give basic information about the personal and political experiences of sexual minorities. Don Clark, one of the first psychologists to write about the gay experience, created a classic in *Loving Someone Gay* (1995). These three books are a useful foundation. Do not overlook the spiritual lives of gay men and lesbians, because for many, spiritual practices may be important sources of support (Barret & Barzan, 1996). It is also vital to recognize that the gay community, like all communities, is composed of various cultures. Attitudes about same-sex relationships vary greatly among different cultures. Learn the specific ways Native American, African American, and Asian American gay men and lesbians respond to their unique cultural backgrounds (Greene, 1997). Being a gay or lesbian person of color often leads to an accentuated experience of oppression. The convergence of strong homophobic cultural norms with sexual identity development creates unique, difficult, and complex struggles (Fukuyama & Ferguson, 2000).

A third essential step toward social action is to find support for yourself. Clearly, those who become connected to the gay rights movement potentially face negative consequences. Emotional responses to homosexuality are deeply ingrained, and most people avoid examining topics that create discomfort. However, in all communities there are gay and nongay persons who are willing to get involved in social activism on behalf of sexual minorities. These individuals provide key support but never totally eliminate the threat of attack from groups or individuals who oppose gay rights. For example, a man who directed an award-winning play that had gay characters was attacked by an elected official and called gay even though he is not. A teacher who listened to a young woman talk about her sexual orientation was admonished by her principal. School boards and other legislative bodies around the country are considering laws that forbid counselors from speaking with young people about sexual orientation without a parent being present. Proceeding carefully and anticipating resistance are essential.

The place to start building support is with the person with the most authority. For example, an intervention to encourage a local newspaper to expand its coverage of the gay and lesbian community began with a letter to the publisher. His encouragement set the tone for what became an ongoing dialogue with editors and reporters that has resulted in a much more realistic presentation of the gay community. In another example, an intervention to encourage a business to include sexual orientation among the protections for all employees began with speaking to the president of the firm and resulted in immediate success. If the person in charge is not afraid, those who work in other responsible positions are also not likely to be afraid.

Changing institutionalized homoprejudice is just one area for activism. Fortunately, within all communities there are abundant opportunities for action that involve changing attitudes before policies.

Among these are the following:

- *Attend a training.* At professional meetings, training on counseling interventions that are useful with gay and lesbian clients is becoming routine. These "starter" experiences enable the beginner to improve direct service delivery. Each summer, the Lesbian and Gay Health Conference, sponsored by George Washington University Medical School, is offered in different parts of the country and provides the most up-to-date mental health information on issues ranging from HIV disease to political oppression.

- *Teach others about gay, lesbian, bisexual, and transgendered issues.* Become an advocate for the inclusion of gay and lesbian counseling in graduate programs. Ask program coordinators to see that this population is included in routine coursework on multiculturalism and diversity. Seek out the gay and lesbian students in your graduate program, ask them to discuss ways they need support, and invite them to speak to faculty and students about their experiences. If no one seems willing, put together a training program and offer it as a unit in formal or informal trainings. Help teachers and other school officials understand the unique needs of gay and lesbian parents as they interact with schools. Check to see if your library carries books that represent gay literature or subjects. If not, give the librarian a list of titles. If so, let the librarian know you appreciate it. Speak to church and civic groups about the need for more inclusive policies.

- *HIV disease has had a major role in the emergence of the gay community.* Learn about HIV and the many ways that gay and nongay persons who are influenced by this disease need support. Also work to make sure others understand that gay and HIV are not interchangeable. HIV is not a gay disease. Equating the two does a disservice to both.

- *Join AGLBIC, the Association for Gay, Lesbian, and Bisexual Issues in Counseling.* This is the newest and fastest growing division within the American Counseling Association. Members are gay-affirming counselors who work in various settings. This is a good source of information and a networking opportunity through which you can learn about social activism for gay men and lesbians around the country.

• *Contact your local gay community.* Many larger communities have a gay and lesbian switchboard that fields telephone calls. These organizations are excellent sources of information and resources. Contact the one nearest you. If there is not one, look into getting one organized. Find the gay newspaper that covers your town or region. Some may be statewide and others may be local. They are a valuable source of information and resources.

• *Work in your community.* There are an endless number of issues that will enhance the lives of gay men and women. Speak to your coworkers about their experience with gay and lesbian clients. See if there are ways to improve service delivery. How about advertising in local gay community newspapers about the availability of gay-positive counseling services? Or contact gay and lesbian mental health professionals and ask them to conduct a training session in your workplace. Is there a youth group for sexual minorities in your community or school? If so, seek ways you can lend support. If not, consider starting one. Gay and lesbian youth need all the support and advocacy they can find in order to make it through adolescence with a healthy sense of identity.

• *Confront prejudice among your coworkers, friends, and family.* Challenges to seemingly harmless jokes and attitudes are much more powerful coming from a nongay person.

• *Ask about the availability of domestic partner benefits at your place of employment, whether they pertain to you or not.* If they are not available, question the policy and encourage your employer to add sexual orientation as one of the protected classes in employment nondiscrimination policies.

• *Speak to political and religious leaders.* Becoming an advocate for human rights for all persons is one way you can speak up on behalf of gay and lesbian citizens. Contact local elected officials and state your availability to serve as a resource when gay-related issues come up. Encourage school boards to include issues of sexual orientation in human sexuality training and in health education curricula. Write letters to members of your state legislature or Congress. In the summer of 1996, at both the state and federal levels, laws were passed that protected heterosexual marriage from the threat posed by the Hawaii Supreme Court's decision to legitimize homosexual marriage. A federal Employment Nondiscrimination Act that would have outlawed discrimination based on sexual orientation in the workplace failed to pass the U.S. Senate by one vote. This bill was reintroduced. Educate your community about why it is needed and encourage your representatives to vote for it.

• *Understand the diversity within the gay community.* Throughout all your activism, understand that, like all communities, the gay and lesbian community is diverse. There are subgroups based on race, age, gender, particular interests, and even parental status, and these groups often disagree about what needs to be done. Broaden your understanding of these issues. Realize that older gay men and women often experience isolation within their own culture, and that some gay professionals believe that choosing a career that involves working with children is totally inappropriate. Even political groups within the community may be at odds with each other. In spite of all the commotion, there is no "homosexual agenda" that the community as a whole would support.

• *Start a support group.* In many medium- and small-sized cities there are few places for gay men and women to gather and have serious conversations about their lives. Consider starting a support or therapy group that might assist in reducing isolation. Advertise your group so that the larger community understands that gay persons are present and need support services.

• *Contact PFLAG.* Parents and Friends of Lesbians and Gays is an international organization that seeks to provide support. Many of these groups meet regularly in mainstream churches and are invaluable in assisting parents and friends who are trying to understand the ways homosexuality is affecting their lives. If there is no chapter in your community, start one.

• *Speak at city, county, and state official meetings when antigay issues come up.* In many cities and towns, antigay legislation is passed without much discussion. Speaking up against discrimination at meetings where these laws are presented is one of the most effective ways to be gay positive. If you are uncomfortable being so public in your advocacy, call your local officials or take them to lunch and let them know you support the gay community. Encourage local law enforcement officials to gather data on hate crimes against gay men and lesbians. Offer to teach a unit on gay and lesbian issues in police academy training programs.

- *March in gay pride marches or participate in public protests about antigay efforts.* Know that across the nation June is Gay Pride month, and in all larger communities, there will be marches and other celebrations of gay and lesbian freedom. Pay attention on National Coming Out Day (October 11) and congratulate those you see coming out or come out more fully yourself. On National Coming Out Day, put *The Advocate,* an award-winning biweekly magazine about the gay community, in your waiting room. Certainly, your gay and lesbian clients have the right to see their publications there along with other reading material.

- *Put books with gay and lesbian themes on your bookshelf.* Clients will see these books and understand that you are interested in gay issues. Place gay symbols such as rainbow flags, triangles, or the Human Rights Campaign equality sign around your office or on your door. Gay and lesbian clients are likely to feel safer and more willing to talk about their lives when they see supportive books and symbols in your office.

- *Educate yourself about sexual identity development models and be prepared to support your clients in the process.*

Conclusion

There are unlimited opportunities to promote the well-being of gay men and lesbians who live our as neighbors, coworkers, family members, or fellow citizens. Most of us grew up without much accurate information about homosexuality, and the general invisibility of the gay community does not encourage the public to look beyond the negative stereotype that is prevalent. One day, the stigma about being gay or lesbian will lessen. The communities that truly seek diversity will understand that tolerance is several steps away from the ideal in which persons are prized because of their differences and all people enrich our life experiences because of their differences.

Among the many opportunities for counselors to become activists for social change perhaps the most daunting lies in assisting the gay and lesbian community as it attempts to gain social justice. Discrimination and homoprejudice exist in virtually every community as well as within the mental health profession. Counselors are in an ideal situation to assist all of us as we come into fuller understanding of sexual minorities and appreciation for the unique contributions gay men and lesbians make to enrich our culture.

The time for social action on behalf of gay men and lesbians is now. As the gay and lesbian community steps more fully into the light, this movement offers all of us the chance to participate in making our communities more inclusive and stronger because of our diversity. A rare opportunity exists today to further a movement that will make a difference in the way all of us live our lives. As more and more people become familiar with the unique needs of lesbian and gay people, the American spirit of fairness will lead most institutions to change their policies so that all persons are more equal. Get involved in the gay rights movement. Your life and the lives of others will be better because of your contribution.

References

American Academy of Pediatrics. (1994). Homosexuality and adolescence. *Pediatrics, 92,* 631.

American Psychiatric Association. (1993). *Gay and lesbian fact sheet.* Washington, DC: American Psychiatric Association.

American Psychological Association. (1997). *A statement on the effectiveness of reparative therapy for homosexuals.* Washington, DC: American Psychological Association.

Ariel, J., & McPherson, D. (2000). Therapy with lesbian and gay parents and their children. *Journal of Marital and Family Therapy, 26,* 421–432.

Barret, R. L., & Barzan, R. (1996). Spiritual experiences of gay men and lesbians. *Counseling and Values, 41*(1), 4–15.

Barret, R. L., & Robinson, B. E. (1990). *Gay fathers.* Boston: Lexington Books.

Bennett, L. (2002). *State of the family: Laws and legislation affecting gay, lesbian, bisexual, and transgender families.* Human Rights Campaign Foundation. Retrieved January 2, 2005, from http://www.hrc.org

Brodzinsky, D. M., & Patterson, C. J. (2002). Adoption agency perspectives on lesbian and gay prospective parents: A national study. *Adoption Quarterly, 5,* 5–23.

Clark, D. (1995). *Loving someone gay.* Berkley, CA: Celestial Arts.

Dworkin, S., & Gutierrez, F. (1992). *Counseling gay men and lesbians: Journey to the end of the rainbow.* Alexandria, VA: American Association for Counseling and Development.

Edwards, R. (1996). Can sexual orientation change with therapy? *APA Monitor, 27*(9), 49.

Fassinger, R. E. (1991). The hidden minority: Issues and challenges in working with lesbian women and gay men. *The Counseling Psychologist, 19,* 151–176.

Frommer, M. S. (1994). Homosexuality and psychoanalysis: Technical considerations revisited. *Psychoanalytic Dialogues, 4,* 215–233.

Fukuyama, M. A., & Ferguson, A. D. (2000). Lesbian, gay, and bisexual people of color: Understanding cultural complexity and managing multiple oppressions. In R. M. Perez, K. A. DeBord, & K. J. Bieschke (Eds.), *Handbook of counseling and psychotherapy with lesbian, gay, and bisexual clients* (pp. 81–105). Washington, DC: American Psychological Association.

Garnets, L., Hancock, K. A., Cochran, S. D., Goodchilds, J., & Peplau, L. A. (1991). Issues in psychotherapy with lesbians and gay men: A survey of psychologists. *American Psychologist, 46,* 964–972.

Greene, B. (1997). *Ethnic and cultural diversity among lesbians and gay men.* Thousand Oaks, CA: Sage.

Isay, R. A. (1989). *Being homosexual: Gay men and their development.* New York: Avon Books.

James, S. (2002). Clinical themes in gay and lesbian parented adoptive families. *Clinical Child Psychology and Psychiatry, 7*(3), 475–486.

Lambda wins Nobozny case. (1997, Fall/Winter). *The Lambda Update, 14*(1), 1–2.

Lassiter, P., Dew, B., Newton, K., Hays, D., & Yarbrough, B. (2004). *Self-defined empowerment in gay and lesbian parents: A qualitative examination.* Manuscript submitted for publication.

Logan, C. (1996). Homophobia? No. Homoprejudice. Yes. *Journal of Homosexuality, 31,* 31–53.

Marcus, E. (1992). *Making history: The struggle for gay and lesbian equal rights, 1945–1990.* New York: HarperCollins.

Marcus, E. (1993). *Is it a choice?* San Francisco: Harper San Francisco.

Martin, A. (1982). Some issues in treatment of gay and lesbian patients. *Psychotherapy: Theory, Research, and Practice, 19,* 341–348.

McHenry, S. S., & Johnson, J. W. (1993). Homophobia in the therapist and gay or lesbian client: Conscious and unconscious collusion in self-hate. *Psychotherapy: Theory, Research, and Practice, 30*(1), 141–151.

National Association of Social Workers. (1992). *Position statement: "Reparative" or "conversion" therapies for lesbian and gay men.* Washington, DC: National Association of Social Workers' National Committee on Lesbian and Gay Issues.

Perrin, E. (2002). Technical report: Coparent or second-parent adoption by same-sex parents. *Pediatrics, 109*(2), 341–344.

Sheinin, A. (2004, October 4). Gays should not teach, DeMint says in debate. *State Newspaper* (Columbia, SC), p. A1.

Smith, D., & Gates, G. (2001, August 22). *Gay and lesbian families in the United States: Same-sex unmarried partner households (A preliminary analysis of 2000 United States census data)* (A Human Rights Campaign Report). Retrieved December 31, 2004, from http://www.hrc.org

U.S. General Accounting Office. (1997, January 31). *Report B-275860.* Retrieved January 2, 2005, from www.gao.gov/archive/1997/og97016.pdf

Voeller, B., & Walters, P. (1978). Gay fathers. *The Family Coordinator, 27,* 149–157.

Chapter 4

Combating Ageism:
Advocacy for Older Persons

Jane E. Myers

The aging of populations is a worldwide phenomenon that is "unprecedented . . . pervasive . . . enduring . . . and has profound implications" (United Nations, 2002). Within the United States, the *graying of America* is a term often used to describe demographic changes over the past 100 years that have resulted in older persons no longer being a small and relatively insignificant minority but an increasing and significant minority group within the total population. At the same time, popular use of the term *gray-out* suggests that a fading into the background occurs as one grays. These statements suggest two important issues for exploration: Our population is growing older, and growing older may not be a fully positive experience. It is important for counselors to understand these changing demographics from a macro, or societal, perspective as well as from a micro, or individual, perspective.

In this chapter, I explore demographic changes in the United States with a focus on the aging of our population and within-group factors that predispose some older persons to significant personal and social risk. I describe counselors' responses to the graying of America and the consequences of these responses to the needs of older persons. I discuss ageism, an unreasonable prejudice against persons based on chronological age, in relation to its personal impact on older individuals. The chapter concludes with a consideration from both macro and micro perspectives of recommended strategies and actions for counselors, and with suggestions for counselor advocacy and empowerment relative to population aging and the needs of older individuals.

Statement of the Problem

Although only 4% of the U.S. population were over age 65 at the turn of the 20th century, more than 12% were in this age group in the year 2000. Increases in the numbers of older persons have become increasingly dramatic, with a 10.2% increase from 1992 to 2002 compared with a 13.5% increase for the under-65 population and a 38% increase in the number of persons aged 45–64 who will reach age 65 in the next two decades. By the year 2030, the 65 and older population will more than double over the 2000 figure of 35 million and will make up more than 20% of the population, or one in every five persons (Administration on Aging, 2003b). As the population ages, the age structure of our society is changing as well. In the first half of the last century, that structure was diagrammed as a pyramid, with younger persons as the large base, adults in the middle, and older persons as the tapering top. A structure smaller at both top and bottom and with a bulge in the middle is a more accurate picture of our society at present. Eventually, the original structure will invert, with a small base of younger persons and a large top of older adults; in fact, Armbrust (2001) observed that by 2014, for the first time, there will be more older people than younger worldwide.

The increased numbers of older persons are due to a variety of factors, the most obvious one being that people are living longer. Improved medical care, enhancements in our ability to treat chronic disease, the ability of persons with disabilities to live long and productive lives, the eradication of diseases such as polio, and decreased infant mortality are among the factors that have prolonged the human life span. In addition, increased affluence and better public health measures, including controlled water supplies, inspection of foods in grocery stores and restaurants, and universal inoculations against diseases such as tuberculosis and many varieties of the flu have resulted in a better and healthier standard of living for most persons.

Persons born in our country in 1900 could expect an average life span of only 47 years. Persons born in 2001 can expect to live to be more than 77 years of age—30 years longer. Interestingly, a survivorship phenomenon exists in regard to aging, such that the longer a person lives, the longer the person can expect to live. A person reaching age 65 in 2001 could expect to live an additional 18.1 years, for a total of more than 83 years of life. Gender differences in life expectancy change this figure significantly, in that women reaching age 65 may expect to live another 19.4 years while men can expect another 16.4 years. Life expectancy also varies by race, and at birth Whites may expect to live

6 years longer than Black persons. This discrepancy declines with age, perhaps because Blacks who survive to old age may be healthier than their White counterparts (Administration on Aging, 2003a).

Currently, African Americans comprise only 8% of the older population compared to approximately 12% of persons under age 65. About 84% of older Americans are Caucasian, 5% are Hispanic, and 2.3% are Asian. Although the reasons for these differences are complex, a history of poverty, lower socioeconomic status, a lifetime of low-paying employment, lack of access to health care, and poor nutrition are among the reasons for shorter life spans among minority populations. The results of institutional racism do not disappear in the later years, but rather are compounded by the stigma associated with advancing age.

The statistics cited here underscore the fact that aging has become a normative life experience. Interestingly, the negative attitudes toward older persons that have been prevalent throughout history remain in the present day (Nelson, 2002): Although we all have only the two choices of growing old or dying young, if we grow old, all of us will be subject to ageism. Ageism is similar in nature to racism, sexism, disabilityism, and other -isms, and refers to an unreasonable prejudice toward persons based on their advanced age. Similar to all prejudices, ageism functions to limit the daily lives and optimal potential of persons as they grow older.

In the United States today, individuals may expect to live three-fourths or more of their lives as adults and one-third or more as older adults. As a consequence, counselors are in a position in which some of their clients, or the families of their clients, will inevitably be older individuals. In addition, counselors who do not die young may expect to experience aging as a personal process as well. Given these facts, it is important to examine how counselors have responded to aging, and to consider how we may respond in the future as the older population increases in size and the phenomenon of ageism continues its traditional historical path.

Counselors' Responses to Population Aging

Blake and Kaplan, writing in 1975 after a careful study of counselors' responses to aging, stated the situation briefly and unequivocally: "Older people are the forgotten and ignored" of the counseling profession (p. 176). Blake and Kaplan's challenge was accepted by the American Counseling Association, which subsequently contracted with the U.S. Administration on Aging for five grant projects designed to alter counseling training, counseling research, and counseling practice with older persons. Over a span of 14 years, and with funding in excess of $1.2 million, these projects were designed to develop curriculum and training materials as well as provide counseling services to older persons (Myers, 1995).

The first two national projects on counseling older persons developed curriculum resources for graduate-level training and for training paraprofessional service providers to older persons. The third used a train-the-trainers approach that resulted in more than 3,200 practicing professional counselors receiving training in basic aspects of aging and gerontological counseling. The fourth project stressed the need for all counselors to graduate with some knowledge of aging and the needs of older persons, and thus developed curriculum modules for infusion into each of the core areas of counseling preparation specified in the standards of the Council for Accreditation of Counseling and Related Educational Programs (CACREP, 2001). In addition to a curriculum manual, a series of training videotapes were developed and disseminated through the ACA (and are now available through Insight Media Corporation).

The final national aging project targeted counselor training at the pre- and in-service levels through the development of competency statements (see http://www.uncg.edu/~jemyers/jem_info/docs/competencies.htm/). Two sets of statements were developed, the first set addressing the minimum competencies required of all counselors for work with older persons and their families, in both individual and group sessions. The second set of competencies formed the basis for a proposal to the National Board for Certified Counselors (NBCC), which resulted in the National Certified Gerontological Counselor (NCGC) credential. An additional proposal to the board of CACREP resulted in the implementation of a new set of standards for a specialty in gerontological counseling training. By all reports in the early 1990s, coursework in gerontological counseling was the third fastest growing area of counselor preparation, lagging behind only substance abuse and marriage and family counseling. Yet the potential for growth of the specialty, seemingly very positive, did not materialize.

By 1997, only about 200 persons had achieved certification as a NCGC, and as a consequence of lack of interest, NBCC suspended the NCGC credential. Only two counselor training programs have achieved accreditation for their gerontological counseling specialty, and many programs have discontinued gerontological counseling courses due to lack of student and faculty interest. These numbers were far lower than expected, and the trends have not been in the direction predicted by the results of multiple national surveys of professional counselors and of counselor training programs (see Myers, 1995, for a description of these studies). In short, counselors' responses to the aging of our population indicate disinterest.

As an example of this disinterest, it is helpful to look at enrollments in counselor education courses that emphasize gerontological issues. Although studies of these courses have not been conducted, anecdotal evidence gathered at annual meetings of groups such as the Association for Adult Development and Aging, especially the Committee on Standards, and the Association for Counselor Education and Supervision, especially the Adult Development, Aging, and Counseling Interest Network, suggests that enrollments in such courses are uniformly small. The author struggles annually with university enrollment expectations and the threat of course cancellation for low enrollments. For the past 10 years, no more than 3 to 4 counseling students out of 120 in the counselor education program have enrolled in the course entitled "Counseling the Older Adult" or its successor developed in an attempt to increase enrollments, "Counseling for Mid Life and Aging." As a consequence, instructors are forced to open enrollment to persons with various backgrounds who are majoring in a variety of academic disciplines. The result is a need to modify the curriculum and teach a broad-based course focusing on basic gerontology, with counseling interventions taught primarily at the paraprofessional level. Thus even those few students who choose to specialize in gerontological counseling are being shortchanged in the education they receive for this specialty. Though the quality of life of older persons and their families is at stake, sadly, counselors seem uninterested in this very special minority that all of us will one day join.

The Consequences of Professional Neglect

The lack of interest in issues of aging among professional counselors and counselor educators has significant consequences, both professional and personal, large and small. For counselors to assume that the ageism so pervasive in our society either does not affect them or does not apply to them represents a very serious form of denial and makes us all contributors to the problems faced by older persons. Denial of aging until one actually experiences the aging process during the midlife decades and beyond seems to be the norm.

Two excellent examples of denial are found in the work of two major theorists in our field: Donald Super and Erik Erikson. Super's early and widely used career development theory incorporated five stages of career development: fantasy, exploration, establishment, maintenance, and decline. As Super neared the age of 60, his theory underwent significant changes. What emerged was a "life-career rainbow," in which a variety of life roles (e.g., student, parent, worker, leisurite) were defined and shown to be active throughout the life span. In talking with Super about these changes over dinner one evening, he indicated to me the importance of what we learn about life as we grow older. At the time we were celebrating his 80th birthday, and he was planning a series of speaking engagements in the United States and abroad, and a trip to the Soviet Union with his son.

Erik Erikson described eight psychosocial stages of life span development, ending with the challenge of ego integrity versus despair. He described the last stage as a time when healthy older persons look back on their lives and gain a sense of well-being with the life they have lived, and a sense of wisdom relative to the life span and its various challenges. In recent years, research with older persons has suggested that the struggle for integrity is largely resolved in the late 60s and early 70s, which was the end of the life span during the time that Erikson first wrote his theory. When he reached his seventh, eighth, and ninth decades, Erikson began to reconceptualize the later stages of life, suggesting that a stage beyond that of integrity in fact existed. This stage of *very old age* was not fully defined before his death; however, both Erikson's wife and others continue to speculate on the challenges of the ninth stage relative to autonomy, particularly given the many possible physical challenges of the later years.

Every year or so I receive a call from an experienced professional counselor who has, early into her (usually, though sometimes it is a male) retirement years, become greatly concerned about the problems of aging. She is certain that counselors need to respond, and that the way to get this response is to provide training in how to work with older persons. She notes that curriculum materials and videotapes are badly needed. When I express my agreement with her and explain that this very rationale was used successfully between 1977 and 1990 to gain grant funding to develop training materials and projects for counselors, and that all of the materials were disseminated to counselor education programs around the country, her response does not surprise me. Two of the things she will predictably say are "I never heard of your work" and "Isn't that wonderful—but you were ahead of your time. I think people are ready to listen now." Sadly, I have to disagree. People, predictably, have a wonderful capacity for denial, and denial of aging is a major issue in our society.

Crose (1991) alerted us to an important issue in working with older persons: that counselors respond from a personal knowledge base. As a consequence, we may fail to recognize our own stereotypes and misconceptions as they affect our older clients; we may fail to meet effectively the mental health and counseling needs of older persons and their families; and we may—and often will—fail to recognize or actualize opportunities to advocate for the needs of older persons. Can we afford to wait until we ourselves grow old to begin to recognize and deal with these concerns? I suggest that we cannot. Ageism affects all of us now, if we recognize that aging is a part of the life span, not apart from the life span.

Ageism: What, Where, When, How, and Why?

Ageism was defined earlier as an unreasonable prejudice against persons simply because of their chronological age or perceived chronological age. It is important for counselors to understand what ageism is, as well as where, when, how, and why it occurs, as a first step in combating this irrational but pervasive phenomenon.

What Is Ageism?

Robert Butler first described ageism in his 1975 Pulitzer Prize–winning book *Why Survive? Being Old in America*. Numerous studies since that time have confirmed the pervasiveness of negative attitudes toward older people. These attitudes have been identified in persons of all ages, including children, adolescents, young and midlife adults, and older persons themselves. Ageism has been found among a variety of health-care providers, including nurses, psychologists, psychiatrists, and counselors.

Old age is viewed as a time of undesirable physical, emotional, social, and financial losses. Older persons are viewed as a group living with poverty, disability, and depression. In spite of abundant research establishing that four out of five older persons are living above the poverty level, that more than 95% of older persons are living in the community and only about 5% in institutional settings, and that rates of depression peak in middle rather than later life, these stereotypes persist. Older persons are erroneously viewed as emotional and financial drains on their adult children (most support their adult children emotionally as well as financially), as wanting to live with their adult children (what adult wants to give up his or her independence after a lifetime of being in charge?), as being disinterested in sex (there is no age limit to sexuality), and as being chronically ill (86% of older persons experience one or more chronic physical impairments, yet most are able to live actively and independently). These stereotypes persist in spite of recent research suggesting that most older people age "well" and that healthy aging, particularly among the young-old (ages 60–75), is the norm. In fact, even many old-old persons (ages 85+) continue to function independently and enjoy life. In general, older persons are resilient in responding to stress, transitions, and change, and experience a lower incidence of mental illness than younger individuals (Gatz & Smyer, 2001; Myers, 2003).

An interesting and widely held stereotype, supported by clichés such as "you can't teach an old dog new tricks," is that older persons are set in their ways. Research reveals that reaction time slows with age but that intelligence does not decline. Older persons can learn equally well, although the pace of learning and learning styles may need to be modified. After all, sorting through a lifetime of accumulated knowledge in the process of assimilating new information certainly requires more time than sorting through only a few years of information. How great is the fund of knowledge in a person 70 years of age, and how many neurons are involved in information processing for such an individual, compared to the fund of knowledge for a person 50 years younger? We lack research in this area, but the possibilities are intriguing.

Research is available to support the perspective that change is unlikely to occur in later life. A front-page headline in a local newspaper that attracted my attention in this regard read "If You're 30, You're Finished" (Costa, 1992). In the article, Dr. Paul Costa of the National Institute on Aging, a well-known and certainly reputable researcher, reported that "by the time people reach 30, their basic personality traits— anxiety, assertiveness, or openness—are virtually 'set like plaster.'" This somewhat pessimistic view of development seems to argue against the prospects of continued development throughout the life span. If people do not change, what rationale is there for counselors to work with adults over the age of 30? Certainly, change is difficult at any age, so the basic question is whether change is more difficult in later life. I think that as we get older, we become more and more like ourselves and less and less like anyone else. If we are set in our ways when we are young, chances are excellent that we will be this way when we are old. The preponderance of research suggests that personality is consistent with aging, not discontinuous.

The developmental perspective suggests that individuals are capable of change and growth across the life span, even if that change means becoming more firmly who they are. In the process of coping with changing life circumstances, personal change and growth can certainly be an asset. Those who fail to cope, or who continue to try to resolve new problems with old, tried-and-true-but-no-longer-effective coping resources, are likely to be among the older persons who could benefit most from counseling interventions. From an ageist perspective, believing that older persons cannot change relieves service providers of the challenge of trying to help them change. However, multiple studies of mental health interventions reveal that older persons have the capacity for change and continued growth, regardless of chronological age. (See Myers & Harper, 2004, for a review of these studies.)

Ageism: Where, When, How?

Ageism is both formal and informal, obvious and subtle. Formal aspects of ageism, such as mandatory retirement ages in some professions, are relatively easy to identify. I am a private pilot who frequently attends aviation training seminars and reads aviation publications. One of the most important characteristics of a safe pilot is good judgment in dealing with the aviation environment, from weather to mechanical systems to navigation to air-traffic control. Judgment, from all accounts, is gained only through experience. Thus it remains an enigma why federal legislation requires airline pilots, whose reflexes may have slowed a tiny bit from the aging process but whose competence as defined by judgment is at an all-time career high, to retire at the age of 60—with an estimated 20 years of useful life remaining! Quick arithmetic here reveals that these pilots are expected not to work for the remaining 25% of their life span, like it or not.

How many counselors are aware of and responsive to legislation concerning child abuse in their state? The answer should be 100%. Among these same counselors, how many are familiar with the mandatory laws regarding elder abuse, which also exist in each state? How about the laws concerning grandparent visitation rights or age discrimination in employment (which extends to persons between the ages of 40 and 70)? The fact that our mental health system gives far greater attention to the needs of young persons than of old reflects our pervasive lack of public awareness and support for programs for our older population. This is a form of ageism.

The prejudices held by health-care providers likewise limit the choices of older persons. Managed care is a particular case in point because medical treatment and hospital-stay limitations are based on studies with young persons, who are known to heal more quickly and require larger doses of medication than their older counterparts. Many of the medical problems and "dementias" of older persons are thus iatrogenic, or physician-induced, occurring, for example, when prescriptions calibrated for use with young persons, usually males in their 20s, are prescribed for older persons. Fortunately, these problems can be alleviated or reversed with proper medical care, especially under the treatment of trained geriatric physicians.

Family, friends, and neighbors of older persons—the informal support network—also are a source of ageism that acts to limit the lives of older people. Family members often are among the first to suggest to an older person that "you can't do that at your age!" Well-meaning loved ones overprotect older persons, interpret their thoughts, expect them to accept the "facts of aging," and charge them with "getting old" if they cannot remember a name or forget where they placed their keys. The same actions in a younger person cause few if any reactions from the same family members. If younger persons express a legitimate distaste for life when circumstances are undesirable, friends may suggest counseling or offer empathy. With older persons, the same behavior often results in a label of crankiness.

Some time ago I overheard a conversation between a retired father and his 30-something daughter that made an impression on me. Dad was dealing with a difficult situation over home repairs and was trying to work with several builders and insurance agency representatives. He had several conversations in which he tried to accommodate their schedules and restrictions while still trying to make the point of what he needed to have accomplished and when. When the daughter heard about the situation, her suggestion (made forcefully and aggressively) was that he immediately obtain an attorney and a backup statement from a builder she knew to "make" them do what was needed. Dad, a competent and effective problem solver throughout his nearly 60 years of life, indicated he would probably continue on the path he had started. The daughter's response shocked all within earshot: "What's the matter, Dad? Does aging mean you stop producing testosterone?" This statement was clearly ageist, not to mention offensive. However, it was not uncharacteristic of what many younger persons think in relation to aging and older persons, though fortunately most are not quite as outspoken as this young woman was with her father. By the way, Dad's method resulted not only in resolution of all of the problems but also in multiple follow-up calls from supervisors to ensure that he was satisfied with the work.

Ageism is reflected in words, deeds, and actions. It is reflected in the things we do for older persons (e.g., speaking louder or slower than normal to be sure we are heard and understood), our responses to older persons (e.g., becoming visibly frustrated when standing behind them in the grocery line, even though we may experience the same wait behind a mother with small children but not feel annoyed), and the things we fail to do with regard to older persons (e.g., consider them for paid tasks, not just volunteer work opportunities) Whenever we make choices or perform actions based on a person's age, we may have succumbed to ageism.

A special note is necessary concerning the use of language to instill ageist attitudes, beliefs, and behaviors. This is a subtle and extremely pervasive means for the perpetuation of negative stereotypes about older persons. The first and most prominent example of such language use is found in the frequently used term *the elderly. The elderly* implies that all persons who are older share some common characteristic or characteristics, usually with negative connotations as discussed earlier. *The elderly* are often seen as frail, ill, rigid, slow, boring, forgetful, and depressed. In actuality, more than 35 million persons are in this age category, and what they share in common is largely a function of chronological age. One could say that the elderly population consists of persons aged 65 and over, or aged 60 and over, or whatever chronological age one chooses, and that statement would be correct. Other statements concerning the elderly run the risk of being accurate for only a portion of the older population. Thus, use of the term *the elderly* functions to stereotype, label, categorize, and in many instances, denigrate the lives of older persons.

Johnson (1996) found the word *elderly* to be

> dangerous in the sense that armies of elders can ingest the word and start thinking of themselves as "the elderly" rather than as potent, respectful, and quite independent persons of worth . . . costly as well as dangerous . . . by relegating perfectly good elders to the ranks of something less than useful; dependent and generally incapable. Such imputations subvert one's sense of self and contribute to the flight toward a legitimate, but most dependent social role, the role of patient. (pp. 9, 13)

Fortunately, in 2001 the American Psychological Association finally took a stand on this issue and observed in its popular style manual that "*Elderly* is not acceptable as a noun and is considered pejorative by some as an adjective" (p. 69). The power of language cannot be overemphasized. The point has been made that many negative attributes are associated with terms such as *aged, elderly,* and *old.* It is noteworthy that older persons who perceive themselves to be younger than their chronological age, either physically or mentally, report that they feel better and perceive their health status to be better than persons of the same age who self-identify as old. Chronological age is not the issue; rather, subjective age is what seems to correlate with positive mental health and wellness (Degges-White & Myers, in press).

Ageism: Why?

Perhaps it is only human nature that results in ageism. We tend to fear what we do not understand, and the processes of aging are not well understood. We also know most about older persons in institutional settings because those who are independent are far more difficult to access and study. Those in institutional environments tend to be the frailest older persons, and those who experience the most serious and disabling conditions. Not surprisingly, the association of aged with disabled results in fears of aging being equated with fears of disability. Thus, most studies of older persons reveal that loss of independence is the greatest fear associated with aging. In addition, although death may be denied as a relatively remote prospect in the younger years, for older persons it becomes an increasing reality. Fears of death contribute to fears of aging, the aging process, and being old.

Predominant social values that place a high priority on full-time, paid employment also contribute to ageism. Retirement constitutes a loss of employment, and retired persons are viewed, often unconsciously, as unemployed. Thus the retired role, although not well defined, is also not highly valued.

Competition for resources and roles between persons of different ages or generations contributes to ageism. For example, the media frequently remind us that the Social Security system is running out of money, so that younger persons who are paying Social Security taxes today are unlikely to benefit by receiving pensions from this fund in their retirement years. At the same time, the media remind us that today's older persons, who are living longer than expected, are drawing a disproportionate share of Social Security funds. Younger persons reading this information cannot help but reflect on the implication that they are paying for the lifestyles of the older generation while facing an uncertain future in regard to the funding of their own later years of life.

Self-Fulfilling Prophecies: The Personal Impact of Ageism

Although it is important to understand the dynamics of negative social attitudes toward older persons, any discussion of ageism is incomplete without consideration of the personal impact of social devaluation. Pedersen (1999), Sue and Sue (2003), Lee (1997), and others have explained in detail the processes of minority identity development. These authors have postulated that persons who belong to minority groups tend to internalize the predominant social perceptions of their group. Older persons are members of a minority group as well as members of our society. It is normal for them to internalize the predominant views of aging, often holding these views for a lifetime before they reach old age.

The consequences of internalizing negative attitudes include both a dislike of their peers and low self-esteem. Older persons may fail to develop relationships with their age peers and may become isolated because they prefer not to associate with "those old people." When they internalize negative societal beliefs about older persons, a sense of personal devaluation, vulnerability, and decreased sense of self-efficacy is likely to result. When they begin to question their abilities, they may begin to withdraw from normal activities and associations, leading to further loss of self-esteem. This process can become cyclical and devastating.

The social breakdown process, first described by Kuypers and Bengtson (1973), explains how ageism creates a climate in which older persons may be devalued, and where normal responses result in social and psychological withdrawal and decline. At the same time, this process implies a variety of interventions that have the potential to interrupt, halt, or even reverse this process. Ultimately, prevention efforts undertaken from both individual and societal perspectives and across the life span offer the potential for a better quality of life for older people.

Action Strategies for Counselors

Counselors are uniquely positioned to have a positive impact on the lives of older persons. As developmentalists, we recognize and support the possibility of positive growth across the life span. We also recognize and are able to respond to all individuals in need of assistance in coping with the normal circumstances of life, such as career entry, career change, retirement, second career, marriage, divorce, remarriage, parenting, grandparenting—the list could go on for pages. What is important is the arena in which we choose to apply these skills. What I recommend here is a dual approach that includes both a macro, or societal, perspective with the counselor as an agent for social change, and an individual approach that includes the counselor as an individual and as a change agent for other individuals.

The Macro Perspective: Advocacy and Empowerment

Empowerment refers to actions intended to help people help themselves or create personal power, whereas *advocacy*, as used here, refers to actions taken on behalf of others to ensure that empowerment does, in fact, occur. What is important in bringing these two actions together is the intended outcome: to create environments in which individuals are able to live their lives effectively and with a sense of well-being, in which they can choose to change themselves or their life circumstances to achieve their goals and live life more fully. Three aspects of environmental change that counselors can directly affect are policies, services, and accurate information.

Empowerment and Advocacy Through Policies

Laws and policies at all levels—international, federal, state, county, local, agency, business and industry, caregiver—can affect the quality of life of older persons. I provided examples earlier of mandatory retirement laws, elder abuse laws, and grandparent visitation laws, and I could provide numerous other examples. Counselors need to examine laws and policies in all settings with consideration for the needs of persons across the life span. Where laws are restrictive, outdated, or nonexistent, advocacy for change is needed.

Working with policymakers and legislators at all levels must be a priority. Counselors have important input to give in the development of policies and laws about job sharing, second career training, phased retirement, older worker skills, and a variety of additional issues that affect quality of life and opportunities for older persons—if we make ourselves part of the decision-making process. We need to support legislation and policies that enhance the rights of older persons and help to defeat or replace policies that limit the rights of older persons. Those rights, first identified with the passage of the Older Americans' Act (OAA) in the 1960s, are relevant today (see Appendix A). That act continues to set national policy for older Americans. We need to have presence with lawmakers when the OAA is reauthorized. Although the OAA includes provisions for counseling, the counseling specified is specific to legal counseling, nutrition counseling, and health counseling. Professional counseling can and should be added.

In 1977, the ACA introduced a set of proposed revisions to the OAA entitled the Older Persons Comprehensive Counseling Assistance Act of 1977. These revisions proposed, among other things, the development of a national clearinghouse of information on the provision of counseling services to older persons, the development of a plan in each state for providing comprehensive counseling services to older persons, grants to states to provide counseling assistance to older people, grants for training and retraining counselors to work with older people, and research and demonstration projects to identify and develop effective services, interventions, and programs to meet the mental health and counseling needs of a broad array of older people. The bill was unfortunately neither approved nor funded. It was reintroduced several times during congressional sessions in the early 1980s, each time with little success. I use the term *little* here intentionally. Although the amendments were never approved, the repeated introduction of the legislation did serve as a means of information and advocacy for both professional counselors and the counseling needs of the older population. Perhaps at some point this legislation could be reintroduced through coalitions with other mental health service providers, which offers the best hope of success.

Empowerment and Advocacy Through Services

If older persons are to experience the benefits of preventive and remedial mental health services, counselors need to be trained and available to work with them. In the absence of federal legislation that mandates and funds gerontological counselor training and counseling services for older persons, it is up to us to ensure that these things occur.

Counselors have limited opportunities for training in gerontological issues. Infusion of gerontological counseling into counselor preparation has not been uniform. If the current status of counselor training is to change, we need to approach decision makers in the educational arena, specifically counselor educators and educational administrators. Any time we get a chance to fill out a professional development needs assessment form or to comment on the quality of education we received from our alma mater, we have an opportunity to say we need more training in working with older persons.

Counselor educators are in a unique position to advocate for counselor training in gerontological issues. Educators can revise existing curricula to include more courses and curricular units specific to life span and later-life issues. In addition, to promote the infusion model, when choosing texts for core courses counselor educators can take care to select ones that include issues of aging. Doing so will send messages to publishers and textbook authors that life span concerns must be incorporated in effective counselor training.

Although it is important to train counselors to be effective in working with older persons, and also important to encourage accreditation of training programs for specialty training and certification of gerontological counselors, these measures will result in discouraged program graduates if the job market does not provide opportunities for employment commensurate with their training. Social services for older persons grew out of welfare programs for older and disabled persons. These programs traditionally were staffed by social workers. Hence, it is not surprising that many jobs in the aging network list social work training and credentials as prerequisites, and many of these positions are legislatively mandated or enabled. For example, each state has laws relating to long-term-care facilities, formerly known as nursing homes. These laws uniformly require that such facilities employ social workers. Accreditation agencies ensure that these staff are in place. Unfortunately, counselors are not mandated in this legislation.

Counselors, especially gerontological counselors, are relative newcomers to the field of services for older persons. We cannot expect automatic acceptance, especially when positions are legislatively controlled. Again, there is a clear need to advocate for the inclusion of counselors in state and federal job classification systems. We also need to advocate with employers in the community, such as community mental health centers, to ensure that counselors are hired in positions earmarked for geriatric mental health provision. The crossover among training, credentialing, and advocacy is increasingly evident here. We cannot present counselors as the best-trained professionals for such positions in the absence of strong training programs, accreditation, and certification to document our claims. Of course, we must provide effective mental health interventions for older persons and their families, which requires a comprehensive knowledge base relative to this population.

Empowerment and Advocacy Through Accurate Information

The fact that not all older persons are alike has been established; but what *are* older persons like? We know enough about this population to have defined at least three subsets of older persons: young-old, middle-old, and old-old, with some lifestyle and health issues marking the differences between the three groups. We know that ethnic and cultural differences within the older population are significant, and that many of the problems of ageism are less apparent or not relevant for older minority individuals within the family and cultural environment. But minority individuals who also are old are placed in a situation of double jeopardy, being subject simultaneously to the effects of -isms related to age as well as race. The addition of disabling conditions, gender, and sexual orientation as factors increases the potential for discrimination.

If counseling practice is to be informed, it must be informed with accurate information. Support for research on effective interventions and outcomes for a variety of circumstances that older persons experience is essential. To the extent that older persons are like persons of other ages, counseling research will inform work with this population. However, there is some evidence that strategies and techniques vary in effectiveness among older people, and that some interventions may be more effective at certain times and with certain older persons. (See Myers & Harper, 2004, for a discussion of evidence-based practice with older persons.) Outcome research studies are essential if we are to learn what works, when, with which older persons, experiencing which conditions, and under what circumstances. We also need to develop interventions that help older persons conceptualize and develop lifestyles oriented toward health and wellness in their later years.

The Micro Perspective: The Counselor as Change Agent

Someone has to implement those strategies for reducing the effects of ageism just discussed, and that someone could be a professional counselor. To be effective as advocates for social change, counselors must first determine their own needs for attitudinal change. Then, in addition to receiving training to prepare them for work with older individuals and groups, counselors may find opportunities to advocate on an individual basis for older persons.

Counselor: Know Thyself

As members of an ageist society, we counselors are likely to hold negative views of older persons or negative perceptions of the potential of older clients for growth and change. It is imperative that we explore those attitudes prior to beginning work with older clients. Awareness training is available at professional conferences as well as in graduate coursework. This training should include adequate opportunities for personal exploration and discussion in a safe environment where group members are available to challenge gently our mistaken beliefs and perceptions about older clients. We need also to explore our own fears and feelings about the processes of growing older, and of death and dying. Again, this may occur in professional training or through individual or group counseling.

   Those of us who wish to work with older persons need to examine our motivations so as to ensure that our goal is to empower, not to patronize or "do for" older people what they seemingly cannot accomplish for themselves. If we find that we feel sorry for our older clients, it will be hard to help them. If transference is an issue, in that our older clients may remind us of older relatives or friends, then we are unlikely to accept our clients as individuals and to respect them enough to confront their issues caringly and challenge them to continue to grow. Do we discriminate between older relatives and older clients, between older friends and older persons in general? If we find that we tend to treat all older persons alike, then we may be experiencing transference. If we find that we think all older persons are like the ones we know best, then we are likely to be engaging in stereotyping and ageism—for better or for worse. As part of our professional development as counselors, we should meet, learn about, and work with a variety of older persons, those who are independent as well as those who are frail or ill.

Finally, we need to examine our language when we speak with and about older persons. The words we use, the phrases we choose, and the intonations we unconsciously employ reflect the real meanings behind what we say. We need to become more aware of what we say, how we say it, and what we really mean; that is, what our true attitudes toward our older clients are. Some suggestions for revising our language so as to avoid stereotyping older persons are found in Appendix B. These suggestions require and can result in significant attitudinal changes, thus helping to reduce ageist beliefs and attitudes in ourselves and in those with whom we interact when speaking with and about older persons.

Advocacy: Daily Opportunities to Be an Agent for Change
We each have opportunities on a daily basis to be advocates for change. We need to become more aware of these opportunities and take advantage of them for ourselves and our older clients. When recommending individuals for paid or volunteer positions or for advisory and governing boards, we have the choice to recommend only people who are younger or to include people who are older. When we decide for older persons that they "would not be interested," "would not want to use their time in that way," "would not have the energy," or "would not be able to present new and creative ideas," then we must catch ourselves being ageist and take a different approach. Perhaps it is the older people we know who are not appropriate choices. If so, the problem could be that we don't know enough older people to make a good choice. We may need to broaden our social and professional networks and actively create opportunities to interact with a variety of older people. To do so will enrich our lives as well as theirs.

Conclusion

The effects of ageism, or prejudice against older persons, are pervasive. Negative attitudes and stereotypes function to deny older persons the right to engage fully in the benefits of life in our country, demeaning their sense of self-efficacy and resulting in a lower overall quality of life. Ageism is perpetuated by individuals as well as organizations.

Counselors have vital roles to play as change agents working both with and on behalf of older persons. We need to view ourselves as advocates who can effect changes in laws, policies, and society. At the same time, we can help older persons live more effective lives through developmental interventions aimed at helping them live life more fully throughout the life span. To be effective agents of change, we first need to examine our personal beliefs and biases, and develop healthy, respectful, positive, wellness-enhancing attitudes toward older persons. Because aging is a universal experience, all our efforts to assist this population will result in significant personal as well as professional gains. We will realize the ultimate benefits both vicariously, as we watch our clients change and grow, and personally, as we ourselves experience the joys and challenges of the processes of aging.

References

Administration on Aging. (2003a). *Facts and figures: Statistics on minority aging in the U.S.* Retrieved February 3, 2005, from http://www.aoa.gov/prof/Statistics/minority_aging/facts_minority_aging.asp#LifeExpectancy/

Administration on Aging. (2003b). *A profile of older Americans.* Washington, DC: Author. Available online at http://www.aoa.gov/prof/Statistics/profile/2003/profiles2003.asp/

American Association of Retired Persons (AARP). (1984). *AARP's truth about aging: Guidelines for publishers.* Washington, DC: Author.

American Psychological Association. (2001). *Publication manual of the American Psychological Association* (5th ed.). Washington, DC: Author.

Armbrust, R. (2001). Professional women dedicate confab to arts/media ageism. *Backstage, 42*(39), 3–4.

Blake, R., & Kaplan, L. S. (1975). Counseling the elderly: An emerging area for counselor education and supervision. *Counselor Education and Supervision, 15,* 156–157.

Butler, R. (1975). *Why survive? Being old in America.* New York: Harper and Row.

Council for Accreditation of Counseling and Related Educational Programs. (2001). *The CACREP Standards*. Alexandria, VA: Author.

Crose, R. (1991). What's special about counseling older women? *Canadian Journal of Counselling, 25*(4), 617–623.

Costa, P. (1992). If you're 30, you're finished. *Greensboro (NC) News and Record*, p. 1.

Degges-White, S., & Myers, J. E. (in press). Transitions, wellness, and life satisfaction: Implications for counseling midlife women. *Journal of Mental Health Counseling*.

Gatz, M., & Smyer, M. (2001). Mental health and aging at the outset of the 21st century. In J. E. Birren & K. W. Schaie (Eds.), *Handbook of the psychology of aging* (5th ed., pp. 523–544). San Diego, CA: Academic Press.

Johnson, R. (1996, winter). Chronologically endowed vs. elderly: One gerontological counselor's pet peeve. *Adultspan*, pp. 9–13.

Kuypers, J. A., & Bengtson, V. L. (1973). Competence and social breakdown: A social-psychological view of aging. *Human Development, 16*, 37–49.

Lee, C. (1997). *Multicultural counseling: New approaches to diversity* (2nd ed.). Alexandria, VA: American Counseling Association.

Myers, J. E. (1995). From "forgotten and ignored" to standards and certification: Gerontological counseling comes of age. *Journal of Counseling & Development, 74*, 143–149.

Myers, J. E. (2003). Coping with caregiving stress: A wellness-oriented, strengths-based approach for family counselors. *Family Journal, 11*, 1–9.

Myers, J. E., & Harper, M. (2004). Evidence-based effective practices with older adults: A review of the literature for counselors. *Journal of Counseling & Development, 82*, 207–218.

Nelson, T. (2002). Ageism: Stereotyping and prejudice against older persons. Cambridge, MA: MIT Press.

Older Americans' Act of 1965, Pub. L. No. 89–73.

Pederson, P. (Ed.). (1999). *Multiculturalism as a fourth force*. Philadelphia: Brunner/Mazel.

Sue, D., & Sue, S. (2003). *Counseling the culturally diverse: Theory and practice* (4th ed.). New York: Wiley.

United Nations. (2002). *World population ageing: 1950–2050*. New York: Author. Available online at http://www.un.org/esa/population/publications/worldageing19502050/index.htm

Appendix A

Rights and Obligations of Older Americans: 1961 White House Conference on Aging

Rights of Senior Citizens

Each of our senior citizens, regardless of race, color, or creed, is entitled to

1. the right to be useful;
2. the right to obtain employment, based on merit;
3. the right to freedom from want in old age;
4. the right to a fair share of the community's recreational, educational, and medical resources;
5. the right to obtain decent housing suited to needs of later years;
6. the right to the moral and financial support of one's family so far as is consistent with the best interest of the family;
7. the right to live independently, as one chooses;
8. the right to live and die with dignity; and
9. the right of access to all knowledge as available on how to improve the later years of life.

Obligations of Aging

The aging, by availing themselves of educational opportunities, should endeavor to assume the following obligations to the best of their ability:

1. the obligation of each citizen to prepare himself or herself to become and resolve to remain active, alert, capable, self-supporting, and useful so long as health and circumstances permit and to plan for ultimate retirement;
2. the obligation to learn and apply sound principles of physical and mental health;
3. the obligation to seek and develop potential avenues of service in the years after retirement;
4. the obligation to make available the benefits of his or her experience and knowledge;
5. the obligation to endeavor to make himself or herself adaptable to the changes added years will bring; and

6. the obligation to attempt to maintain such relationships with family, neighbors, and friends as will make him or her a respected and valued counselor throughout his or her later years.

Appendix B

Changing Our Ageist Language

Strategies for changing our ageist language include attention to vocabulary and phrases and statements. The following suggestions are taken from *AARP's Truth About Aging: Guidelines for Publishers*, 1984.

Avoid words and phrases which

- demean—such as *old maid, old codger, old fool, over-the-hill, has-been;*

- patronize—such as *cute, sweet, dear,* and *little;*

- stereotype older persons—such as *passive, dependent, nagging,* and *shrewish* as applied to older women, and *dirty old men* and *leches* as applied to older men—or are negative physical descriptors—such as *deaf, dentured, fragile, frail, withered, doddering.*

Replace ageist statements with nonageist statements. For example:

Ageist: At 72, she is confused, apathetic, withdrawn, taking no interest in anything.
Nonageist: All her life she has been confused, apathetic, withdrawn, taking no interest in anything. No wonder she's that way at 72.

Ageist: What does an old man like that want with a sports car?
Nonageist: Now that his children are on their own, he can have that sports car he has always wanted.

Ageist: That man she's with must be half her age!
Nonageist: Men of all ages find her attractive.

Ageist: Ask my grandmother. I'm sure she'll do it. She always has plenty of time!
Nonageist: Ask my grandmother. She always tries to make time to help others.

Chapter 5

Counselor Advocacy for Access: Addressing the Challenges of Disability

Ellen S. Fabian

Two challenges to understanding disability in a social justice context are that disability itself has no consensual definition and that even an individual's perception of his or her own disability can fluctuate throughout the life span. A second aspect that differentiates disability as a status from race or gender is that an individual may be born with a physical or mental impairment; may develop one through a variety of chronic illnesses throughout life; or may traumatically acquire one through an accident, war injury, or disease. Scholars in disability studies have commented that disability is a universal experience, in that "if we are not disabled now, we probably will be if we live long enough" (Albrecht & Bury, 2001, p. 585).

One consequence of these issues is that whereas it is easy to distinguish and count people by gender, age, or some other enduring characteristic, it has proven difficult to define and count individuals with disabilities. As a result, estimates of the number of people with disabilities, even in the United States, vary markedly from 14 million to more than 50 million, depending on the definition used and the source of the "count" (Burkhauser & Houtenville, 2003). Although there may be disagreement about the number of individuals with disabilities, one sustaining feature of disability in the United States and the rest of the world is the link between it and poverty. In other words, no matter how disability is counted, estimates from the United States and from the United Nations suggest that, worldwide, people with disabilities are the most impoverished group of people in any society (Schriner, 2001). In the United States, for example, 73% of single mothers with disabilities are living in poverty. Even when employed, people with disabilities earn on average only 63% as much as their nondisabled counterparts, and more than 10% of full-time workers with significant disabilities fall below the poverty line, a rate more than three times that of people without disabilities (LaPlante, Kennedy, Kaye, & Wenger, 1996).

These facets of disability provide a context, or lens, through which counselors from different backgrounds can begin to understand the disability experience in America. The purpose of this chapter is to describe the historical and contemporary context of disability and rehabilitation in the United States, and to examine how counselor roles and functions need to change in response to a changing social and political context for disability. To accomplish this, the chapter presents the context of disability and rehabilitation in the United States; reviews the major models of disability; describes the competing nature of rehabilitation counselors' roles; and emphasizes the importance of a social justice paradigm for rehabilitation counselors.

Context of Disability

Disability affects individuals from all racial, ethnic, and socioeconomic groups. However, the incidence of disability differs among different cultural and ethnic groups in the United States, with the highest rates being among Native Americans (21.8%), followed by African Americans (21.7%) (Bradsher, 1996). A number of reasons have been put forth to explain these differences, including poverty, inadequate access to preventive health care, physical environments that place individuals at higher than average risk for accidents and disease, and genetic predispositions (Alston, 2004; Smart & Smart, 1997). In addition, the impact that a disability has on an individual's life can be mediated through socioeconomic circumstances or cultural background. For example, a college professor with a spinal cord injury who uses a wheelchair will experience less financial and social impact from that disability than would a food service worker or maid. The differential effect of disability in this example suggests that the idea of disability needs to be examined from an environmental and social context, a notion that has important implications for social advocacy.

Until the 1960s, disability in the United States was defined and treated as an impairment or problem located within an individual that could not be "cured" but could be ameliorated through medical intervention, use of prostheses or other devices, or specialized training. An individual who became (or was born) blind, for example, was equipped with a guide dog and a cane and provided orientation and mobility training to manage the physical world. An individual who was unable to use her legs was provided a wheelchair or braces and perhaps retrained to work at home or within limited accessible locations. Starting in the 1960s, the disability rights movement catalyzed, and with it came an emphasis on redefining disability as a problem in the social and built environment, rather than as a problem or impairment in the individual (Hahn, 1985). So, for example, the "treatment" for the individual who was blind or used a wheelchair became not simply canes or guide dogs, but ramps, talking stoplights, curb cuts, and a thousand other features designed to eliminate barriers that impeded people with disabilities from full participation in the community. In other words, the disabling aspect of any particular impairment became the social and environmental barriers that prevented access. Similar to the civil rights movement and the resulting laws that were enacted to address barriers to full participation for ethnic minorities, the disability rights movement pushed for enactment of federal laws that began to strip away barriers to full participation and access. The passage of the Americans With Disabilities Act in 1990 (P.L. 101–336), with its mandates requiring accessibility in the physical environment as well as antidiscrimination measures in employment, is frequently heralded as equal to the major civil rights legislation enacted for minority groups in the United States.

Models of Disability

The shift in redefining disability as a civil rights issue rather than a medical problem was described as a paradigm shift in the general understanding of disability and the treatment of individuals with disabilities. This paradigm shift had implications for how services were prescribed and provided, as well as how professional services, such as rehabilitation counseling, were perceived. The lingering effects of the medical model, however, have had significant consequences for rehabilitation counseling and service provision. Therefore, it is useful to examine some of these in order to understand how the field can evolve within a social justice paradigm.

The Medical Model

The impairment model of disability, also called the medical model, treats disability as a disorder of the person, and treatments are provided to attempt to alter the individual through medical intervention, skills training, psychological counseling, and so on (Scotch & Schriner, 1997). The medical model has had a number of enduring consequences that have important implications for social advocacy today. One of these consequences was the explosion of the disability and rehabilitation treatment sector, and the second was the growth of the disability benefits system.

One consequence of the medical model can be seen in the proliferation of medical and psychosocial treatment services and interventions for people with disabilities. This growth has been particularly phenomenal in the past two decades or so, during which time public and private funding sources for disability services grew dramatically (Albrecht, 1992). This growth was essentially the result of a number of legal, social, and demographic trends that continue to influence treatment and service delivery. In terms of demographics, people in the United States (and around the world) live longer and thus are more likely to experience disability at some time in their lives. In addition, new diseases, unhealthy lifestyles, and violence contribute to an ever-growing population of individuals with disabilities. In terms of the legal and social arena, federal laws and policies were enacted to provide specialized services or treatment to people with disabilities through injuries as a result of work situations (via the Occupational Safety and Health Administration, or OSHA), through the aging process (via the Social Security Administration, or SSA), through wars or conflict (via the Veterans Administration, or VA). These contributed to an explosion of health- and rehabilitation-related businesses designed to treat the resulting illnesses or disabilities. In fact, estimates are that the health-care sector providing medical and rehabilitation treatment will generate more than $2 trillion in 2007 (Gold, 1999). Naturally, access to these health-care resources is highly correlated with socioeconomic status, education, and ethnic minority background factors—with those who have the most to gain from such treatment services having the least access to the best (Albrecht & Bury, 2001). In the context of the medical, or impairment, model of disability, the explosion of the disability business sector has paired profit with acceptance of the "sick or disabled role" (Albrecht & Bury, 2001; Parsons, 1951); thus encouraging an identity that emphasizes incapacity rather than inclusion.

Another force that has sustained the medical model of disability is the disability compensation system. Although the complexity of the system is beyond the scope of this chapter to describe, it may be important from a social justice standpoint to understand some of the basic mechanisms. Essentially, there are two sources of disability compensation: public and private. The most prevalent public source is the Social Security Administration, which provides compensation in the form of disability insurance payments to children and adults who are found to be totally incapacitated to perform work or social roles.

The explosion in disability compensation benefits over the past decade or so is frequently mentioned as a national economic problem (Mead, 2004), with more than $75 billion annually going for disability income transfer programs (Mitra & Brucker, 2004). Research on disability insurance beneficiaries has found that receipt of such benefits functions as a disincentive to employment, in that individuals are generally fearful of losing their benefits if they return to work (Killeen & O'Day, 2004). As a result, less than 1% of disability beneficiaries leave the rolls each year to return to work (Mitra & Brucker, 2004), not a surprising statistic given the fact that eligibility determination requires that the individual be found "totally incapacitated." It should be noted, however, that such programs, particularly Supplemental Security Income (SSI), which is payment to disabled beneficiaries who have never worked, provide subsidies well below federal poverty guidelines (Burkhauser & Stapleton, 2004).

In the private sector, disability compensation programs are obtained from insurance companies, typically through employer-provided insurance plans (Brodwin, 2001). As with the publicly provided programs, beneficiaries of such programs need to document their inability to return to work due to a medical condition that has lasted 6 months or longer. Although the benefit amounts and nature of these programs differ depending on the specific company, the insurance plan, and state regulations, most disability cash payments tend to be very modest, and also probably contribute to the correlation between disability and poverty cited earlier in the chapter.

The Civil Rights Model

The civil rights model of disability is based on the assumption that disability is the product not of the individual but of environment barriers, social stigma, and discrimination (Scotch, 1988). The root of the civil rights model of disability is social activism, and it emerged in tandem with the civil rights movements of the 1960s, growing out of a similar sense of social, financial, and community discrimination and stigma (Hahn, 1985). Some people with disabilities experienced similar types of extreme social stigma and sanctions as other did ethnic minority groups in the United States. These included incarceration in state institutions without recourse to constitutional due process protections (Fink, 1992), forced sterilization and other extreme medical procedures without informed consent (Pfeiffer, 1999), and denial of certain civil rights (such as the rights to vote and marry), that are the cornerstones of a free society (Barnartt, Schriner, & Scotch, 2001).

The civil rights model was also a backlash against the medical model and its assumptions regarding functional deficits and inadequacies, its paternalistic values regarding the role of the professional in the helping process, and its neglect of self-determination in service delivery systems (Bichenbach, 2001). Not only was the civil rights model of disability concerned with environmental and political inequities, it was also a reaction to social stereotyping and stigma. The comment, "My disability is how people respond to my disability" (Gill, 2001, p. 362), captures the idea that social attitudes toward an individual with a disability are more salient than the actual functional issues in preventing access and opportunity.

The civil rights model of disability, like the civil rights movement for ethnic minorities, rested on the assumption that the enactment of various antidiscrimination and equal opportunity laws could level the playing field for people with disabilities. Civil rights advocates felt that physical barriers preventing access to community, social, employment, and other domains were an expression of social stigma and discrimination policies that prevented people with disabilities from living, learning, and working in society on an equal basis with nondisabled people (Hahn, 1985). The preamble to the Americans With Disabilities Act (P.L. 101–336) reflects this model of disability by stating that people with disabilities constitute a "discrete and insular minority," thus making the case that individuals with disabilities are similar to other minority groups. Although the civil rights, or minority group, model of disability presents a social activist framework for challenging political, economic, and social inequalities, there are several significant issues unique to the disability community.

First, the degree of social stigma and discrimination depend to a large extent on the type and nature of the disabling condition. Studies have shown that people with psychiatric disabilities, for example, encounter significantly more social stereotyping than those with spinal cord injuries (Wahl, 1999). Second, apart from the deaf community, there is really no unifying culture or language among people with disabilities; in fact, people with disabilities are a heterogeneous group in terms of ethnicity, gender, age, religion, culture, and so forth. The intersection of disability with some of these other characteristics, such as race, presents a complex picture of individual identity and social and political consequences. The experience of a poor African American male with a significant physical disability, for example, is going to be substantially different from that of a White male with a back injury, even though both may be disability compensation program beneficiaries (Smart & Smart, 1997).

Another difference is that, unlike people from different ethnic minorities, the majority of people with disabilities have an acquired condition and have not experienced marginalization and social stereotyping from birth; thus, they may r eject the notion of belonging to a minority group. Even though Fine and Asch (1988) found that 74% of the Americans with disabilities who responded to their survey report a sense of common identity as a minority group, other researchers have found a reluctance among people with disabilities to be identified by stigmatizing labels with frequently negative connotations (e.g., *retarded, lame, blind*). Related to this latter point is the fact that the Americans With Disabilities Act, as well as other disability nondiscrimination laws, require that individuals with disabilities meet a medical incapacity standard ("a physical, mental or emotional impairment that substantially limits functioning in one or more major life activities"). Thus, individuals with disabilities who are seeking civil rights protection need to rely on standards associated with the medical model in order to achieve the protections guaranteed by these equal rights laws (Bichenbach, 2001).

Social and Cultural Construction of Disability

Although the civil rights, or minority group, model of disability remains predominant in the United States, it doesn't entirely account for the fact that disability is a construct whose meaning shifts depending on each individual's perspective, environmental background, and social and cultural context (Banks, 2003; Marshall & Largo, 1999; Neath, 1997). The social construction of disability considers these perspectives in suggesting that the definition of disability hinges on the social and cultural context in which it occurs. "Culture determines the meaning of a disability; the impact it has on the person with the disabilities . . . and the community" (Banks, 2003, p. 380). This perspective has important implications for cross-cultural and multicultural approaches to understanding and counseling individuals with disabilities, as well as for identity development.

For example, on a cross-cultural basis, what one society or culture defines as disability may have no meaning in another culture. Groce (1998) pointed out that the categorical term *disability* does not exist across cultures. Although other cultures may have terms for blindness, deafness, or other physical and psychological impairments, they may lack one umbrella term encompassing all conditions. In India, Bengali families use the term *inconvenienced* to describe disability, thus avoiding negative connotations or stereotypes associated with terms such as *impaired* or even *disabled* (Rao, 2001). Not only do the nature and definition of disability vary across cultures, but beliefs regarding the causes of disability are equally diverse. For example, in some cultures chronic illness or disability is seen as a form of punishment toward those who have sinned or violated a taboo (Banks, 2003). This type of cultural belief contributes to family feelings of guilt and shame regarding a disabled child or other family member.

Another cultural value embedded in many Western rehabilitation approaches is the individual emphasis, as opposed to a collective or community focus (Groce & Zola, 1993). Most rehabilitation service delivery systems define the individual with the impairment as the client, and most have as their goal individual improvement measured by indicators such as employment, independent living, and integration in the community (Szymanski, Parker, & Patterson, 2005). Although these goals are not deleterious to the individual, they may impede use of rehabilitation services, particularly among individuals whose cultural values and beliefs emphasize collectivity or family (Bellini, 2003). Moreover, the focus on individualized, professional services limits the transferability of rehabilitation service delivery systems from Western countries to developing ones (Fabian, McInerney, & Rodrigues, 2005).

Competing Roles for Rehabilitation Counselors

Perhaps no other counseling specialty has faced the complexity of philosophical issues and discourse regarding professional role and function as much as rehabilitation counseling has. As I described earlier in the chapter, the traditional role of the rehabilitation counselor fit within the medical model of disability, treating the client's impairment and trying to assist the individual to "fit in," rather than advocating for changes in the environment. The new paradigm of disability emerging from the civil rights model and the social construction of disability refocused attention on disability as a "product of the interaction between the characteristics of the individual (e.g., conditions, or impairments, functional status, or personal and social qualities), and the characteristics of the natural, built, cultural, and social environments" (National Institute on Disability and Rehabilitation Research [NIDRR], 2000, pp. 8–9). Implicit in this new paradigm is that the role of the rehabilitation counselor is not simply to change the individual, but to advocate for and promote changes in the economic, social, and political environment in order to eliminate barriers to full participation in society. These two paradigms entail conflicting roles for rehabilitation counselors.

Traditionally, rehabilitation counseling has been associated with the medical, or impairment, model of disability. To some extent, most counseling specialties have evolved similarly, particularly as most have their roots in psychology or medicine (Cottone, 1992). Rehabilitation counseling is unique in that it traces its origins to federal legislation passed in the early 1920s that authorized and funded what became the Vocational Rehabilitation Services Program (Fabian & MacDonald-Wilson, 2005). The Vocational Rehabilitation Services Program is a state-federal partnership program with offices in every state and the District of Columbia annually serving approximately 1 million adults with disabilities (Rehabilitation Services Administration, 2004). The emphasis within this program is on individualized case finding, eligibility determination, and fee-for-service arrangements. As a result of the link to federal legislation and the emphasis on return to work, the historical origin of the field is associated with vocational issues and job placement (Fabian & MacDonald-Wilson, 2005).

Rehabilitation counseling is also unique in that it was the first counseling specialty to seek professional certification status, and subsequently the Commission on Rehabilitation Counselor Certification (CRCC) was established in the 1970s (Szymanski et al., 2005). One consequence of the early move to certification was the emphasis on empirically based role and function studies of rehabilitation counseling (Leahy, Chan, & Saunders, 2003; Muthard & Salomone, 1969; Wright, Leahy, & Shapson, 1987). This sequence of empirical studies demonstrated the enlargement of the scope of the field from a pure concern for vocational and return-to-work strategies to more contemporary functions that include clinical services, diagnosis, treatment planning, and so forth. Today, the scope of practice for the profession emphasizes the medical model, as the functions incorporate those identified previously, as well as individual and group counseling and individualized service evaluation (Szymanski et al., 2005). Client advocacy does, however, remain an item within the professional scope of practice statement, as well as an obligation under the rehabilitation counselor code of ethics (CRCC, 2003).

Although the need for rehabilitation counselors to function as client advocates is recognized, the role demands in the professional scope of practice statement are in sharp contrast to the perspective regarding individuals with disabilities that emerges from the civil rights model (Szymanski et al., 2005). Within the medical model, for example, rehabilitation counselors are perceived as functioning within the "rehabilitation paradigm which contains the dependency inducing potential of the physical-patient or professional-client relationship" (Nosek, 1992, p. 110). This dichotomy is a critical issue in the field, within which disability rights advocates criticize the individualistic assumptions underlying professional practice, stating that "this individual focus is a politically conservative approach to disability— one that first stops short of confronting and challenging the structural and attitudinal barriers that keep disabled people and other disadvantaged groups from being fully integrated into society" (Schriner, 2001, p. 653).

The current conflict for the rehabilitation counselor is played out in the sharply contrasting views of disability implicit in the various models. Table 5.1 summarizes some of these differences.

Table 5.1. Contrasting Paradigms of Rehabilitation Counseling

	Traditional rehabilitation paradigm	Social justice paradigm
Paradigm	Medical model	Civil rights model
Theoretical derivation	Psychology, adjustment, sociology	Political science, economics, sociology
Focus of attention	Individual	Environment
Service provider	Rehabilitation counselor, psychologist	Consumers, peers, grassroots self-help groups
Locus of service	Professional offices, treatment centers, rehabilitation facilities	Independent living centers, grassroots advocacy organizations and associations
Types of intervention	Counseling, assessment, diagnosis, case management, career and job counseling	Peer mentoring, self-help, political advocacy, self-determination
Types of social action	Individual advocacy, employer intervention	Collective political action, lobbying, political protests
Types of organizations	Professional counseling associations, rehabilitation organizations	Collective action groups (National Council on Disability, National Alliancefor the Mentally Ill)
Publications	Professional journals in the field	*Disability Rag, Mouth* (Internet resources)

Rehabilitation Counselors in a Social Justice Paradigm

Because of the historical roots of rehabilitation counseling practice, together with the marginalization of people with disabilities in the United States and throughout the world, rehabilitation counselors face unique challenges in combining the functions of the roles displayed in Table 1. It is clear, however, that the profession is moving in the direction of adopting a social justice perspective and working collaboratively with disability rights organizations to achieve a truly integrative agenda. Support for this assumption can be found in several sources. One is federal legislation authorizing consumer self-determination and informed consent in the vocational rehabilitation process, as mandated by the state systems of rehabilitation services, which passed in 1992 as part of the Rehabilitation Act Amendments; another is the passage of antidiscrimination legislation described earlier in the chapter. Yet another source of support is increased attention in the literature to empowerment theory and subsequent strategies that should be implemented to support the development of people with disabilities (Emener, 1991; Kosciulek, 1999). The emergence of a social justice perspective in rehabilitation counseling is hinted at in numerous studies that have documented unequal access to and results from traditional rehabilitation service delivery systems (Bellini, 2003; Wilson, 2002). Years of research in rehabilitation and related areas, such as mental health, provide substantial evidence of treatment and outcome disparities (Fabian & Edwards, 2005). Finally, the Rehabilitation Counseling Code of Ethics, perhaps unique among counselor codes, specifically addresses the obligation for client advocacy.

However, the gap between the two models—the medical and the civil rights approach—in terms of reconceptualizing the role and function of the professional rehabilitation counselor remains largely unaddressed in the rehabilitation literature (Szymanski et al., 2005), even though disability rights advocates and disability studies scholars have called for action (Groce, 1998; Nosek, 1992; Schriner, 2001). This circumstance probably exists for several reasons. One is that some of the assumptions of the new paradigm may be threatening to the field in that they challenge the unique expertise of the counselor. A second is that few practicing rehabilitation counselors (or counselor educators) are individuals with disabilities; thus, we are missing the "insider perspective" (Nosek, 1992; Schriner, 2001). A third is that disability issues and disability studies are not generally included in social justice literature or social justice agendas (Davis, 2001), thus further marginalizing individuals with disabilities by excluding them from consideration within the social justice movements and demands of other groups. Finally, transformation is a slow process—it is only in the past two decades that the civil rights model of disability has been well articulated and widely endorsed. Now that its underlying assumptions have been widely adopted by federal agencies (e.g., NIDRR), the disability rights movement (Hurst, 2003), and the World Health Organization (2004), changes may follow more rapidly.

A few recommendations for changes in the role of the rehabilitation counselor have appeared in disability studies texts (e.g., Schriner, 2001), as well as the rehabilitation literature (e.g., Szymanski et al., 2005). The following are suggestions culled from the literature that are based on the new paradigm of disability and that identify specific steps and strategies for incorporation into rehabilitation counseling and counselor education to assist the rehabilitation counselor become a social justice advocate.

> 1. *Engage in reflective practice through education and awareness building.* An emerging body of literature calls for the transformation of rehabilitation counseling practice (Schriner, 2001; Szymanski et al., 2005). The call for change results from advocacy by disability rights advocates, the impoverished circumstances of the majority of people with disabilities around the world, research on disparities in rehabilitation outcomes for ethnic minority groups, and the growth of the international disability rights movement. In order to maintain rehabilitation counseling as a vital and viable resource within the disability world, counselors and educators need to broaden their awareness of these movements, enlarge their knowledge of the scope of disability studies scholarship, and expand their scholarship to include journals such as *Disability Studies* and consumer journals such as *Disability Rag*.

> 2. *Engage in multidisciplinary thinking and behaving.* The roots of rehabilitation counseling are in vocational education, psychology, and medicine. In contrast, the disability studies field emerges from a much different and broader theoretical and academic background, encompassing sociology, anthropology, economics, and community development (Schriner, 2001). Our educational efforts, as well as our research and writing, need to consider these broader perspectives and ensure that they are included in our disciplinary thinking and education programs. For example, courses related to

political action, community development, or non-Western approaches to rehabilitation service delivery may be important topics in designing a social justice paradigm approach to counselor training.

3. *Practice inclusion in all policy, educational, and service delivery domains.* It would be unthinkable for a group of men to design a women's studies curriculum without including any women in the design and development of the course. Yet, policy, programs, and curriculum in rehabilitation have often been developed and implemented without the perspective of individuals with disabilities or with just a token individual being present. Although disability is a porous category, unlike gender, the perspective of the insider is unique and contemporary in terms of policy development, intervention design, and so forth. "Nothing about us without us" (Charlton, 1998) is one of the famous slogans of the disability rights movement, and it needs to be a value underscoring policy and practice.

4. *Elevate attention to society as well as the individual.* As I described earlier in this chapter, the new paradigm of disability moves toward defining disability not as residing in the individual, but in the interaction between the individual and the environment (NIDRR, 2000). This implies not only the built, or physical, environment, but the social, cultural, and economic environments as well. It is within these arenas that the future of rehabilitation services and disability empowerment will be found. Also, only through a society-level focus will rehabilitation counseling be viewed as relevant within different cultures in the United States as well as in different countries around the world.

5. *Adopt a systems focus.* Relevant to the third point, in order to analyze and plan contextually, the counselor must think and plan systemically (Cottone, 1992). Early family counseling theorists realized that changing the individual had no effect whatsoever if the family in which the individual lived was ignored. Systemic thinking for social justice requires that counselors think not only about the individual's specific environmental barriers and supports,

but also about how modifying or changing either part of this equation—individual or environment—affects and modifies the system. An example of the failure of nonsystems thinking can be seen in the disability beneficiary programs offered through the Social Security Administration. At the same time that the impairment focus of these programs requires that individuals be declared "totally incapacitated" for work, additional provisions contain various incentives to persuade people to get a job! This type of paradox presents significant dilemmas for people with disabilities, particularly those from other cultures who may distrust the bureaucracies that are sponsoring these paradoxical policies (Alston, 2004).

6. *Transform rehabilitation practice.* Kay Schriner (2001) wrote about the need for transformative rehabilitation practice in order to align the rehabilitation profession with the disability rights movement. She also noted that transformative rehabilitation practice would elevate the demand for political and civil rights and parity, reconstruing the role of the rehabilitation counselor as an advocate, a lobbyist, and an educator. For example, she pointed out that the transformed rehabilitation practitioner might lobby for political candidates who have a disability, would advocate for legislation and regulatory change, would conduct voter registration drives, and so on. Szymanski and colleagues (2005) called for a redefinition of the field of rehabilitation counseling to incorporate transformative elements, such as comanagement of the vocational rehabilitation process, and systems thinking, which would view the individual within his or her social, cultural, and political environments.

Conclusion

In this chapter I reviewed the context of disability and rehabilitation in the United States, as well as the major models and paradigms for viewing disability. I also described the challenges that rehabilitation counseling and rehabilitation counselors encounter as they integrate social advocacy and social justice practices within their roles and functions.

Schriner (2001) used a metaphor to describe the way that rehabilitation practice needs to change within a social justice arena

> If we believe that society is, metaphorically speaking, throwing disabled people into the river of employment, then why are we picking them out of the river one at a time rather than running upstream to stop them from being thrown in in the first place? (p. 654)

Her question underscores much of what is being considered and what needs to be considered in moving toward a social justice paradigm for rehabilitation counseling.

References

Albrecht, G. L. (1992). *The disability business: Rehabilitation in America*. Newbury Park, CA: Sage.

Albrecht, G. L., & Bury, M. (2001). The political economy of the disability marketplace. In G. L. Albrecht, K. D. Seelman, & M. Bury (Eds.), *Handbook of disability studies* (pp. 585–609). Thousand Oaks, CA: Sage.

Alston, R. J. (2004). African Americans with disabilities and the Social Security Administration's return to work incentives. *Journal of Disability Policy Studies, 14,* 216–221.

Americans With Disabilities Act of 1990, 42 U.S.C. ß 12101 *et seq.*

Banks, M. E. (2003). Disability in the family: A life span perspective. *Cultural Diversity and Mental Health, 9*(4), 367–384.

Barnartt, S., Schriner, K., & Scotch, R. (2001). Advocacy and political action. In G. L. Albrecht, K. D. Seelman, & M. Bury (Eds.), *Handbook of disability stud*ies (pp. 430–449). Thousand Oaks, CA: Sage.

Bellini, J. (2003). Counselors' multicultural competence and VR outcomes in the context of client racial similarity and difference. *Rehabilitation Counseling Bulletin, 46,* 64–173.

Bichenbach, J. E. (2001). Disability human rights, law, and policy. In G. L. Albrecht, K. D. Seelman, & M. Bury (Eds.), *Handbook of disability studies* (pp. 565–584). Thousand Oaks, CA: Sage.

Bradsher, J. E. (1996, January). *Disability among racial and ethnic groups* (Disability Statistics Abstract No. 10). Washington, DC: U.S. Department of Education, National Institute on Disability and Rehabilitation Research.

Brodwin, M. (2001). Rehabilitation in the private for-profit sector: Opportunities and challenges. In S. Rubin & R. Roessler (Eds.), *Foundations of the vocational rehabilitation process* (5th ed., pp. 475–495). Austin, TX: PRO-ED.

Burkhauser, R. V., & Houtenville, A. J. (2003). Employment among working-age people with disabilities: What current data can tell us. In E. M. Szymanski & R. M. Park™ er (Eds.), *Work and disability: Issues and strategies in career development and job placement* (2nd ed., pp. 53–90). Austin, TX: PRO-ED.

Burkhauser, R. V., & Stapleton, D. C. (2004). The decline in the employment rate for people with disabilities: Bad data, bad health, or bad policy? *Journal of Vocational Rehabilitation, 20*, 185–201.

Charlton, J. T. (1998). *Nothing about us without us: Disability oppression and empowerment*. Berkeley: University of California Press.

Commission on Rehabilitation Counselor Certification (CRCC). (2003). *Code of professional ethics for rehabilitation counselors*. Retrieved November 19, 2004, from http://www.crccertification.com/code.html

Cottone, R. R. (1992). *Theories and paradigms of counseling and psychotherapy*. Boston: Allyn & Bacon.

Davis, L. J. (2001). Identity politics, disability, and culture. In G. L. Albrecht, K. D. Seelman, & M. Bury (Eds.), *Handbook of disability studies* (pp. 535–545). Thousand Oaks, CA: Sage.

Emener, W. (1991). An empowerment philosophy for rehabilitation in the 20th century. *Journal of Rehabilitation, 57*, 7–12.

Fabian, E., & Edwards, Y. E. (2005). Community mental health and African Americans. In D. A. Harley & J. M. Dillard (Eds.), *Contemporary mental health issues among African Americans* (pp. 225–236). Alexandria, VA: American Counseling Association.

Fabian, E., & MacDonald-Wilson, K. (2005). Professional practice in rehabilitation service delivery systems and related system resources. In R. M. Parker, E. M. Szymanski, & J. B. Patterson (Eds.), *Rehabilitation counseling: Basics and beyond* (4th ed., pp. 55–88). Austin, TX: PRO-ED.

Fabian, E., McInerney, J., & Rodrigues, P. S. (2005). *International education in rehabilitation: A collaborative approach.* Unpublished manuscript, University of Maryland.

Fine, M., & Asch, A. (1988). *Women with disabilities: Essays in psychology, culture, and politics.* Philadelphia: Temple University Press.

Fink, P. J. (1992). *Stigma and mental illness.* Washington, DC: American Psychiatric Association.

Gill, C. J. (2001). Divided understandings: The social experience of disability. In G. L. Albrecht, K. D. Seelman, & M. Bury (Eds.), *Handbook of disability studies* (pp. 351–372). Thousand Oaks, CA: Sage.

Gold, R. (1999). Healthcare: Facilities. *Standard & Poor's Industry Surveys.* New York: McGraw-Hill.

Groce, N. E. (1998). Women with disabilities in the developing world. *Journal of Disability Policy Studies, 8,* 177–193.

Groce, N. E., & Zola, I. K. (1993). Multiculturalism, chronic illness, and disability. *Pediatrics, 91,* 1048–1055.

Hahn, H. (1985). Toward a politics of disability: Definitions, disciplines, and policies. *Social Science Journal, 22*(4), 87–105.

Hurst, R. (2003). The international disability rights movement and the ICF. *Disability and Rehabilitation, 25,* 572–576.

Killeen, M. B., & O'Day, B. L. (2004). Challenging expectations: How individuals with psychiatric disabilities find and keep work. *Psychiatric Rehabilitation Journal, 28,* 157–163.

Kosciulek, J. (1999). The consumer-directed theory of empowerment. *Rehabilitation Counseling Bulletin, 42,* 196–213.

LaPlante, M. T., Kennedy, J., Kaye, H. S., & Wenger, B. L. (1996). *Disability and employment* (Disability Statistics Abstract No. 11). Washington, DC: U.S. Department of Education, National Institute on Disability and Rehabilitation Research.

Leahy, M., Chan, F., & Saunders, J. (2003). Job functions and knowledge requirements of certified rehabilitation counselors in the 21st century. *Rehabilitation Counseling Bulletin, 46,* 66–81.

Marshall, C. A., & Largo, H. R. (1999). Disability and rehabilitation: A context for understanding the American Indian experience. *Lancet, 354,* 758–760.

Mead, P. (2004). The Social Security Administration tries a new deal for disability. *Workforce Management, 83,* 73–76.

Mitra, S., & Brucker, D. (2004). The early intervention project: An innovative initiative to return disability insurance applicants to work. *Journal of Disability Policy Studies, 15,* 159–167.

Muthard, J. E., & Salomone, P. R. (1969). The roles and functions of the rehabilitation counselor. *Rehabilitation Counseling Bulletin, 13* (1-SP), 81–168.

National Institute on Disability and Rehabilitation Research (NIDRR). (2000). *U.S. Department of Education, Office of Special Education and Rehabilitation Services, National Institute on Disability and Rehabilitation Research, Long Range Plan.* Washington, DC: Author.

Neath, J. (1997). Social causes of impairment, disability, and abuse: A feminist perspective. *Journal of Disability Policy Studies, 8,* 195–230.

Nosek, M. A. (1992). Independent living. In R. M. Parker & E. M. Szymanski (Eds.), *Rehabilitation counseling: Basics and beyond* (2nd ed., pp. 103–133). Austin, TX: PRO-ED.

Parsons, T. (1951). Illness and the role of the physician: A sociological perspective. *American Journal of Psychiatry, 21,* 452–460.

Pfeiffer, D., (1999). Eugenics and disability discrimination. In R. P. Marinelli & A. E. Dell Orto (Eds.), *The psychological and social impact of disability* (pp. 12–31). New York: Springer.

Rao, S. (2001). "A little inconvenience": Perspectives of Bengali families of children with disabilities on labeling and inclusion. *Disability and Society, 16,* 531–548.

Rehabilitation Act Amendments of 1992, 106 Stat. 4344.

Rehabilitation Services Administration, U.S. Department of Education, Office of Special Education and Rehabilitation Services. (2004). *Research and statistics*. Retrieved January 16, 2006, from http://www.ed.gov/rschstat/eval/rehab/statistics.html

Schriner, K. (2001). A disability studies perspective on employment issues and policies for disabled people: An international view. In G. L. Albrecht, K. D. Seelman, & M. Bury (Eds.), *Handbook of disability studies* (pp. 642–662). Thousand Oaks, CA: Sage.

Scotch, R. K. (1988). Disability as a basis for a social movement: Advocacy and the politics of definition. *Journal of Social Issues, 44,* 159–172.

Scotch, R. K., & Schriner, K. (1997). Disability as human variation: Implications for policy. *Annals of the American Academy of Political and Social Science, 549,* 148–159.

Smart, J. F., & Smart, D. W. (1997). The racial/ethnic demography of disability. *Journal of Rehabilitation, 63,* 9–15.

Szymanski, E., Parker, R. M., & Patterson, J. B. (2005). Beyond the basics: Sociopolitical context of rehabilitation counseling practice. In R. M. Parker, E. M. Szymanski, & J. B. Patterson (Eds.), *Rehabilitation counseling: Basics and beyond* (4th ed., pp. 395–412). Austin, TX: PRO-ED.

Wahl, O. F. (1999). *Telling is risky business: Mental health consumers confront stigma*. New Brunswick, NJ: Rutgers University Press.

Wilson, K. B. (2002). Exploration of VR acceptance and ethnic minorities: A national investigation. *Rehabilitation Counseling Bulletin, 45*, 168–176.

World Health Organization. (2004). *International classification of functioning, disability, and health (ICF)*. Retrieved November 20, 2004, from http://www.who.int/classifications/icf/en

Wright, G. J., Leahy, M. J., & Shapson, P. R. (1987). Rehabilitation skills inventory: Importance of counselor competencies. *Rehabilitation Counseling Bulletin, 31*, 107–130.

Chapter 6

Challenging Sexism:
Promoting the Rights of Women
in Contemporary Society

Judy A. Lewis

Counselors who are oriented to a social justice perspective always eschew the microscope in favor of the wide-angle lens. Instead of using the psychological equivalent of a microscope to magnify and define the deficits within their clients, they seek the widest possible view of the context within which their clients' development takes place. The need for such an expansive view is especially clear when we consider the lives of women. Women's oppression is a global phenomenon that crosses all national and cultural boundaries. Women are not only subject to human rights violations on the basis of their sex alone, but may also be victimized by multiple oppressions, with racism, heterosexism, ageism, religious discrimination, and poverty all taking their toll. It is only when we take notice of this reality that we can even begin to help the individual women who seek our assistance.

The Global Oppression of Women

Even people of good faith who view themselves as advocates and multiculturalists may think that a global perspective involves looking through a wider lens than they have in their possession. One rationale for this retreat behind national borders is a valid concern that confronting practices in distant places might imply an unwarranted interference in the worldviews that are central to other cultures. Another reason for this distancing may be found in the less valid belief that there is a sharp differentiation and separation between the oppression faced by women in other countries and the lives of women in the more progressive environment of the United States.

Global Sexism and the Multiculturalist

In North Africa, 6,000 women are genitally mutilated each day. This year, more than 15,000 women will be sold into sexual slavery in China. Two hundred women in Bangladesh will be horribly disfigured when their spurned husbands or suitors burn them with acid. More than 7,000 women in India will be murdered by their families and in-laws in disputes over dowries. Violence against women is rooted in a global culture of discrimination which denies women equal rights with men and which legitimizes the appropriation of women's bodies for individual gratification or political ends. Every year, violence in the home and the community devastates the lives of millions of women. (Amnesty International, 2001)

As horrifying as these figures are, multiculturalists have often been hesitant to make judgments on what they assume to be the accepted norms of cultures that are not their own. Nussbaum (1999, 2000) put this conflict into perspective:

On the one hand, it seems impossible to deny that traditions, both Western and non-Western, perpetrate injustice against women in many fundamental ways, touching on some of the most central elements of a human being's quality of life—health, education, political liberty and participation, employment, self-respect, and life itself. On the other hand, hasty judgments that a tradition in some distant part of the world is morally retrograde are familiar legacies of colonialism and imperialism and are correctly regarded with suspicion by sensitive thinkers in the contemporary world. To say that a practice endorsed by tradition is bad is to risk erring by imposing one's own way on others. . . . To say that a practice is all right whenever local tradition endorses it as right and good is to risk erring by withholding critical judgment where real evil and oppression are surely present. To avoid the whole issue because the matter of proper judgment is so fiendishly difficult is tempting but perhaps the worst option of all. (Nussbaum, 1999, p. 30)

Saying that "the situation of women in the contemporary world calls urgently for moral standtaking" (1999, p. 31), Nussbaum chose justice over tradition. Among the salient points she made are that a way of life should not be preserved intact if it causes real pain to human beings; that women who are victimized by harmful traditional practices have not necessarily been asked whether these practices meet with their approval; that in every culture there can be found instances of women's protest movements, belying the notion that women approve of their treatment; and that norms calling for withholding rights from women have been "purveyed . . . through male texts and the authority of male religious and cultural leaders, against a background of women's almost total economic and political disempowerment" (Nussbaum, 2000, p. 42).

Although Nussbaum's case for confronting human rights violations is strong, it should not be confused with the suggestion that women should be pressured to give up traditional values in favor of Westernization. The important point is that women should be able to choose the kinds of lives they desire for themselves and their families.

The U.S. Piece of the Globe

Amnesty International (2005) has pointed out that a "global culture of discrimination against women allows violence to occur daily and with impunity." No country in the world is exempt from this pandemic of violence against women—certainly not the United States, where a woman is raped every 6 minutes and a woman is battered every 15 seconds. Despite all evidence to the contrary, U.S. citizens often perceive that violations of women's human rights are limited to other countries and stop short of our own borders.

> Many Americans understand that internationally accepted standards can help to serve as guides in foreign countries where women are not granted the same level of rights as men; however, it is more difficult for Americans to see the benefit of these international principles within U.S. borders. (American Bar Association Section of Individual Rights and Responsibilities, 1998)

We should think of discrimination and violence against women as global issues that need to be confronted on every front, at home and abroad. Yet, there is striking evidence that the United States has failed to take part in actions that could interrupt oppressive practices. We need look no further than the fact that the United States is the only industrialized country—and, in fact, one of the very few members of the United Nations—that has not ratified the UN Convention on the Elimination of All Forms of Discrimination Against Women (CEDAW).

Discrimination is defined in the convention as

> any distinction, exclusion, or restriction made on the basis of
> sex which has the effect or purpose of impairing or nullifying
> the recognition, enjoyment, or exercise by women, irrespective
> of their marital status, on a basis of equality of men and women,
> of human rights and fundamental freedoms in the political,
> economic, social, cultural, civil or any other field. (United
> Nations Division for the Advancement of Women, 2005, para.
> 2)

The treaty requires signatories to condemn discrimination against
women, take steps to eliminate such discrimination, and submit regular
reports of their progress to the United Nations. States that endorse the
convention are expected to "incorporate the principle of equality of
men and women in their legal system, abolish all discriminatory laws,
and adopt appropriate ones prohibiting discrimination against women"
(para. 4). This document, perhaps surprisingly, goes beyond legal issues
to address cultural matters as well. "The Convention is the only human
rights treaty which affirms the reproductive rights of women and targets
culture and tradition as influential forces shaping gender roles and family
relations" (para. 8).

Why should the United States join the rest of the world in ratifying
the convention? The American Bar Association Section of Individual
Rights and Responsibilities (1998) made the answer clear:

> Ratification would help support the United States' role as an
> international leader on human rights issues and would
> demonstrate that the United States is indeed a part of the
> international community. Moreover, the treaty not only would
> provide women in America with yet another tool for combating
> discrimination, but also would help guard against any future
> efforts to circumscribe already established rights.

Americans must remain vigilant both about worldwide concerns
and about threats to equality at home. The American Bar Association is
absolutely on target about the need to guard against circumscription of
rights that have been seen as etched in stone. The current situation in
the United States is not one that should engender peace of mind. In
2005, for instance, the U.S. Bureau of Labor Statistics proposed
dropping gender data from its Current Employment Statistics Survey.
As Equal Rights Advocates and the cosigners of their letter of protest

pointed out, women remain underrepresented in a number of employment fields, and the wage gap between women and men continues to widen.

> Discontinuing reporting by gender sends one of two troubling messages: Either women no longer experience workplace discrimination or gender discrimination is not important enough to warrant an employer's time on a single question in a 7-minute survey. The first message is inaccurate, and the second is at odds with the federal government's own stated goal of economic opportunity for women in the workplace. (Equal Rights Advocates, 2005b)

Equal Rights Advocates also pointed out that "women overwhelmingly occupy the low-wage positions of the retail, restaurant, and hotel industries" and that these workers are very vulnerable to sexual harassment. Moreover, "deeply embedded patterns of discrimination work to bar women's access to promising careers historically considered nontraditional for women, like construction and firefighting." In Silicon Valley, Asian and Latina immigrants work in "high-tech sweatshops." Even in higher education, "female faculty and administrators . . . face widespread gender discrimination in hiring, compensation, tenure awards, and post-tenure promotions" (Equal Rights Advocates, 2005a).

The United States' failure to make progress in the area of economic opportunity shows up clearly, not only when we look at women's career options, but also when we look at issues such as health care—or the lack of it.

> Women's health is likely to be a silent victim of the combination of the recent downturn in the economy and rapidly increasing health care costs. In response to these major forces, employers may be more likely to drop dependent coverage, switch to less expensive and/or more limited plans, or raise worker costs for care. Because women are likely to be low-income and also rely on dependent coverage more often than men, they may have much to lose. Stable coverage will thus be likely to continue to elude many women. (Salganicoff, Beckerman, Wyn, & Ojeda, 2002)

In the United States, women face violence, economic deprivation, and lack of access to health care. U.S. women may face a different degree of deprivation than their sisters in nondemocratic, developing countries, but the basic nature and intent of oppression is the same. The United States takes its place in the world not as a model of virtue, but as a participant in the culture of oppression.

National Commitment to Action

Once the national condition of denial has ended, policymakers and advocates can begin to focus on a commitment to action against discrimination and inequity. A document known as the *Contract With Women of the USA* (Center for Women Policy Studies, 2005) provided a good model for such a commitment. Developed by the Center for Women Policy Studies and the Women's Environment and Development Organization, the contract has been signed by numerous public officials and policymakers who have pledged to work toward equality and empowerment for U.S. women. The document is organized around the following 12 general principles:

1. empowering women;
2. sharing family responsibilities;
3. ending the burden of poverty;
4. providing high-quality, affordable health care;
5. guaranteeing sexual and reproductive rights;
6. guaranteeing workplace rights;
7. creating educational equity;
8. ending violence against women;
9. protecting a healthy environment;
10. supporting women as peacemakers;
11. honoring international commitments and ratifying the CEDAW; and
12. implementing a long-term national plan to achieve equality.

This contract provides a fine model because it is organized around clear goals and implicitly recognizes that we have a great deal of work to do in order to meet those goals. As all signers of the contract state,

> We pledge to work together to overcome discrimination based on sex, race, class, age, immigration status, sexual orientation, religion, and disability. We seek to end social, economic, and political inequities, violence and the human rights abuses that still confront millions of women and girls in our country. (Center for Women Policy Studies, 2005)

We should also notice that the goals, language, and spirit of this statement are a good fit for the counseling profession. As counselors, it is appropriate—and necessary—to devote ourselves to the elimination of injustices that affect all of our students and clients. The American Counseling Association's own *Advocacy Competencies* (2003) can help to lead the way.

Counseling and Advocating for Women's Rights

The social justice perspective does, of course, emphasize the counselor's role in social and political advocacy. Because of their work with clients and students, counselors see firsthand how much the individuals they serve are affected by their immediate environments and by the political and economic policies and cultural norms that characterize the broader social context. We know that female clients are affected by injustices even at the national and global levels, but it is because we know our clients as people that we bring to the process of advocacy a perspective and an expertise that are unique to our profession. Counselors should never feel that they have to choose between helping individual clients and advocating on their behalf in the national or international arenas. The role of direct helper and the role of advocate are complementary. Effective counselors use their wide-angle lenses whether they happen to be counseling in their offices, lobbying at the Capitol, or marching for justice.

Client Empowerment

The first principle of the *Contract With Women of the USA* (Center for Women Policy Studies, 2005) related to empowerment of women. Fortunately, counselors are in a good position to act on that principle. In fact, the ACA's *Advocacy Competencies* (2003) have conceptualized client empowerment as one aspect of the process of advocacy.

An advocacy orientation involves not only systems-change interventions but also the implementation of empowerment strategies in direct counseling. Advocacy-oriented counselors recognize the impact of social, political, economic, and cultural factors on human development. They also help their clients and students understand their own lives in context. This process lays the groundwork for self-advocacy.

This conceptualization is especially helpful when counselors work with members of oppressed groups. When it comes to women's issues, advocacy-oriented counselors realize that sexism and cultural assumptions about gender have a major impact on their clients' lives. It is not enough, however, for the counselor to know this. It is also important for the client to see her life in context. Not just counselors but clients and students as well need those wide-angle lenses.

Because of the messages about gender that females receive from their earliest years, women often make assumptions about themselves and what they can expect from life. The gender-based limitations that a culture might prescribe become so deeply engrained that women come to accept these limitations as though they were part of nature rather than socially constructed. The fact that gender stereotyping is a worldwide phenomenon makes it even more likely that ideas born of oppression will be internalized. Advocacy-oriented counselors help their clients move past this internalized oppression. They also help clients and students recognize that social, economic, political, and cultural factors affect their lives in ways that they must understand in order to overcome. Counselors are often taught that they should help clients focus on those aspects of their lives that they can control. Unfortunately, many counselors take this stricture to mean that they should pressure clients to avoid talking about external factors that have affected their lives and limited their choices. How many clients have been steered away from discussing racism, sexism, or heterosexism under the assumption that these phenomena are uncontrollable and therefore beyond the bounds of the counseling process? Nothing could be further from the truth! In fact, empowerment is all about helping clients understand that they are powerfully affected by the environment, particularly oppression, and that they can overcome these limitations only after they have moved beyond unquestioning acceptance of racist or sexist or heterosexist stereotypes. In discussing the impact of racism on African American families, Franklin (1993) pointed out that

> once the pervasive impact of racism is acknowledged as a force in a Black family's experience, the family can move on to confront other issues. But if the impact of racism is ignored, it's unlikely that therapy will go anywhere. (p. 36)

This principle applies across oppressions and forms the basis for an empowerment approach to helping. What are the differences between empowerment and disempowerment? Table 6.1 shows the contrasting characteristics of empowered versus disempowered clients. Many women lack awareness that the boundaries confining them are constructed as part of the apparatus of oppression. Without this awareness, they become mired in self-blame. "Why," they ask, "can't I get a job that's good enough to support my kids?" "What is it about me that makes me so disorganized that I can't seem to do my job, take care of the house, be patient with my children, and take better care of my aging parents?" "What should I have done differently to keep my husband from hitting me?" "Why did I make the mistake of going to a place that put me in danger of being raped?" "Why do other people seem to be able to take action and get what they need when I can't?" "Why am I stuck?"

Table 6.1. Characteristics of Empowerment Versus Disempowerment

Empowerment	Disempowerment
Awareness of context, including oppression	Self-blame
Skills for self-management	Lack of self-management skills
Mutual support	Isolation
Self-esteem	Victimization
Ability to recognize options and make choices	Lack of choices

Empowerment involves, first, recognizing that these problems do not stem from a defect within the individual woman but instead are violations of her selfhood. Perhaps what the client needs to be asking is, "How can we get past a situation where women's salaries are a fraction of White men's?" "How can we get past a situation where women are expected to carry out all of these family roles alone and without support from the community?" "Why do government leaders question even unpaid family leave?" "How can women and men work together to end the culture of violence and victimization?" "Now that I realize these things that have happened in my life are not my fault, how can I get out of being stuck and take action?"

Although it may not seem intuitively correct, the fact is that counselors who are willing to help their clients explore the oppressions that affect them are also increasingly able to help their clients move toward self-responsibility and personal action. The ACA advocacy competencies suggest that, in carrying out direct interventions, the counselor should be able to

- identify strengths and resources of clients and students;
- identify the social, political, economic, and cultural factors that affect the client/student;

- recognize the signs indicating that an individual's behaviors and concerns reflect responses to systemic or internalized oppression;
- at an appropriate developmental level, help the individual identify the external barriers that impede his or her development;
- train students and clients in self-advocacy skills;
- help students and clients create self-advocacy action plans; and
- assist students and clients in carrying out action plans.

This approach involves a major change in the culture of counseling! If we consider the ways counselors work with women, it is a positive thing to note that most of us have gotten past the sexism of the past. School and career counselors no longer insist that students choose supposedly gender-appropriate career plans. Interest inventories are not printed in pink for women and blue for men. Couples counselors do not insist that women accept traditional gender roles within their families. Mental health counselors do not believe that assertiveness in women is a diagnosable illness. Moving beyond blatant sexism, however, is only a first step. Simply trying to be nonsexist falls far short of where we need to be, which is working toward the kind of empowerment/feminist/gender-aware counseling that helps women get unstuck.

Consider the contrasting counseling models shown in Table 6.2. From a social justice perspective, simply thinking of oneself as nonsexist falls far short of the mark. Suppose a school counselor has learned to avoid imposing stereotyped gender roles on his or her students, but doesn't notice that internalized oppression has already brought these students to a recognition that male students go to premedical majors and female students to nursing school. Suppose a family counselor has learned to avoid overtly sexist assessment instruments but doesn't realize that questions about what it means to be a man or a woman in a family might be important. Effective counselors know that "the process of oppression is insidious because targeted people must face a lethal combination of overt bigotry, covert discrimination, and a socialization process that encourages internalization of negative self-views" (Carlson, Sperry, & Lewis, 2005, p. 126). Effective counselors know that their job involves taking an active role in recognizing and confronting oppression.

**Table 6.2.Contrasts Between Nonsexist Versus Feminist,
Gender-Aware Counseling Models**

Nonsexist counseling	Empowerment/feminist/ gender-aware counseling
Does not reinforce stereotyped gender roles	Helps clients recognize the impact of social, economic, political, and cultural factors on their lives
Encourages clients to consider a wide range of choices, especially in regard to careers	Helps clients transcend limitations resulting from gender stereotyping
Avoids use of sexist assessment instruments	Includes gender-role analysis as a component of assessment
Treats male and female clients equally	Recognizes and addresses the fact that male and female clients live in different worlds
Does not consciously impose oppressive values on clients	Recognizes the influence of the counselor's own cultural background and values; counselor remains open to learning

Social and Political Advocacy

The ACA's *Advocacy Competencies* (2003) encourage counselors to engage in social and political advocacy as a direct outgrowth of their professional roles:

> Counselors regularly act as change agents in the systems that affect their own students and clients most directly. This experience often leads toward the recognition that some of the concerns they have addressed affect people in a much larger arena. When this happens, counselors use their skills to carry out social/political advocacy.

In order to influence public policy in the public arena, the advocacy-oriented counselor needs to be competent in carrying out the following actions:

- distinguishing those problems that can best be resolved through social and political action;
- identifying the appropriate mechanisms and avenues for addressing these problems;
- seeking out and join with potential allies;
- supporting existing alliances for change;
- with allies, preparing convincing rationales for change supported by data;
- with allies, lobbying legislators and other policymakers; and
- maintaining open dialogue with communities and clients to ensure that the social and political advocacy is consistent with their goals.

As the advocacy competencies make clear, the choices counselors make about the particular policies or pieces of legislation they will address often come from their recognition of the problems their clients are facing. Sometimes counselors will be at the forefront of legislative action. More often, they will join or support existing alliances. At any given time, a number of issues will be on the table, all of which might have real impact on women's lives. The key, then, is to be vigilant in order to recognize the best time for action. At the time I am writing this chapter, advocates for women have to be particularly vigilant. Many of the current debates are more about protecting existing rights than pressing for new ones. Examples of just a few important current issues are the following (National Organization for Women, 2005):

- February 2005 marked the 10th anniversary of the United Nations Fourth World Conference on Women, which was held in Beijing. The Beijing Platform for Action called for guaranteeing women's freedom of political participation; increasing their access to education, employment, and health care; and protecting their human rights. At a conference marking the 10-year anniversary, the U.S. delegation tried to amend the platform by adding antiabortion language.
- The Abortion Non-Discrimination Act became law in 2004 through being added as an amendment to the final appropriations bill. Under this law, Medicare, health maintenance organizations, insurance companies, and hospitals can bar doctors from providing abortion referrals, performing abortions, or even counseling

patients about their options—even if the patient asks for the information.

- Scientific panels of the U.S. Food and Drug Administration (FDA) recommended that over-the-counter sales of emergency contraception be allowed, but the FDA overruled this advice. Women's advocacy groups are working to get this ruling changed so that women over 16 would have access to such drugs.
- The proposed Federal Marriage Amendment to the Constitution, currently under consideration, would ban same-sex marriages and might also mean the end of civil unions and domestic partnerships. This discriminatory amendment would institutionalize the denial of equal protection to lesbian, gay, bisexual, and transgendered couples.

There's always something to work on! We should remember, however, that narrowly defined issues rise and fall but the larger battles sometimes go on for years. One example of this is the quest to ratify, at long last, the Equal Rights Amendment to the U.S. Constitution. The long-forgotten (by some) Equal Rights Amendment reads as follows:

> Section 1. Equality of rights under the law shall not be denied or abridged by the United States or by any State on account of sex.
> Section 2. The Congress shall have power to enforce, by appropriate legislation, the provisions of this article.
> Section 3. This amendment shall take effect 2 years after the date of ratification.

The Equal Rights Amendment is still being championed—and rightly so—by some political leaders and many women's advocates. As Congressman Jesse Jackson Jr. (2001) stated,

> The lack of a clear constitutional guarantee of equality for women leaves America's democratic promise unfulfilled for half the population. It is a shameful truth that 225 years after this nation was established, equality between the sexes remains more hope than reality. The disadvantaged status of women is so pervasive and so supported by cultural mandates that many people—women and men—see these conditions as "normal" and accept them. But in fact our entire society suffers greatly from

> the subjugation of women, maintained and perpetuated by the threat or reality of men's violence against women. That injustice is widespread and institutionalized does not make it less abusive. (p. 351)

Jackson also pointed out that nothing short of a constitutional amendment can bring about the necessary degree of change:

> A national dialogue leading to adoption of an amendment that would prohibit discrimination based on sex will have the most profound impact yet in reshaping the legal and economic landscapes. For if women—who constitute the majority of the population—were to have their basic human right to equal treatment under the law, every aspect of their current disadvantaged status would be forever changed. (p. 351)

Significantly, Jackson included his statements on equal rights for women in a book that also highlighted the need for guarantees of full employment, of universal health care, of affordable housing, and of a quality public education. The breadth of the subject matter does not make his statements about women's oppression any less valid or less important. On the contrary, Jackson was right in recognizing that extending human rights to everyone does not lessen the rights of some. In the final analysis, all of the isms are part of the same phenomenon of systemic oppression, and competing oppressions are the last things we need.

> White women who are victims of sexism are socialized to accept and participate in racism. By the same token, men of color who are victims of racism are socialized to accept and participate in sexism, which degrades women of color as well as White women. The inability to see the parallels and intersections of racism and sexism keeps both in place. (Arnold, 1997, p. 42)

References

American Bar Association Section of Individual Rights and Responsibilities. (1998). *Eliminating discrimination against women: The push for an international treaty.* Retrieved March 2005 from http://www.abanet.org/irr/hr/sum98ktonuge.html

American Counseling Association. (2003). *Advocacy competencies.* Alexandria, VA: American Counseling Association.

Amnesty International. (2001). *Shattered minds: Torture and ill treatment of women.* Retrieved March 2005 from http://www.amnestyusa.org/women/violence/

Amnesty International. (2005). *Amnesty International USA home page.* Available online at http://www.amnestyusa.org

Arnold, M. S. (1997, May). The connection between multiculturalism and oppression. *Counseling Today, 39,* 42.

Carlson, J., Sperry, L., & Lewis, J. A. (2005). *Family therapy techniques: Integrating and tailoring treatment.* New York: Routledge.

Center for Women Policy Studies. (2005). *Contract with women of the USA.* Retrieved March 27, 2005, from http://www.centerwomenpolicy.org/contract.htm

Equal Rights Advocates. (2005a). *Legal advocacy and policy projects.* Retrieved March 2005 from http://www.equalrights.org/professional/prof_main.asp

Equal Rights Advocates. (2005b, February 22). *Women and civil rights organizations call upon U.S. Bureau of Labor Statistics to continue tracking gender inequity.* Retrieved February 24, 2005, from www.equalrights.org

Franklin, A. J. (1993, July/August). The invisibility syndrome. *Family Networker,* 33–39.

Jackson, J. L., Jr. (2001). *A more perfect union: Advancing new American rights.* New York: Welcome Rain.

National Organization for Women. (2005). *The truth about George: Women's rights*. Retrieved March 1, 2005, from http://www.thetruthaboutgeorge.com/women/

Nussbaum, M. C. (1999). *Sex and social justice*. New York: Oxford University Press.

Nussbaum, M. C. (2000). *Women and human development: The capabilities approach*. Cambridge, UK: Cambridge University Press.

Salganicoff, A., Beckerman, J. Z., Wyn, R., & Ojeda, V. D. (2002). *Women's health in the United States: Health coverage and access to care* (Kaiser Women's Health Survey, May 2002). Menlo Park, CA: Henry J. Kaiser Family Foundation.

United Nations Division for the Advancement of Women. (2005). *Convention on the elimination of all forms of discrimination against women*. Retrieved March 1, 2005, from http://www.un.org/womenwatch/daw/cedaw/

Chapter 7

Promoting Healthy Male Development:
A Social Justice Perspective

Mark S. Kiselica and Mark S. Woodford

In recent years, the challenging yet rewarding work of counseling boys and men has received increased attention in the counseling literature. Within this literature, a growing number of mental health professionals have recognized that the process of helping boys and men to reach their full potential often requires a social justice approach to counseling, which demands that counselors move beyond the domain of traditional, individual counseling and attempt to help boys and men in three ways. First, counselors work to eradicate sexist attitudes that adversely affect male development (Brooks & Silverstein, 1995). Second, counselors support the rights of boys and men who have been neglected and disparaged by society (Beymer, 1995). Third, counselors confront fellow professionals who subscribe to harmful stereotypes about the emotional lives of males that can undermine the counseling process with this population (Kiselica, 2001, 2003a, 2003c; Kiselica & O'Brien, 2001).

The purpose of this chapter is to describe these challenges and to suggest advocacy and systems-change strategies that build upon male strengths and foster the optimal development of boys and men. We begin with an overview of social justice counseling and its value as an approach to promoting healthy male development. A discussion of how sexist attitudes about women hurt boys and men in their interpersonal relationships follows. We then suggest how counselors can work with feminist and male advocacy organizations to change systems so that they foster psychologically healthy male development. Next, we describe and critique myths about the emotional lives of males and offer suggestions for challenging misguided assumptions about boys and men.

A Social Justice Perspective Regarding the Problems
of Boys and Men

A social justice approach to counseling and psychotherapy (also referred to as advocacy counseling or social action counseling) uses all the methods of counseling and psychology to confront injustice and inequality in society (Mays, 2000; Strickland, 2000). Key aspects of social justice counseling include serving as a advocate for a client or social cause, pleading on behalf of a client, working in the social contexts in which a client's problems occur, and negotiating with systems to eliminate or reduce social problems, such as poverty, unequal access to opportunity, and various forms of prejudice (Kiselica & Robinson, 2001). Social justice counseling involves "helping clients challenge institutional and social barriers that impede academic, career, or personal-social development" (Lee, 1998, pp. 8–9). The provision of direct services to clients is complemented by indirect forms of helping, including consciousness-raising activities, which involve influencing the people and institutions that affect clients' lives (Bradley & Lewis, 2000; Kiselica, 2004; Kiselica & Robinson, 2001). Thus, competent social justice counselors are well-rounded practitioners who can use traditional individual interventions with nontraditional systems-change strategies flexibly and simultaneously in order to respond to their clients' most pressing needs (Kiselica, 2004).

The sexist socialization of males, the neglect and maltreatment of particular populations of boys and men, and the misconceptions about males by many mental health professionals are three problems that warrant social justice interventions by counselors. Regardless of the particular setting in which he or she is employed, each counselor who works with troubled boys and men is likely to be confronted again and again with issues associated with sexism, injustice, and erroneous assumptions about males that cannot be resolved simply through change within the individual. A crucial first step counselors can take toward addressing these issues is to understand the powerful and deleterious effects of sexism, unjust practices, and stereotypes about the emotional lives of boys and men. We discuss these three sets of issues and our proposed solutions for them within a social justice framework.

Social Justice Counseling With Boys and Men

In order to help boys and men effectively, counselors must combine social justice interventions that are focused on changing systems, institutions, and policies with traditional forms of individual and group counseling that have been developed to ameliorate intrapsychic and interpersonal problems. It is beyond the scope of this chapter to describe traditional counseling processes and interventions with males, but several excellent publications exist on the subject. For example, the *Handbook of Counseling Boys and Adolescent Males,* edited by Horne and Kiselica (1999), is a comprehensive guide to developmental, multicultural, and clinical counseling with numerous special populations of male youth. *Men in Groups,* by Andronico (1996), is a superb resource for understanding the process of working with boys and men in groups. Finally, *The New Handbook of Psychotherapy and Counseling With Men,* by Brooks and Good (2001), is a fine two-volume resource on counseling boys and men in various settings and with various modalities. Counselors can interweave the male-oriented individual and group counseling interventions described in these books with our social justice recommendations for understanding and eliminating sexism toward women, maltreatment of boys and men, and erroneous assumptions and stereotypes about males. In this chapter, we limit our discussion to individual counseling with boys and men aimed at helping them to understand the impact of sexism on their lives.

Understanding and Eliminating Sexism Toward Women

Sexism has been broadly defined as the "differential treatment of people based on their biological status as male or female" (Kilmartin, 1994, p. 24). How men choose to treat women (and other men) is based largely on what they have seen and experienced through participating in life as males, specifically through the male gender socialization process. Traditional sex role differentiation views men and women in stereotypical ways: for example, (a) men are seen as more "active and strong," whereas "women are viewed as passive and weak"; (b) men are viewed as being "high on dominance, autonomy, aggressiveness, exhibition, achievement, and endurance," whereas women "are viewed as more deferent, abasing, nurturant, and affiliative" (Glicke & Fiske, 1999a, pp. 378–379). The worldwide prevalence of these stereotypes is evidenced by a study of 25 different countries that included "considerable geographic, economic, and cultural diversity" (Best & Williams, 1993, as cited in Glicke & Fiske, 1999a). Sexist attitudes are rooted in the traditional gender role socialization process (Russell & Trigg, 2004), and can not only hurt the development of healthy interpersonal relationships of boys and men but also lead to powerful and deleterious effects on women.

How Sexism Toward Women Hurts Females and Males

In a sexist culture that bases social approval on a man's ability to live out traditional masculine characteristics and behaviors, it is virtually inevitable that men will experience negative emotional consequences, such as anxiety and depression (Kilmartin, 1994). At best, men can work to become more conscious of the impact of this socialization process on their lives and choose to transcend these constrictive notions about masculinity. At worst, these stereotypes and their concurrent sexist attitudes result in what Brooks and Silverstein (1995) called "multiple shortcomings of traditional masculinity" and the "dark side of masculinity" (p. 281). Examples include "violence, sexual abuse and sexual harassment, substance abuse, and self-destructive behavior . . . and relationship inadequacies, absent fathering, and social-emotional withdrawal" (p. 281).

Glicke and Fiske (1999b) have argued that the traditional male socialization process leads males to develop ambivalent sexism, which refers to male dependency on and power over women. Glicke and Fiske described two forms of ambivalent sexism: benevolent and hostile. Benevolent sexism refers to the feeling of protecting and providing for women, which presumes that females are "the weaker sex . . . in need of men's protection" (p. 211). Hostile sexism is conceived as an attitude of superiority of men over women that can manifest as a "competitive drive to differentiate and dominate" (p. 211).

Feeling superior and dominating "the weaker sex" can cause men to isolate themselves from others and hurt their interpersonal relationships. For example, if a male is trained to believe that women are the weaker sex because they show their emotions more readily, then he may remain disconnected from his own emotional life out of fear of being perceived as weak (not only by other males, but also by women). As a result, he may be unaware of the emotional undercurrents of his life, and his feelings of sadness or fear may surface as anger and aggression—emotions that fit with his gender training. Levant (1995) has stated that men who view the world in this way "pour out their vulnerable emotions through the channel of anger" (p. 237).

In terms of interpersonal relationships, the total effects of sexist training on women and men cannot be measured, but we know from the literature on sex discrimination and sexual harassment that the impact is great, particularly on women. According to Benokraitis (1997), blatant sex discrimination is the intentional treatment of women in a harmful way that manifests in our society as "sexual harassment, sexist language and jokes, physical violence (rape, incest, wife abuse), and other forms of obviously unequal treatment in the family, employment, education, politics, religion, law, and other areas" (p. 7). Reported incidences of sexual harassment, defined as "unwelcome sexual advances, requests for sexual favors, and other verbal or physical conduct of a sexual nature" (U.S. Equal Employment Opportunity Commission, 2005, para. 2) are on the rise. For example, data compiled nationally by the Office of Research, Information, and Planning from EEOC's charge data system indicated that the number of sexual harassment charges filed with EEOC rose from 10,532 in 1992 to 13,566 in 2003. This is an indication of an increase in either the prevalence of sexual harassment or the reporting of such incidents.

The data concerning violence against women are staggering. In terms of domestic violence, the number of reported incidents in the United States alone "is estimated to be anywhere from 960,000 cases of violence against a current or former spouse, boyfriend, or girlfriend" (U.S. Department of Justice, 1998b) to "3 million women who are abused by their husband or boyfriend" (The Commonwealth Fund, 1999). Additionally, the U.S. Department of Justice (1998b) reported that "while women are less likely than men to be victims of violent crimes overall, women are five to eight times more likely than men to be victimized by an intimate partner." Additionally, Heise, Ellsberg, and Gottenmoeller (1999) reported that worldwide "at least one in every three women has been beaten, coerced into sex, or otherwise abused during her lifetime." Women of all races are about equally vulnerable to violence by an intimate partner (Bureau of Justice Statistics, 1995). Lastly, 30% of Americans surveyed reported that they knew at least one woman who had been physically abused by her husband or boyfriend in the past year (Lieberman Research, 1996).

Pregnant women are not immune to domestic violence. For example, Horon and Cheng (2001) reported that women who are pregnant or recently pregnant are more likely to die from homicide than from any other cause of death. In fact, estimates are that approximately one-third of all deaths among pregnant women are related to injuries sustained in domestic violence situations, making homicide the leading cause of death among these women, followed by cancer, respiratory problems, motor vehicle collisions, cardiomyopathy, drug overdose, and suicide (Nannini, Weiss, Goldstein & Fogerty, 2002).

Between 3 and 10 million children witness some form of domestic violence each year (Carlson, 1984), and there is an association between spouse abuse and child abuse. For example, a national survey of more than 6,000 American families revealed that 50% of the men who have frequently assaulted their wives also have frequently abused their children (Strauss, Gelles, & Smith, 1990).

In addition to the social-emotional and physical costs to women and children, there are also enormous financial costs to society in terms of health care. The Centers for Disease Control and Prevention (2003) estimated that rape, physical assault, stalking, and homicide committed by intimate partners cost Americans in excess of $5 billion each year. Of that amount, nearly $4 billion go to direct medical and mental health-care services, and nearly $2 billion are indirect costs of lost productivity or wages.

Domestic violence by adult males against women has an apparent impact on adolescent male behavior against adolescent females. For example, a poll of girls ages 14 to 17 indicated that 40% of those surveyed reported knowing someone of the same age who had been either hit or beaten by their boyfriend (Children Now/Kaiser Permanente poll, December 1995). Additionally, more recent data indicated that approximately one in five high school girls has been physically or sexually abused by a dating partner (Silverman, Raj, Mucci, & Hathaway, 2001).

An astonishing 76% of women who reported having been physically assaulted or raped since turning the age of 18 stated that the assault was committed by a current or former spouse, a cohabiting partner, or someone with whom they were on a date (U.S. Department of Justice, 1998a). More recent data have supported these findings. For example, according to government statistics from 2001, 41,740 women were victims of rape or sexual assault committed by an intimate partner (Bureau of Justice Statistics Crime Data Brief, 2003).

Stalking behavior also appears to be associated with physical assault of intimate partners. For example, 80% of women who are stalked by former husbands reported being physically assaulted by that partner, and 30% are sexually assaulted by that partner (Center for Policy Research, 1997). Additionally, Tjaden and Thoennes (2000) have reported that 503,485 women are stalked by an intimate partner annually in the United States.

Lastly, some have suggested that the proliferation of pornography and the sexual objectification of women has an influence on the increasing numbers of women reporting sexual harassment, assault, and rape (Donnerstein & Linz, 1987). Pornography is a billion-dollar industry in the United States, and hard-core pornography may include violence against women, whereas soft-core porn may provide sexual misinformation to males who are educated about sex primarily through pornographic materials (Brooks & Silverstein, 1995).

The detrimental effects of sexism on women and society—death, sexual harassment, assault, rape, and domestic violence—do not fit with the notion of healthy male development, specifically healthy interpersonal relationships between boys or men and women. If we look at the sexist notions of males needing to be dominant and aggressive over women to be "real men," then we can easily make a case for a correlation between sexist training and the maltreatment of women.

Likewise, the qualities of valuing closeness and connection and being intimate do not fit with traditional male gender stereotypes. Pittman (1993) has described the traditional socialization process of males as a "careful and deliberate process" that is "sometimes brutal, always dehumanizing" and has the end product of "cutting away large chunks of ourselves" (p. 32). These isolating features have an impact on the development of healthy interpersonal relationships by boys and men and lead to powerful and deleterious effects on women. If "men have been specialized and trained to sacrifice their emotions and even their lives for what they have been told is their duty as men" (p. 33), then they will remain isolated from themselves and, consequently, from others.

Kilmartin (1994) explained how men can become more conscious of the male socialization process and the sexist attitudes that result from it. This work requires "psychological mindedness, non-defensiveness, introspection, and a willingness to listen to another's point of view" (p. 94). Challenging constrictive notions about masculinity and prescriptive notions about how women are supposed to behave (at the individual and cultural level) will help counselors and their clients to confront the very heart of sexism.

Individual Counseling to Help Males Understand the Impact of Sexism

Sometimes counselors working with males whose problems are linked to sexism rush into the counseling process with an ardent desire to "cure" the male of his sexism. This is a big mistake. Although challenging the client's dysfunctional attitudes and behavior is important, it is equally important to work to establish rapport with the client first, in order not to alienate him. With regard to the rapport-building process, Kiselica (2001, 2003a, 2003c, in press) has recommended that the counselor practice a "male-friendly" approach to counseling boys and men. A male-friendly approach involves using process skills that are tailored to the ways that boys and men tend to develop friendships. For example, it is common for boys and men to become close through mutual participation in instrumental activities, such as working on projects or playing sports. Accordingly, effective counselors have flexible session schedules, work with boys and men in the gym, toss a football while talking about serious matters, interject humor into their conversations about clinical issues, and self-disclose personal information as ways of establishing and maintaining rapport with male clients. Also, although addressing issues pertaining to sexism may be part of the therapeutic agenda, competent counselors are attuned to the client's agenda for counseling, being sure to address his most pressing need (Kiselica, 2001, 2003a, 2003c, in press). By relating to the client in his preferred relational style and making sure to address his priorities, the counselor is likely to earn the client's trust and respect, which can serve as the foundation for exploring issues related to sexism.

A crucial aspect of the helping process—as is the case with any client—is to refrain from passing judgment on the client as the subject of sexism becomes a topic during counseling. The counselor can avoid judgmental thinking by adopting a systems perspective on the client's difficulties, trying to help the client to see not only his contributions to problems related to sexism, but also systemic factors that might have contributed to his sexist attitudes and behaviors. Erickson (1993) offered some pertinent and prudent advice for counselors engaged in this process:

> In order for therapists, especially female therapists who may have their own biases and beliefs about men to begin with, to be able to work effectively with men, we need to see beyond a man's blatant contribution to the problem, to search also for everyone else's part, rather than to lay blame for all relationship breakdowns only at his feet. (p. 210)

Approaching the client from a systems perspective can reduce the odds that he will become defensive in counseling. Communicating a systems framework also can help the client to consider the ways that sexism hurts him.

Allen and Gordon (1990) have offered numerous helpful suggestions for exploring with male clients the impact of sexism on men's lives. They recommend a nonthreatening, educational approach that includes the following activities:

- identifying the beliefs the client holds about masculinity;
- identifying the sources of these beliefs in societal institutions and in the family of origin;
- identifying some of the potentially harmful results of these beliefs;
- connecting beliefs to the presenting problems;
- emphasizing that these were not freely chosen beliefs, they are not "carved in stone," and they can be changed should he choose to do so (p. 138).

Although these activities can help boys and men to understand the role of society and the socialization process in the development of sexist ideology and behaviors, they do not excuse males from taking responsibility for any misdeeds they might have done. On the contrary, the counselor must challenge the client to change dysfunctional ways of relating. Furthermore, as Kupers (1993) has noted, although it can be beneficial to help the client to discover the qualities and dilemmas he shares with other men, the counselor also must help the client to understand and change his idiosyncratic flaws.

Most of the literature on helping boys and men echoes the recommendations of Allen and Gordon (1990) and Kupers (1993) pertaining to the process of addressing sexism with male clients. A shortcoming of this literature is that the subject of building upon male strengths is rarely mentioned. There are some notable exceptions to this trend, however. For example, to his credit, Andronico (1996, 2001) has noted that men have a long history of developing bonds and doing great deeds through their work in groups such as boy scout troops, armed services units, work groups, and athletic teams. Because boys and men are accustomed to group relations, Andronico urges counselors to use group modalities to tap into the capacity of men to rely on each other for help while achieving their goals. Consistent with this recommendation, we urge counselors to use profeminist men's groups, male advocacy organizations, and mythopoetic gatherings as means to assist boys and men.

Working With the Profeminist Men's Movement

Fortunately, many conscientious men recognize that sexism harms both the women who are the targets of it and the males who perpetrate it. In an attempt to eliminate sexism, members of a profeminist men's movement have embraced the ideals of feminism in their work to help men lead more fulfilling lives. Numerous organizations consisting either entirely or primarily of men have joined the women's rights movement to confront male violence toward women, homophobia, sexual harassment, and gender gaps in hiring practices and wages. Some of these groups are volunteer service organizations. For example, the White Ribbon Campaign (WRC) is a worldwide organization of men working to end violence against women through the development of consciousness-raising and educational forums about a wide range of subjects, including partner abuse and what men can do to stop other men from hurting women. Other profeminist organizations, such as the American Men's Studies Association (AMSA) and the International Association for Studies of Men (IASOM), support and promote multidisciplinary studies of men while eschewing sexism, homophobia, and other forms of oppression. The Society for the Psychological Study of Men and Masculinity (SPSMM) is a national organization of pro-feminist and gay-affirming psychologists whose mission is to advance knowledge regarding the psychology of men through research, education, training, public policy, and improved clinical services for men.

Social justice counselors can contribute to the work of these and other similar organizations in several ways. For example, members of the WRC work to create awareness about, and work toward the elimination of, violence against women in institutions and communities. Counselors can volunteer their services to WRC campaigns to help WRC members craft policies denouncing violence and affirming women's rights in educational institutions. At the community level, counselors can organize White Ribbon events whose purpose is to raise community awareness about rape and the battering of women. In both institutional and community settings, counselors can serve as facilitators of workshops designed to help boys and men develop nonsexist attitudes and ways of relating to girls and women. Counselors also can join academic and professional organizations, such as SPSMM, AMSA, and IASOM, and can engage in studies designed to understand and change sexist attitudes toward women.

Understanding and Eliminating Injustice Toward Boys and Men

Counselors should recognize that profeminist groups have sometimes been criticized for directing too much attention to the ways males hurt women at the expense of understanding the troubles that men have. For example, Kupers (1993) stated,

> Profeminist men risk becoming too one-sidedly political and losing sight of the psychological pain and spiritual vacuum that plagues so many men. Men who are hurting might not be interested in running to the aid of women who are oppressed, and this is especially the case if a man believes his pain was caused by a woman's rejection.... There is danger that political, profeminist men will be viewed as self-righteous and judgmental, and will thereby lose many potential supporters of the antisexist men's movement. (p. 152)

Kupers' point is well taken. Society in general and profeminist organizations in particular have devoted too little substantive attention to the struggles of many populations of boys and men. For example,

African American boys (see Lee, 2003), teenage fathers (see Kiselica, 1995, in press), blue-collar males (see Kupers, 1993), and noncustodial fathers (see Kupers, 1993) — to name just a few — are all groups of males who are disempowered in the United States. Their needs are rarely mentioned in profeminist circles. Consequently, it behooves the counselor to understand and work with male advocacy organizations dedicated to addressing injustice toward boys and men.

Working With Male Advocacy Groups

Counselors should be aware that many male advocacy organizations were founded as a backlash against feminism. Our own experiences of searching the Internet and talking with many of these groups have confirmed that some men's groups have an irrational fear of and anger toward women. At the same time, we have learned that some male advocacy movements were founded out of a genuine concern for particular populations of boys and men whose needs have been dismissed by society. Although space limitations prevent us from discussing all of these advocacy organizations, we have chosen three for discussion here as illustration of male advocacy initiatives. First is the mythopoetic men's movement, a loosely organized group of men who participate in activities designed to address a void of masculine mentorship in contemporary American society. Other groups are dedicated to helping divorced men with their efforts to be awarded custody of their children and to advocating for the child visitation rights of noncustodial fathers. There are also numerous groups that support men with the process of being a good parent. We describe several of these groups here and suggest ways that a counselor can work with these groups to address some of the significant problems that boys and men experience.

The Mythopoetic Men's Movement

The mythopoetic movement represents an attempt by men to capture longstanding mythological images of men in an effort to define what it means to be a man. These images include both the feminine, or soft, side of being a man and the "deep male," which is the source of life and power (Kupers, 1993). Mythopoetic men experience and embrace these images through special ritualistic gatherings where they beat drums, tell stories, read poetry, and engage in physical movement and imagery exercises. Participating in these rituals allows men to experience male bonding and experimentation with male gender roles in a safe place (Andronico, 2001; Williams & Myer, 1993).

Several writers have suggested that counselors can use mythopoetic events as an adjunct to traditional counseling. For example, Williams and Myer (1993) reported a case study in which they used participation in mythopoetic gatherings to help a 35-year-old man with a history of alcohol addiction, marital discord, and conflicted feelings toward his father to bond with men, risk emotional vulnerability, and establish a more intimate and caring relationship with his wife. Andronico (2001) observed that although mythopoetic retreats are not counseling, they do have therapeutic value. As an adjunct to counseling and psychotherapy, Andronico continued, mythopoetic gatherings can help men who have trouble expressing their feelings in words to express them nonverbally through drumming and movement.

Because mythopoetic groups appeal to many troubled men, it behooves counselors who work with men to consider how they can tap into the valuable experiences that mythopoetic groups have to offer. Andronico (2001) recommended that counselors become more familiar with the mythopoetic movement both by reading about the movement and by attending mythopoetic events. Although this movement is very loosely organized and does not have a central organization akin to other male advocacy groups, we can recommend some useful Internet Web sites that list mythopoetic events and other similar events. For example, www.menweb.org is an online magazine that publicizes mythopoetic and other men's gatherings, and www.mankindproject.com features New Warrior activities, which are like mythopoetic events in that they are designed to help men to understand both the dark and positive sides of masculinity, to embrace their duties as men, and to accept the consequences of their actions through outdoor, adventure-based experiences.

Kupers (1993) raised an important caution about mythopoetic events. Although mythopoetic groups can produce positive outcomes, such as providing men with a sense of brotherhood, they will fall short in helping men to achieve maximally satisfying lives if they do nothing to end sexist relations. Thus, as Andronico (2001) has advised, counselors must help men to take the lessons they have learned from mythopoetic experiences and apply them in their lives. For example, one of the positive features of mythopoetic men's gatherings is that they are usually characterized by egalitarian relations among the participants. Andronico urged counselors to challenge men to practice the same egalitarian way of relating in their homes.

Men's Advocacy Groups Pertaining to Child Custody and Visitation
One of the most emotionally charged issues for men pertains to child custody decisions and fathers' visitation rights. U.S. Census Bureau

(2002) data have indicated that custodial mothers represent 85.1% of all custodial parents while the remaining 14.9% were fathers; these percentages have remained unchanged since 1994. Other data document that many noncustodial fathers are denied their right to visit their children. For example, anywhere from one third (see Ellman, 2004) to eight tenths (see American Coalition for Fathers and Children, 2000) of noncustodial fathers reported that they have been denied access to their children due to tensions between the fathers and their former wives. Supporting these findings are reports from mothers who have admitted interfering with visitation to punish their former spouse. For example, 40% of the custodial mothers participating in a study of 400 families affected by divorce acknowledged having thwarted their former spouse's access to their child (Braver & O'Connor, 1998).

These findings document that a vast majority of divorced men are noncustodial fathers and that a significant percentage of them have been denied the right to visit with their children. Other findings from a national survey conducted by the American Coalition for Fathers and Children (2000) in conjunction with the University of California at Berkeley suggested that the legal system is unlikely to assist men who have experienced access and visitation denial. For example, in 82% of the cases in which men making child support payments had reported child access and visitation interference, the courts did not do anything to enforce visitation.

The forced severing of father-child contact can have devastating effects on both the child and the father. The chronic exclusion of a child from his or her father's life can cause significant emotional damage to the child and place the child at higher risk for a host of adjustment difficulties, including behavioral problems, chemical abuse, teenage pregnancy and parenthood, school dropout, juvenile delinquency, runaway, and suicide (see Center for Children's Justice, 2005). Caring fathers who are denied access to their children experience a host of reactions, including sadness, depression, and anger (Kiselir, her In severe cases where a mother engages in malicious periods former spouse, such as deliberately turning a see the child is father and denying the father visits with child relationship of time, fathers can suffer from to hurt men and children characterized by the fathe CFC) was formed to promote withdrawing emot custody and access decisions. (Rand, 1997

wl

C

Accentuating a positive and noninflammatory tone in its work and consisting of local chapters across the United States, the ACFC sponsors advocacy initiatives and provides informative reports, educational kits, and announcements about events pertaining to shared parenting.

Because ACFC embraces the consciousness-raising and systems-change strategies of social justice counseling, it is a fitting organization for counselors interested in men's issues to contact. Counselors can work with the ACFC and other organizations that support a nonsexist view of parenting in several ways. First, counselors can facilitate meetings of local ACFC chapters, thereby providing disaffected fathers with a supportive atmosphere to discuss their frustrations regarding child custody and visitation. Second, counselors can join forces with ACFC members to lobby for much-needed changes in the justice system, including the education of judges about the important role of fathers in child development (see Hawkins & Dollahite, 1997; Lamb, 1997; Snarey, 1993) and the positive effect that the provision and protection of child visitation rights has on child support payments (see U.S. Census Bureau, 2000). Third, all parties advocating for men's rights should press for the creation of government-funded social support and legal aid programs for fathers who have been denied court-approved visits with their children.

Groups That Promote and Support Responsible Fatherhood
Historically, the role of the father in child development has been a neglected topic in the counseling and psychology literature and in public policy pertaining to families. Consequently, the mental health professions and society have offered fathers meager or no guidance about parenting. So men had to prepare for fatherhood on their own, often basing their conceptions of fatherhood almost exclusively on their experiences with their own fathers (Peters & Day, 2000). Over the past 30 years, however, there has been an increased awareness about the ~ds of fathers and the importance of fathers in their children's lives. o¹~mitant with the growing interest in fatherhood, numerous Initiat¹~s dedicated to promoting and supporting responsible NFI and merged. Among them are the National Fatherhood fathering, related to fath~ National Center for Fathering (NCF). Both the in public policy ~ sites providing extensive information on in their children's workshops regarding special topics Counselors can¹ and local policymakers for changes and NCF in their respe~ ~port the participation of fathers Dollahite, 2001). ~lationships with NFI ~men. Counselors

assisting fathers can turn to NFI and NCF for numerous resources pertaining to special fathering circumstances—such as divorced fathers, new fathers, and fathers with special-needs children—and suggest that fathers visit these organizations' Web-based discussion groups where they can ask for and give advice and communicate with other fathers nationally and internationally (Grant et al., 2001). Counselors also can contact NCF about enrolling in its exciting Train the Trainer program, which instructs volunteers in how to teach dads a variety of fathering skills (National Center for Fathering, 2005). Because counselors are trained in group facilitation skills, they are ideal candidates to serve as NCF instructors with fathers interested in enhancing their parenting skills.

Understanding and Eliminating Myths Regarding Boys and Men

There has been an explosion of publications regarding the emotional lives of boys and men over the past 10 years, much of it appearing in the pop psychology literature. Although this burgeoning literature has produced many positive results, such as an increased awareness about males and the special problems they experience, it also has fostered some erroneous assumptions about boys and men that have the potential to impede the process of helping males (Kiselica, 2001, 2003a, 2003c, in press; Kiselica & O'Brien, 2001). For example, in a series of conference presentations and publications about the emotional lives of boys, Pollack (1995, 1997, 1998, 2000) has claimed that boys experience a normative, forced, premature emotional separation from their mothers and develop disabling levels of emotional constriction due to the combined effects of this separation and a harsh male socialization process. Emotional constriction in boys and men is so great, Pollack added, that males suffer from low to moderate levels of alexithymia, which Sifneos (1973) and Krystal (1982) defined as a clinical condition characterized by significant deficits in the ability to access, identify, and express feelings.

Although Pollack's assumptions about male development have received extensive media coverage, there is very little to no empirical support for his claims. For example, if it were true, as Pollack has contended, that boys experience a forced, premature, and emotionally damaging separation from their mothers, one would find a significantly higher proportion of boys relative to girls who suffer from attachment disorders. However, a review of empirical research findings from the attachment literature has indicated that males are no more likely than females to be insecurely attached to their mothers or to have insecure attachment styles that are associated with problems in their interpersonal relationships (see Kiselica & O'Brien, 2001). Furthermore, both young boys and adult males are just as likely as girls and women to have secure attachments (see Kiselica & O'Brien, 2001). Similarly, if it is normative for boys and men to develop alexithymia, then a significantly higher percentage of males than females should be alexithymic, yet the bulk of the pertinent empirical data have suggested that there are no consistent gender differences in alexithymia (see Kiselica & O'Brien, 2001). Collectively, these data challenge the claim that boys experience the normative trauma of a forced separation from their mothers and indicate that the capacity of boys and men to express emotions and to recognize the emotional states of others appears to be within the normal range. Furthermore, other research findings have indicated that sex differences in emotions tend to be small and inconsistent and challenge the assumption that males and females are emotionally different (see Wester, Vogel, Pressly, & Heesacker, 2002).

Another problematic assumption about males is the equating of aggression with masculinity. Many scholars have used the term *hypermasculinity* to describe males who display a pattern of toughness, emotional insensitivity, and lack of empathy (Brooks & Gilbert, 1995). For example, Kilmartin (1994) has stated that "violence, physical risk taking, and hostility directed toward women and gays" (p. 31) are examples of hypermasculinity. Similarly, Lisak (2001) has proposed that hypermasculinity is a feature of men who degrade women, while Brooks and Silverstein (1995) have suggested that aggression, rape, and violence against women as well as sexual harassment, sexual excess, promiscuity, and pornography are all manifestations of hypermasculinity. Although we commend these authors for their efforts to raise awareness about the abhorrent behaviors of some men, we have serious concerns about their use of the term *hypermasculinity* to categorize those behaviors. Although it is true that violence, homophobia, and sexual assault are very serious social problems that are often committed by men and supported by a sexist culture, it is also true that these types of problematic behaviors are not unique to males. Using hypermasculinity as an umbrella term for these vexing problems implies that being a male means being physically and sexually aggressive and homophobic to some degree, and that being "very male" means being extremely assaultive and homophobic. The use of hypermasculinity also ignores the fact that men differ greatly in the ways they view their masculinity and the ways they behave. Although many boys and men are aggressive, misogynist, and homophobic, many other men consider caring for people to be central to their conception of what it means to be a man. In support of this claim, considerable research has shown how men care for their children and their wives and partners and contribute to their work worlds and society, and that these forms of generativity are important aspects of identity for many males (see, e.g., Hawkins & Dollahite, 1997; Lamb, 1997; Snarey, 1993).

Adopting erroneous, deficit models of male development and masculinity can pose a serious threat to the helping process. Data from analog research about couples counseling reveal that counselors who view men as hypoemotional are likely to blame men for couples' problems and to view male clients as more pathological than they really are (Heesacker et al., 1999). Other anecdotal data reveal that helpers who view boys as hypermasculine and hypoemotional tend to overestimate the degree to which boys are resistant to getting true help, thereby alienating boys from counseling (Kiselica, 2003c, in press). If professionals continue to embrace these stereotypes, they are likely to see boys as flawed and treat them as unwhole beings who need to be fixed, rather than as people who want to be helped.

A social justice perspective demands that professional counselors think critically about dubious models of male development and disparaging language about boys and men. In addition, counselors must challenge their fellow mental health professionals to acquire accurate information about males and their emotional makeup and to use more positive language in their discussions about some of the bad things that boys and men do. For example, counselors must inform their colleagues and school personnel and parents that most boys and men are reasonably well-adjusted human beings who seek and maintain connections in their relationships and whose capacity for emotional expression is within the normal range (Kiselica, 2001, 2003b; Kiselica & O'Brien, 2001). In addition, counselors must use nonsexist language when describing boys and men who demonstrate adjustment difficulties. For instance, when referring to a husband who beats his wife, it is more appropriate and accurate to refer to that individual as a batterer who needs help to learn anger management skills than it is to label him as hypermasculine. Finally, counselors must raise awareness about true gender differences in adjustment problems. For example, whereas it is untrue that boys are more likely than girls to have insecure attachments or alexithymia, it is true that boys are significantly more likely than girls to be the target of a physical assault at school, to experience a learning disability or a developmental delay that adversely affects their academic adjustment, to drop out of school, to commit delinquency offenses, and to commit suicide (Kiselica & Horne, 1999). Counselors must work to raise awareness about these problems that many males are at higher risk of suffering, and to develop and provide service programs addressing the actual problems that boys and men tend to have.

Conclusion

We are fortunate that we live in an era of heightened awareness regarding the harm that sexism toward females does to boys and girls and men and women. We hope that counselors will use the suggestions we have offered in this chapter to create systemic changes that will reduce sexist practices toward women in our society. We also challenge counselors to recognize that awareness about the particular ways that men have been hurt by societal neglect and by inaccurate assumptions and disparaging language about males lags far behind societal understanding regarding sexism toward women. Advocacy for women's rights must be balanced by advocacy for the rights of boys and men. By thinking about and working to change injustice toward both females *and* males, counselors will help boys and men to maximize their potential and lead more fulfilling lives.

References

Allen, J. A., & Gordon, S. (1990). Creating a framework for change. In R. L. Meth & R. S. Pasick (Eds.), *Men in therapy: The challenge of change* (pp. 131–151). New York: Guilford Press.

American Coalition for Fathers and Children. (2000). *Child support statistics—ACFC survey 8/2000*. Retrieved March 4, 2005, from http://www.facenj.org/stats/cs/ACFC-CS.HTM

Andronico, M. P. (Ed.). (1996). *Men in groups: Insights, interventions, and psychoeducational work*. Washington, DC: American Psychological Association.

Andronico, M. P. (2001). Mythopoetic and weekend retreats to facilitate men's growth. In G. R. Brooks & G. Good (Eds.), *The handbook of counseling and psychotherapy with men: A guide to settings and approaches. Vol. 1* (pp. 43–58). San Francisco: Jossey-Bass.

Benokraitis, N. V. (1997). *Subtle sexism: Current practice and prospects for change*. Thousand Oaks, CA: Sage.

Beymer, L. (1995). *Meeting the guidance and counseling needs of boys*. Alexandria, VA: American Counseling Association.

Bradley, L., & Lewis, J. (2000). Introduction. In J. Lewis & L. Bradley, (Eds.), *Advocacy in counseling: Counselors, clients, and community* (pp. 3–4). Greensboro, NC: ERIC Clearinghouse on Counseling and Student Services.

Braver, S. L., & O'Connor, D. (1998). *Divorced dads: Shattering the myths*. New York: Tarcher.

Brooks, G. R., & Gilbert, L. A. (1995). Men in families: Old constraints, new possibilities. In R. F. Levant & W. S. Pollack (Eds.), *A new psychology of men* (pp. 252–279). New York: Basic Books.

Brooks, G. R., & Good, G. E. (Eds.). (2001). *The new handbook of psychotherapy and counseling with men: A comprehensive guide to settings, problems, and treatment approaches*. San Francisco: Jossey-Bass.

Brooks, G. R., & Silverstein, L. (1995). Understanding the dark side of masculinity: An interactive systems model. In R. F. Levant & W. S. Pollack (Eds.), *A new psychology of men* (pp. 280–336). New York: Basic Books.

Bureau of Justice Statistics. (1995, August). *Violence against women: Estimates from the redesigned survey*. Washington, DC: U.S. Government Printing Office.

Bureau of Justice Statistics Crime Data Brief. (2003, February). *Intimate partner violence, 1993–2001*. Washington, DC: U.S. Government Printing Office.

Carlson, B. E. (1984). Children's observations of interpersonal violence. In A. R. Roberts (Ed.), *Battered women and their families* (pp. 147–167). New York: Springer.

Center for Children's Justice. (2005). *Effects on children of removing a father from the life of a child*. Retrieved February 4, 2005, from http://www.childrensjustice.org/fatherlessness1.htm

Center for Policy Research. (1997, July). *Stalking in America*. Syracuse, NY: Syracuse University Press.

Centers for Disease Control and Prevention. (2003). *Costs of intimate partner violence against women in the United States.* Atlanta, GA: Author.

The Commonwealth Fund. (1999, May). *Health concerns across a woman's lifespan: 1998 Survey of Women's Health.* New York: Author.

Donnerstein, E., & Linz, D. (1987). Mass-media sexual violence and male viewers: Current theory and research. In M. S. Kimmel (Ed.), *Changing men: New directions in research on men and masculinity* (pp. 198–215). Newbury Park, CA: Sage.

Elman, I. M. (2004). Should visitation denial affect the obligation to pay support? In W. Comanor (Ed.), *The law and economics of child support payments.* Cheltenham, UK: Edward Elgar.

Erikson, B. M. (1993). *Helping men change: The role of the female therapist.* Thousand Oaks, CA: Sage.

Glicke, P., & Fiske, S. T. (1999a). Gender, power dynamics, and social interaction. In M. M. Ferree, J. Lorber, & B. B. Hess (Eds.), *Revisioning gender.* Thousand Oaks, CA: Sage.

Glicke, P., & Fiske, S. T. (1999b). Sexism and other isms: Interdependence, status, and the ambivalent content of stereotypes. In W. B. Swann, J. H. Langlois, & L. A. Gilbert (Eds.), *Sexism and stereotypes in modern society.* Washington, DC: American Psychological Association.

Grant, T. R., Hawkins, A. J., & Dollahite, D. C. (2001). Web-based education and support for fathers: Remote but promising. In J. Fagan & A. J. Hawkins (Eds.), *Clinical and educational interventions with fathers* (pp. 143–170). New York: Haworth Clinical Practice Press.

Hawkins, A. J., & Dollahite, D. C. (Eds.). (1997). *Generative fathering: Beyond deficit perspectives.* Thousand Oaks, CA: Sage.

Heesacker, M., Wester, S. R., Vogel, D. L., Wentzel, J. T., Mejia-Millan, C. M., & Goodholm, C. R. (1999). Gender-based emotional stereotyping. *Journal of Counseling Psychology, 46,* 483–495.

Heise, L., Ellsberg, M., & Gottenmoeller, M. (1999, December). Ending violence against women. *Population Reports*, Series L, No. 11.

Horne, A. M., & Kiselica, M. S. (Eds.). (1999). *Handbook of counseling boys and adolescent males: A practitioner's guide*. Thousand Oaks, CA: Sage.

Horon, I., & Cheng, D. (2001). Enhanced surveillance for pregnancy-associated mortality—Maryland, 1993–1998. *Journal of the American Medical Association, 285*, 11.

Kilmartin, C. T. (1994). *The masculine self*. New York: Macmillan.

Kiselica, M. S. (1995). *Multicultural counseling with teenage fathers: A practical guide*. Thousand Oaks, CA: Sage.

Kiselica, M. S. (2001). A male-friendly therapeutic process with school-age boys. In G. R. Brooks & G. Good (Eds.), *The handbook of counseling and psychotherapy with men: A guide to settings and approaches. Vol. 1* (pp. 43–58). San Francisco: Jossey-Bass.

Kiselica, M. S. (2003a, Autumn). Male-sensitive counseling with boys. *Counselling in Education*, 16–19.

Kiselica, M. S. (2003b). *Parenting with the experts series: Parenting boys* [video]. Boston: Allyn & Bacon.

Kiselica, M. S. (2003c). Transforming psychotherapy in order to succeed with boys: Male-friendly practices. *Journal of Clinical Psychology: In Session, 59*, 1225–1236.

Kiselica, M. S. (2004). When duty calls: The implications of social justice work for policy, education, and practice in the mental health professions. *The Counseling Psychologist, 32*, 838–854.

Kiselica, M. S. (in press). Male-sensitive psychotherapy with a teenage father. In M. Englar-Carlson & M. Stevens (Eds.), *In the room with men: A casebook of psychotherapy with men*. Washington, DC: American Psychological Association.

Kiselica, M. S., & Horne, A. M. (1999). Preface: For the sake of our nation's sons. In A. M. Horne & M. S. Kiselica (Eds.), *Handbook of counseling boys and adolescent males* (pp. xv–xx). Thousand Oaks, CA: Sage.

Kiselica, M. S., & O'Brien, S. (2001, August). Are attachment disorders and alexithymia characteristic of males? In M. S. Kiselica (Chair), *Are males really emotional mummies: What do the data indicate?* Symposium conducted at the Annual Convention of the American Psychological Association, San Francisco, CA.

Kiselica, M. S., & Robinson, M. (2001). Bringing advocacy counseling to life: The history, issues, and human dramas of social justice work in counseling. *Journal of Counseling & Development, 70,* 387–397.

Krystal, H. (1982). Alexithymia and the effectiveness of psychoanalytic treatment. *International Journal of Psychoanalytic Psychotherapy, 9,* 353–379.

Kupers, T. A. (1993). *Revisioning men's lives: Gender, intimacy, and power.* New York: Guilford Press.

Lamb, M. E. (Ed.). (1997). *The role of the father in child development* (3rd ed.). New York: Wiley.

Lee, C. C. (1998). Counselors as agents for social change. In C. C. Lee & G. R. Walz (Eds.), *Social action: A mandate for counselors* (pp. 3–16). Alexandria, VA: American Counseling Association.

Lee, C. C. (2003). *Empowering young Black males III: A systematic modular training program for young Black children and adolescents.* Alexandria, VA: American Counseling Association Foundation and ERIC/CASS.

Levant, R. F. (1995). Toward the reconstruction of masculinity. In R. F. Levant & W. S. Pollack (Eds.), *A new psychology of men* (pp. 229–251). New York: Basic Books.

Lieberman Research. (1996, July–October). *Tracking survey conducted for the Advertising Council and the Family Violence Prevention Fund.*

Lisak, D. (2001). Homicide, violence, and male aggression. In G. R. Brooks & G. E. Good (Eds.), *The new handbook of counseling and psychotherapy with men* (pp. 278–292). San Francisco: Jossey-Bass.

Mays, V. M. (2000). A social justice agenda. *American Psychologist, 55*, 326–327.

Nannini, A., Weiss, J., Goldstein, R., & Fogerty, S. (2002). Pregnancy-associated mortality at the end of the 20th century: Massachusetts, 1990–1999. *Journal of the American Medical Women's Association, 57*, 23.

National Center for Fathering. (2005). *Train the trainer: Programs overview.* Retrieved February 9, 2005, from http://www.fathers.com/training/ttt01overview.html

Peters, H. E., & Day, R. D. (2000). Editor's introduction. In H. E. Peters, G. W. Peterson, S. K. Steinmetz, & R. D. Day (Eds.), *Fatherhood: Research, interventions, and policies* (pp. 1–10). New York: Haworth Press.

Pittman, F. S. (1993). *Man enough: Fathers, sons, and the search for masculinity.* New York: Putnam's.

Pollack, W. S. (1995). No man is an island: Toward a new psychoanalytic psychology of men. In R. F. Levant & W. S. Pollack (Eds.), *A new psychology of men* (pp. 33–67). New York: Basic Books.

Pollack, W. S. (1997, August). Lost boys: Finding boys' voices. In W. S. Pollack (Chair), *Rescuing Ophelia's brothers: What about boys?* Symposium conducted at the Annual Convention of the American Psychological Association, Chicago, IL.

Pollack, W. S. (1998). *Real boys: Rescuing our sons from the myths of boyhood.* New York: Random House.

Pollack, W. S. (2000, August). *Real boys' voices: Listening to America's sons, saving Ophelia's brothers.* Paper presented at the Annual Convention of the American Psychological Association, Chicago, IL.

Rand, D. C. (1997). The spectrum of parental alienation syndrome. *American Journal of Forensic Psychology, 15.*

Russell, B. L., & Trigg, K. Y. (2004, April). Tolerance of sexual harassment: An examination of gender differences, ambivalent sexism, social dominance, and gender roles. *Sex Roles, 50,* 565–573.

Sifneos, P. E. (1973). The prevalence of "alexithymic" characteristics in psychosomatic patients. Topics of Psychosomatic Research, 9th European Conference on Psychosomatic Research, Vienna, 1972. *Psychother, Psychosom, 22,* 255–262.

Silverman, J. G., Raj, A., Mucci, L. A., & Hathaway, J. E. (2001). Dating violence against adolescent girls and associated substance use, unhealthy weight control, sexual risk behavior, pregnancy, and suicidality. *Journal of the American Medical Association, 286,* 5.

Snarey, J. (1993). *How fathers care for the next generation: A four-decade study.* Cambridge, MA: Harvard University Press.

Strauss, M. A., Gelles, R. J., & Smith, C. (1990). *Physical violence in American families: Risk factors and adaptations to violence in 8,145 families.* New Brunswick: Transaction.

Strickland, B. R. (2000). Misassumptions, misadventures, and the misuses of psychology. *American Psychologist, 55,* 331–338.

Tjaden, P., & Thoennes, N. (2000). *Extent, nature, and consequences of intimate partner violence.* Washington, DC: National Institute of Justice.

U.S. Census Bureau. (2000, October). *More custodial parents receive full amount of child support, Census Bureau reports.* Retrieved February 3, 2005, from http://www.census.gov/Press-Release/www/releases/archives/children/00533.html

U.S. Census Bureau. (2002, October). *Custodial mothers and fathers and their child support: 1999.* Retrieved February 3, 2005, from http://www.census.gov/prod/2002pubs/p60–217.pdf

U.S. Department of Justice. (1998a). *Prevalence, incidence, and consequences of violence against women: Findings from the National Violence Against Women Survey.* Washington, DC: U.S. Government Printing Office.

U.S. Department of Justice. (1998b). *Violence by intimates: Analysis of data on crimes by current or former spouses, boyfriends, and girlfriends.* Washington, DC: U.S. Government Printing Office.

U.S. Equal Employment Opportunity Commission. (2005). *Sexual harassment.* Retrieved February 3, 2005, from http://www.eeoc.gov/

Wester, S. R., Vogel, D. L., Pressly, P. K., & Heesacker, M. (2002). Sex differences in emotion: A critical review of the literature and implications for counseling psychology. *The Counseling Psychologist, 30,* 629–651.

Williams, R. C., & Myer, R. A. (1993). The men's movement: An adjunct to traditional counseling approaches. *Journal of Mental Health Counseling, 3,* 393–404.

Chapter 8

Promoting Ethnic/Racial Equality Through Empowerment-Based Counseling

Cheryl Holcomb-McCoy and Natasha A. Mitchell

Undeniably, racial discrimination and social inequality have had a profound influence on the social and emotional development of ethnic minority persons (Ridley, 1995; Sue, 1977). Fundamentally, these conditions are rooted in the social organization of our society and evolve from the relations among racial, class, and gender groups in the United States. The notion that the problems of ethnic minority persons lie outside of the individual and are rooted in society creates a dilemma for counselors and mental health professionals because it diminishes the focus on the cultural processes of counseling and shifts the focus to the complex interrelationships of social structures and cultural processes in society. It is this paradigm shift that challenges counselors and requires nontraditional counseling strategies, theories, and techniques.

In order to make this paradigm shift, counselors must first address the cycle of oppression that has predominated the history of many ethnic groups. In contrast to the traditional definition that denotes colonialism and conquest, oppression in a counseling context designates the disadvantage and injustice some people suffer not because tyrannical power coerces them, but because of the everyday practices of a society. Oppression in this sense is embedded in unquestioned norms, habits, and symbols; in the assumptions underlying institutional rules; and in the collective consequences of following those rules.

Young (1990) suggested that a group is oppressed if it is subject to one or more of five conditions: exploitation, marginalization, powerlessness, cultural imperialism, and violence. Exploitation refers to the steady transfer of the results of the labor of one social group to the benefit of another. Marginalization refers to the process whereby individuals or groups of people are permanently confined to lives of social marginality because they are not perceived as attractive or acceptable to people in the dominant culture. Young emphasized that marginalization is particularly harmful to people because it means being both expelled from participation in social life and subjected to material deprivation. Powerlessness is defined as having to take orders without having the right to give them. Cultural imperialism refers to the dominance of one group's experiences and culture and its establishment as the norm. Young claimed that cultural imperialism occurs when the experiences and perspectives of oppressed groups seem invisible to the dominant group. And paradoxically, the oppressed group is stereotyped and marked out as the other. And lastly, violence is a manifestation of oppression because of the social context that makes violence possible and, in some cases, acceptable. Violence is viewed as systemic because it is often directed at members of oppressed groups simply because they are members of that group.

As most counselors are aware, one's mental health is affected by experiences of oppression. Research has indicated that an individual's negative racial experiences and exposure to oppressive environments can influence his or her mental health (Loo, 1994). Traditional counseling, however, has focused on working with clients on internal issues (e.g., depression, stress management) as opposed to external forces (e.g., racism, oppression, discrimination) that create stressors and disempowerment. We believe that counselors need to extend their work to address external forces in order to alleviate ethnic minority clients' negative internal conditions. As such, we focus in this chapter on the unique experiences and social status of ethnic minorities in today's society. We believe understanding the complexities and historical status of minority communities is necessary in order to assist ethnic minority persons in making lasting changes in their lives. We also discuss empowerment and advocacy-based interventions. These interventions ultimately shift the focus of counseling from a traditional model to more of a social action approach in which counselors are acting in the role of advocate and community change agent.

Historical Overview of Oppression Experienced by Ethnic Minorities

Historically, minorities in the United States have experienced institutionalized oppression based mostly on racism. Over the course of U.S. history, Whites have systematically oppressed Asians, Africans, Latinos, and Native Americans (Axelson, 1999; Locke, 1998; Saenz,

1999; Wright, 1992). We present a brief historical overview of the oppression experienced by each of the four major U.S. minority groups in an effort to demonstrate the connection between the oppressive historical experiences of minorities and their current experiences of inequity and injustice.

Asian Americans

Asian Americans have experienced economic and legal oppression since the time of their migration to the United States. Chinese people migrated to the United States mostly between 1850 and 1882, and Japanese people arrived in large numbers between 1890 and 1908 (Axelson, 1999). The gold rush in California created a demand for cheap labor for building the transcontinental railroad (Locke, 1998), and the U.S. government encouraged Chinese immigration to meet this demand. By 1870 Chinese people had become 8.6% of the total population and 25% of the wage-earning force in California; however, slowing economic conditions also made them competitors with Whites for scarce jobs (Takaki, 1979). In response, the U.S. government passed legislation to bar Chinese immigration, thereby ensuring more jobs for Whites. Not only were Chinese workers used as a cheap labor force when needed and then denied access to economic resources when Whites became fearful that their privileged status was being infringed upon, they were also characterized as morally inferior, savage, childlike, and lustful to justify these oppressive measures (Takaki 1979). The 1882 Chinese Exclusion Act prohibited Chinese people from immigrating, and those who already resided in the United States were barred from becoming citizens (Lin, 1999; Takaki 1979). This act and other exclusionary laws were extended to Japanese Americans in 1907 (L. C. Lee, 1989) and remained in effect until 1943 (Lin, 1999; Locke 1998).

Before the exclusion acts were extended to them in 1907, Japanese people were brought to the United States to fill the need for cheap labor caused by the exclusion of Chinese immigrants. As soon as Japanese workers began to move from working as low-paid laborers to succeeding in small-truck farming, their ability to immigrate to the United States was halted by the signing of the 1906 Gentlemen's Agreement (Axelson, 1999; L. C. Lee, 1989). Arguably, one of the most egregious acts of racial oppression meted out against Japanese Americans was their internment in camps during World War II. In 1942 an executive order forced 120,000 Japanese Americans into internment camps because they were viewed as a threat to U.S. national security. First- and second-generation Japanese Americans were forced to leave their homes, land, businesses, and communities to exist in internment camps for 3 years only to return to urban areas where they were now relegated to jobs as gardeners, secretaries, domestics, and industrial workers (Fujiwara & Takagi, 1999). Interestingly enough, though the United States was also at war with Germany and Italy during World War II, German and Italian Americans were never interned. It is clear that Asian populations have had their access to resources limited by White Americans through the systematic implementation and execution of oppressive laws and economic policies; we turn now to the African American population in the United States, which has also experienced this type of institutionalized oppression.

African Americans

The majority of African Americans were forcibly transported to the United States as chattel from Africa (Axelson, 1999; Herring, 1999). The first Africans arrived in Virginia in 1619 and served as indentured servants who by law could be whipped by their masters. As the demand for labor increased, Virginia gave official statutory recognition to slavery in 1661 (Giddings, 1996). African Americans were deemed to be socially, intellectually, and morally inferior, thereby justifying their enslavement (Locke, 1998; Takaki, 1979). Enslaved Africans were (a) brutalized culturally through systematic attempts to sever their connection to their African heritage; (b) brutalized physically through whippings, mutilations, and sanctioned rapes; (c) brutalized socially through the deliberate separation of family members from each other; and (d) brutalized emotionally through repeated messages that reinforced the idea that to be African is to be inferior.

The enslavement of Africans lasted until the passage of the 13th Amendment in 1865, which officially ended slavery in the United States. The institution of slavery had provided the United States with 204 years of free, back-breaking African American labor that allowed the young country quickly to acquire great economic wealth, stability, and world political power (Herring, 1999). After the institution of slavery was ended, Blacks in the United States experienced decades of legalized segregation until the passage of a series of civil rights acts between 1957 and 1968 (Axelson, 1999; Giddings, 1996; Turner, Singleton, & Musick, 1984). Many have argued that this 386-year legacy of oppression has significantly contributed to the inequities that Blacks experience in the United States today (Estrada, García, Macías, & Maldonado, 1981; Locke, 1998; Takaki, 1979; Turner et al., 1984).

Latino Americans

Latinos have also experienced oppression in the United States. The experience of Mexican and Puerto Rican Americans, the two largest subgroups within the Latino population, provide clear examples of political and economic oppression. Puerto Rico became an occupied territory of the United States in 1898 with the end of the Spanish-American War. At the onset of World War I, Puerto Ricans were granted U.S. citizenship, and the passage of the 1917 Jones Act facilitated their migration to the industrial areas of the northeastern United States (Axelson, 1999; Torrecilha, Cant, & Nguyen, 1999). This encouraged migration provided the United States with cheap domestic labor during World War I (Bonilla & Campos, 1981). Today, Puerto Rico is a U.S. commonwealth where the residents cannot vote for the U.S. president and have no elected representation in Congress; however, they can be drafted to go to war for the United States (Axelson, 1999).

Similarly, Mexicans in the United States have experienced land acquisition and exploitation as cheap labor. The Mexican War (1846–1848) ended with the Treaty of Guadalupe Hidalgo, under which Mexico lost half of its national territory to the United States (Saenz, 1999). Arizona, California, Colorado, New Mexico, Texas, Nevada, Utah, and parts of Kansas, Oklahoma, and Wyoming were established out of the acquired territory (Estrada et al., 1981). Many Mexicans chose to stay on their land and accept U.S. sovereignty with ostensible guarantees of their property rights; however, due to federal policies designed to dispossess Mexicans of their land, they were increasingly relegated to being a mobile, colonized labor force (Estrada et al., 1981). For example, the Chinese Exclusion Act of 1882 increased White dependence on cheap Mexican labor in the mining industry. Pay scales for miners showed that White miners made $3.25 per day plus board, while Mexican miners were paid $1.75 per day plus a ration of flour (Takaki, 1979). Thus, Mexican miners made almost half the income of White miners but had the additional daily expense of providing food and housing for themselves. This kind of deliberate reinforcement of the economic hierarchy fortified Latinos' status as an oppressed minority group in the United States. Unfortunately, Native American populations had similar experiences.

Native Americans

Native Americans were the first people to settle in the geographical area now referred to as North America. It is believed that Native

Americans entered this continent from Asia approximately 15,000 to 35,000 years ago across a land bridge located where the Bering Strait now exists (Snow, 1979; Wright, 1992). The term *Indian* came into use when Columbus in his travels to find India landed in North America and mistakenly called the people of the sovereign Native American nations Indians. Countless Native Americans were killed by diseases spread by European settlers or were murdered in wars and battles with the newly created nation; those that survived were subjected to assimilationist policies that promoted the denigration of Native American culture and the illegal appropriation of their land (Wright, 1992). Through legislation and U.S. Supreme Court decisions between 1824 and 1887, Native Americans were removed from their land and forcibly relocated to government-designated areas (Green, 1999). One of the most notorious examples of this relocation was the Trail of Tears in which 16,000 Cherokee Nation members were forced to leave their land in Georgia and walk to resettle in what is now Oklahoma (Wright, 1992). These systematic acts sanctioned by the U.S. government allowed for European-dominated development of the land, which ultimately led to wealth accumulation among European Americans and denied Native Americans commensurate access to land and wealth (Green, 1999; Locke, 1998).

Common Threads

Minority groups in the United States have similar experiences of being marginalized and oppressed at the hands of White Americans. Members of all four of the major minority groups have been used as cheap or free labor and have aided in the development of the nation without adequate compensation or acknowledgement of their contributions. Additionally, the Whites who benefit under the structure provided by oppressive systems (Turner et al., 1984) have justified this treatment of minority populations through systematic, negative characterizations of these groups as being stupid, lazy, childlike, untrustworthy, violent, animalistic, and morally inept (Axelson, 1999; Takaki, 1979; Wright, 1992). In essence, the general belief was that the abusive nature of oppressive structures was necessary for the development of these wayward peoples. These beliefs and structures have persisted over time and continue to relegate modern-day members of minority groups to circumstances and realities in which they are believed to be, and in essence have become, second-class citizens in their own nation.

The Legacy of Oppression: Economic and Educational Inequities

Currently, minorities in the United States face many similar issues, most born out of their shared experience of oppression predicated primarily on race (Axelson, 1999; Cohen & Northridge, 2000; Organista, Chun, & Marín, 1998). This history of oppression manifests in members of minority groups continuing to experience inequities in access to and quality of education, as well as in job earnings and labor participation (Axelson, 1999; Estrada et al., 1981; Rury, 2005). In addition, the systemic and repeated nature of these oppressive experiences has had a cumulative effect on the socioemotional state of minorities in the United States (Clark, Anderson, Clark, & Williams, 1999; Rollock & Gordon, 2000).

Economic and Occupational Inequities

The majority of statistics indicate that U.S. minority populations disproportionately experience poverty and low incomes. U.S. Census (2000) data indicated that the median personal income for Whites was $23,640, compared to $20,200 for Asian Americans, $16,300 for African Americans, $14,500 for Native Americans, and $14,400 for Latinos (Le, 2005a). Given that Whites have the highest median personal income, it stands to reason that they would also have the lowest poverty rates. The poverty rates for the five major U.S. racial/ethnic groups are as follows: 9.4% for Whites, 11.9% for Asian Americans, 21.4% for Latinos, 24.9% for African Americans, and 25.1% for Native Americans (Le, 2005a).

One reason for these economic disparities among minorities is that they are heavily concentrated in labor, service, and clerical positions that tend to pay lower wages than the managerial, professional, and technical fields where Whites are heavily concentrated (Green, 1999; National Urban League, 2005). Even when a minority group (such as Asian Americans who are erroneously dubbed the model minority for their apparent economic and educational success) has a strong presence in professional fields, inequities still exist (Le, 2005a). A closer look reveals that Asian Americans, 34.6% of whom are engaged in professional work, still earn less than their White counterparts in these fields, even when they are equally qualified (Le, 2005a). It is widely acknowledged that racism and lack of access to educational opportunities tend to segregate minorities into lower-paying occupational fields (Axelson, 1999; Herring, 1999; Locke, 1998). The result of hundreds of years of minorities not being paid or being underpaid for their valuable labor has increased poverty and diminished wealth in minority communities. In 2002, the median wealth of White households was $88,651, whereas for Latino households it was $7,932, and for African American households it was only $5,988 (Pew Hispanic Center, 2005b). Compounding the lack of access to economic resources, minority groups also experience an educational system fraught with bias, inequity, and lowered expectations of minority students (Kozol, 1991; Rury, 2005).

Educational Inequities

Although many statistics indicate an improvement in minority educational attainment over time (National Center for Education Statistics [NCES], 2004b, 2004d), the achievement gap between minority and White populations still exists (Dworkin & Dworkin, 1999) and has been well documented (NCES, 2004b). Between 1992 and 2002, the average math and reading proficiency scores for White students have remained higher than those for Black students in the 12th grade (NCES, 2004d). Results of the 2003 Trial Urban District Assessment (TUDA) indicated that in 9 of the 10 urban school districts assessed (Atlanta, Boston, Charlotte, Chicago, Cleveland, District of Columbia, Houston, Los Angeles, New York City, and San Diego) the percentages of eighth-grade students possessing below basic math skills ranged from 46% to 71%, which is a significantly greater percentage than the national average of 33% of students (NCES, 2004a).

The gap in test scores is not the only area for concern; dropout figures among minority students are equally troubling. In 2000, the high school dropout percentages for Whites, Blacks, Latinos, and Asians were 6.9%, 13.1%, 27.8%, and 4% respectively (NCES, 2004b; Pew Hispanic Center, 2005a). Although it may appear that there is little cause for concern about dropout rates among Asian Americans, when Asian American dropout data are disaggregated by ethnic group, it reveals that an extremely high percentage of Southeast Asian Americans are not completing high school. According to the U.S. Census Bureau (2000), 52.7% of Cambodian, Hmong, and Laotian Americans have not earned a high school diploma (Le, 2005b).

Whereas the situation is dire for those minority students who drop out of school, the situation is equally troubling for those who stay in school and attempt to attend college.

Minority high school students tend to enroll in less rigorous classes than White students. In 2000, 47% of White graduates had completed advanced math courses, whereas only 31% of Latino, 32% of African American, and 29% of Native American graduates had done so (NCES, 2004c). This disparity in the quality of high school education minority students obtain contributes to disparities observed in achievement at the collegiate level. Of the 1,291,900 bachelor's degrees conferred during the 2001–2002 academic year, 70.8% went to Whites, 8.6% went to Blacks, 6.1% went to Latinos, 6.1% went to Asians, and 0.7% went to Native Americans. The disparity is quite disturbing when one considers the impact of this inequality on income and economic stability. In 2000, the average income for both male and female high school graduates was $29,637; for males and females with a bachelor's degree the average income was $48,375 (NCES, 2004a). So, given that Whites constitute more than two thirds of the total population of bachelor's degree earners, one can argue that they are two thirds more likely to earn higher incomes over their lifetime and to maintain more economic stability in their families and communities as a result.

The existence of historical oppression and current inequities for minorities is analogous to the running of a marathon in which the White competitor is given a 1-hour head start and allowed to use both legs to complete the race, whereas all the minority competitors are required to run the marathon with one leg and start 1 hour after the White competitor. Under these circumstances it becomes almost impossible to catch up to the White competitor, much less win the race. Certainly, among minorities there are many examples of resistance to oppression, success in the face of adversity, and resilience of spirit. As Harrell (2000) noted, however, "there remain far too many examples of despair, dysfunction, isolation, hopelessness, destructiveness, and spiritual depletion" (p. 42). It is this prolonged reality of the minority experience that has such detrimental effects on their socioemotional functioning.

The Socioemotional Impact of Injustice and Inequity

The connection between the injustice of racism and the socioemotional health of minorities has been well documented in the literature (Clark et al., 1999; Harrell, 2000; hooks, 1995; Rollock & Gordon, 2000). Minorities are repeatedly exposed to racist environmental stimuli that are sources of particularly toxic chronic and acute stress (Clark et al., 1999). Racial oppression not only affects the well-being of minority groups through the actual experience of stress, it also limits minorities' access to resources that could serve as mediators of stress (Harrell, 2000). Further injury is levied upon the psyche of minorities when others call into question the existence of oppression and related injustices. In essence, minorities experience other people's constant refusal to validate and acknowledge their personal and systemic experience of being oppressed (Franklin & Boyd-Franklin, 2000; Harrell, 2000). Race-related stress can be defined as "the race-related transactions between individuals or groups and their environment that emerge from the dynamics of racism, and that are perceived to tax or exceed existing individual and collective resources or threaten well-being" (Harrell, 2000, p. 44).

Minorities often exert enormous amounts of cognitive and emotional energy on combating racism and racism-related stress. Specifically, they may second-guess their personal observations and perceptions, try to explain an experience of bias to others, mentally replay a hostile situation over and over again, engage in mental role-playing to prepare for a potentially hostile future situation (Harrell, 2000), negotiate their public presentation so as not to be perceived as overly ethnic and risk negative treatment, and cope with being marginalized in public arenas that systematically engage in noninclusion and nonacknowledgement of minority contributions. These are just some of the ways in which racism-related stress can take a toll on the psychoaffective functioning of minorities.

Racial oppression also impedes the formation of identity among minority individuals. More specifically, racism can lead to difficulties in healthy identity development especially on dimensions of race and ethnicity (Cross, 1991; Helms, 1990). Oppression can lead minority individuals to (a) internalize oppressor-defined negative identities, which can be detrimental to healthy identity development; (b) deny and denigrate culturally centered values and beliefs that are an inextricable part of the minority existence; and (c) have lowered self-confidence and self-efficacy due to the repeated psychological attacks associated with oppression (Van Voorhis, 1998).

bell hooks (1995) best summed up the importance of acknowledging and addressing the socioemotional impact of minority oppression, specifically with regard to African Americans:

> Collective failure to address adequately the psychic wounds inflicted by racist aggression is the breeding ground for a psychology of victimhood wherein learned helplessness, uncontrollable rage, and/or feelings of overwhelming powerlessness and despair abound in the psyches of Black folks yet are not attended to in ways that empower and promote holistic states of well-being. (p. 137)

As counselors committed to combating oppression and promoting social justice, it is imperative that we use a systemic approach that empowers minorities while redressing the inhumane legacy of injustice.

Empowerment and Advocacy-Focused Counseling Interventions

Professional counselors can play a pivotal role in combating racism and assisting clients who belong to historically oppressed racial/ethnic groups (Bolyard & Jensen-Scott, 1996; Gibbs, 1998). In order to begin the process of combating oppression, however, counselors must recognize that traditional counseling is embedded in White, Eurocentric culture and is possibly cross-culturally limited. Counselors typically lack specific training in modifying their counseling strategies to meet the needs of diverse clients. Moreover, many counselors are unaware of the problems and effects of oppression on clients of color. Therefore, a first step is for counselors to become knowledgeable about their clients' history of oppression. Next, they can initiate empowerment and advocacy-focused interventions.

Advocacy, empowerment, and social action are not new to the counseling field. In the 1970s, the growth of community counseling brought advocacy and community organizing to the attention of the counseling profession (Toporek & Liu, 2001). Scholars such as Bryant (1994) described the facilitation of changes in the client's environment as a necessary and appropriate role for counselors. As part of the multicultural counseling competencies and standards, Arredondo and colleagues (1996) directed counselors to assess the appropriateness of intervening on clients' behalf. They stated that culturally competent counselors "can describe concrete examples of situations in which it is appropriate and possibly necessary for a counselor to exercise institutional intervention skills on behalf of a client" (p. 71). Although the counselor's role as an advocate has appeared in the literature, for the most part discussions of advocacy, empowerment, and social action have remained on the periphery.

We define *advocacy* as action a counselor takes to facilitate the removal of external and institutional barriers to clients' well-being. *Empowerment* is one end of the advocacy continuum and consists of interpersonal interactions between the counselor and client working within the sociocultural and sociopolitical context. McWhirter (1994) viewed empowerment as a dimension of advocacy in which the counselor initially becomes involved in the client's environment in order to help him or her achieve goals, with the ultimate goal being that the client will act independently.

Rappaport (1987) noted that empowerment is easy to define by its absence but difficult to define in action as it takes on different forms in different people and contexts. In general, empowerment can be defined as a process of increasing personal, interpersonal, or political power so that individuals, families, and communities can take action to improve their situations. It is a process that fosters power (that is, the capacity to implement change) in disenfranchised and powerless groups of people, for use in their own lives, their communities, and their society, by acting on issues that they define as important. Interestingly, the word *empowerment* can be disempowering when it is understood to mean the powerful giving power to the powerless. Therefore, the appropriate role of the counselor is to help clients build their own power base.

Empowerment occurs at the individual and the community levels. By definition, it is a social process because it occurs in relationship to others. One important implication of this definition of empowerment is that the individual and community are fundamentally connected. Counselors can, therefore, combat oppression by using empowerment strategies at both levels when counseling clients of historically oppressed racial backgrounds.

Individual Empowerment

Although the literature on empowerment theory describes empowerment as a method that can incorporate multiple levels of intervention, most of the current work has focused on individual or interpersonal empowerment (Gutierrez, 1995; Parsons, 1991). The literature has discussed methods and strategies for moving individuals to a point where they feel a sense of personal power. One such strategy is the development of critical consciousness (Zimmerman, 2000). Critical consciousness has been described as involving three psychological processes: (a) group identification, which includes identifying areas of common experiences and concern with a particular group; (b) group consciousness, which involves understanding the differential status of power of groups in society; and (c) self- and collective efficacy, which is described as perceiving oneself as a subject (rather than as an object) of social processes and as capable of working to change the social order. For individuals to understand that their problems stem from a lack of power, they must first comprehend both their group's status in society and the overall structure of power in society. At the individual level, counselors can empower ethnic minority clients by facilitating discussions about their group identification and how it has affected their life circumstances. Paulo Freire (1973) indicated that the disempowered already know a great deal about the sources of their oppression and what must be done to overcome it. What they do not have is an organized approach to translating this knowledge into action. Clients can empower themselves by taking responsibility for their own learning, by increasing their understanding of the communities in which they live, and by understanding how they as individuals are affected by current and potential policies and structures. Equipped with this greater understanding and with new confidence in themselves, ethnic minority clients can develop new life strategies that better meet their needs.

An empowerment approach to counseling requires that counselors provide clients with the knowledge and skills to think critically about their problems and to develop strategies to act on and change problems (J. A. Lee, 2001). Counselors and clients must work collaboratively toward the goal of clients taking charge of their own lives. For instance, clients can define their problems then engage in a decision-making process to solve them. Counselors can facilitate problem solving and decision making by building on clients' strengths. The problem-solving process can include problem identification, selection of one problem, the choosing of a goal to solve or minimize the problem, generation of activities to achieve the goal, and identification of available resources to assist in goal attainment (Gutierrez & Ortega, 1991).

Advocacy and helping clients mobilize resources are critical aspects of empowerment-focused counseling. Counselors may draw on the work of Amidei (1992), which outlines specific types of advocacy (e.g., self-advocacy, administrative or regulatory advocacy, legislative advocacy) and which types of advocacy work best in which situations. Amidei suggested that counselors can make a difference for vulnerable people in a community by following three steps: (a) be informed, (b) be involved (e.g., volunteer, attend a conference, sit on a board), and (c) be an advocate (e.g., make calls, write letters, design a campaign to educate voters). Counselors can use Amidei's framework to teach clients how to advocate for themselves and how to build a collective advocacy base. In short, providing ethnic minority clients with information about building a collective advocacy base is essential in empowerment-focused counseling practice.

Ethnic minority clients can realize and extend their power through networking with others, both inside and outside of their particular social groups. Counselors can develop and implement "power groups" to assist clients in networking and helping one another. Small groups such as power groups promote dialogue and critical thinking among their members. According to J. A. Lee (2001), participants in small empowerment groups go beyond the "sharing of experiences and catharsis" to "think, see, talk as well as act for themselves" (p. 37). Participants in the small group may focus on helping one another, offering social support to one another, taking collaborative social actions, and developing problem-solving skills and competencies.

Community Empowerment

Counselors must recognize that most ethnic minority communities and families have been involved in a struggle against oppressive structures and that the struggle has required much strength. As such, counselors must first recognize how a given family and community have survived and identify the strengths of that community. These strengths can then serve as the foundation of community organization strategies. Community organizing involves mobilizing people to combat common problems and to increase their voice in institutions and decisions that affect their lives and communities. Community-based service provision involves community-level efforts to deliver counseling and social services (e.g., career counseling, parenting skills, employment counseling) that will improve people's lives and opportunities within a community.

Community organizing includes methods that create social environments which support social justice through influencing policies, developing programs, or governing locally. The concept of social justice is central to the practice of community organizing. Social justice refers to equity, equality, and fairness in the distribution of societal resources (Flynn, 1995). Social justice includes a focus on the structures and outcomes of social processes and how they contribute to equality. The counselor's role in community organizing is to develop practices that contribute to these aforementioned goals. For instance, counselors might reach out to community members and organizations in order to develop services that are closely aligned with the community's goals.

Considering that most of America's population growth in the next century will be among immigrant and ethnic minority groups (Megbolugbe & Simmons, 1995), linking these individuals to the larger American community constitutes a major challenge for counselors. The concept of social capital and its application to empowerment-focused counseling are critical to the practice of counseling.

Social capital commonly refers to the aspect of social networks and norms that facilitate trust and the ability to achieve individual and collective goals. Although the term has been used mostly by sociologists (e.g., Coleman, 1990) and political scientists, social capital provides a useful analytic tool for counselors because it makes a conceptual link between an individual's particular social relationships and the social organization of a larger collective. At the same time, counselors can bring conceptual strength to the study of social capital by adding a focus on the individual's behaviors, development, and psychological functioning.

The first step for counselors, therefore, is to provide ethnic minority clients with knowledge of how to network with diverse people. For example, a study of social networks in Los Angeles showed that being embedded in a racially diverse network has a significant positive effect on the incomes of both Black and Latino men and women. There was a $24,213 difference in income between those with a racial bridge and those who did not have the benefit of such network ties (Johnson & Farrell, 1997). Counselors can facilitate these community contacts and networks to ensure that ethnic minority clients are not cut off from diverse social networks.

Counselors who engage in community empowerment strategies often provide their services through community organizations, and they are often leaders in mobilizing the provision of counseling and mental health services to communities and community organizations (e.g., schools, agencies) that are in need. Community-based services involve efforts to deliver counseling services (e.g., employment counseling, parent education) that will improve ethnic minority persons' lives and opportunities within a community. Possible empowerment strategies on the community level might include supporting community outreach initiatives, advocating for improved media coverage of community initiatives, and advocating for laws and regulations that meet the needs of community members and give communities a voice in larger society.

Conclusion

To bring about change in the lives of ethnic minority clients, counselors must first be willing to challenge their own deeply held assumptions and unconscious attitudes about people of other races or ethnic groups. Furthermore, given the interactive and collective nature of the empowerment-focused counseling discussed in this chapter, counselors must also consider how their own positions, interpretations, and identities influence their ability to assist their ethnic minority clients. Because counselors are often in positions of power in relation to the clients with whom they work, it is especially important that they reflect throughout the counseling process, finding creative ways to share and cede power toward the common goal of social justice.

Finally, it is imperative that counselors challenge and interrupt oppressive and culturally biased practices in their own communities. Lewis and Arnold (1998) stated that the "most difficult—and most necessary—challenge is to become continuously involved in taking an honest inventory of our own lives as community members and as counselors" (p. 59). In other words, in order to assist all clients move toward empowerment, counselors must be willing to challenge racist and oppressive acts in their own communities. No longer should counselors tolerate ethnic group stereotyping, racist jokes, and subtle racial discrimination. Instead they must be willing to be advocates for racial equality in every aspect of their lives.

References

Amidei, N. (1992). *So you want to make a difference? Advocacy is the key.* Washington, DC: OMB Watch.

Arredondo, P., Toporek, R., Brown, S. P., Jones, J., Locke, D. C., Sanchez, J., & Stadler, H. (1996). Operationalization of the multicultural counseling competencies. *Journal of Multicultural Counseling and Development, 24,* 42–78.

Axelson, J. A. (1999). *Counseling and development in a multicultural society* (3rd ed.). Pacific Grove, CA: Brooks/Cole.

Bolyard, K. L., & Jensen-Scott, R. L. (1996). Worldview and culturally sensitive crisis intervention. In J. L. DeLucia-Waack (Ed.), *Multicultural counseling competencies: Implications for training and practice* (pp. 217–236). Alexandria, VA: Association for Counselor Education and Supervision.

Bonilla, F., & Campos, R. (1981). A wealth of poor: Puerto Ricans in the new economic order. *Daedalus, 110*(2), 133–176.

Bryant, B. K. C. (1994). *Counseling for racial understanding.* Alexandria, VA: American Counseling Association.

Clark, R., Anderson, N. B., Clark, V. R., & Williams, D. R. (1999). Racism as a stressor for African Americans: A biopsychosocial model. *American Psychologist, 54,* 805–816.

Cohen, H. W., & Northridge, M. E. (2000). Getting political: Racism and urban health. *American Journal of Public Health, 90,* 841–842.

Coleman, J. S. (1990). *Foundations of social theory.* Cambridge, MA: Harvard University Press.

Cross, W. E. (1991). *Shades of Black. Diversity in African American identity.* Philadelphia: Temple University.

Dworkin, A. G., & Dworkin, R. J. (1999). *The minority report: An introduction to racial, ethnic, and gender relations* (3rd ed.). Fort Worth, TX: Harcourt Brace.

Estrada, L. F., García, C., Macìas, R., & Maldonado, L. (1981). Chicanos in the United States: A history of exploitation and resistance. *Daedalus, 110*(2), 103–131.

Flynn, J. P. (1995). Social justice in social agencies. In R. L. Edwards (Ed.), *Encyclopedia of social work* (pp. 95–100). Washington, DC: National Association of Social Workers Press.

Franklin, A. J., & Boyd-Franklin, N. (2000). Invisibility syndrome: A clinical model of the effects of racism on African American males. *American Journal of Orthopsychiatry, 70,* 33–41.

Freire, P. (1973). *Education for critical consciousness.* New York: Seabury Press.

Fujiwara, L. H., & Takagi, D. Y. (1999). Japanese Americans: Stories about race in America. In A. G. Dworkin & R. J. Dworkin (Eds.), *The minority report: An introduction to racial, ethnic, and gender relations* (3rd ed., pp. 297–320). Fort Worth, TX: Harcourt Brace.

Gibbs, J. T. (1998). Black American adolescents. In J. T. Gibbs, L. N. Huang, & associates (Eds.), *Children of color: Psychological interventions with minority youth* (pp. 171–214). San Francisco: Jossey-Bass.

Giddings, P. (1996). *When and where I enter: The impact of Black women on race and sex in America.* New York: Bantam.

Green, D. E. (1999). Native Americans. In A. G. Dworkin & R. J. Dworkin (Eds.), *The minority report: An introduction to racial, ethnic, and gender relations* (3rd ed., pp. 255–277). Fort Worth, TX: Harcourt Brace.

Gutierrez, L. (1995). Understanding the empowerment process: Does consciousness make a difference? *Social Work Research, 19,* 229–237.

Gutierrez, L., & Ortega, R. (1991). Developing methods to empower Latinos: The importance of groups. *Social Work With Groups, 14,* 23–43.

Harrell, S. P. (2000). A multidimensional conceptualization of racism-related stress: Implications for the well-being of people of color. *American Journal of Orthopsychiatry, 70,* 42–57.

Helms, J. E. (1990). *Black and White racial identity: Theory, research, and practice.* New York: Greenwood Press.

Herring, C. (1999). African Americans in contemporary America: Progress and retrenchment. In A. G. Dworkin & R. J. Dworkin (Eds.), *The minority report: An introduction to racial, ethnic, and gender relations* (3rd ed., pp. 181–208). Fort Worth, TX: Harcourt Brace.

hooks, b. (1995). *Killing rage: Ending racism.* New York: Henry Holt.

Johnson, J. H., & Farrell, W. C. (1997, April 10). *Growing income inequality in American society: A political economy perspective.* Paper presented at the National Policy Association Conference, Washington, DC.

Kozol, J. (1991). *Savage inequalities: Children in America's schools.* New York: Crown.

Le, C. N. (2005a). The model minority image. *Asian-nation: The landscape of Asian America.* Retrieved February 22, 2005, from http://www.asian-nation.org/model-minority.shtml

Le, C. N. (2005b). Socioeconomic statistics and demographics. *America.* Retrieved February 22, 2005, from http://www.asian-nation.org/demographics.shtml

Lee, J. A. (2001). *The empowerment approach to social work practice: Building the beloved community* (2nd ed.). New York: Columbia University Press.

Lee, L. C. (1989). *Cultural transformation in higher education: The case of Asian America.* Unpublished manuscript, Cornell University.

Lewis, J. A., & Arnold, M. S. (1998). From multiculturalism to social action. In C. C. Lee & G. R. Walz (Eds.), *Social action: A mandate for counselors* (pp. 51–66). Alexandria, VA: American Counseling Association.

Lin, J. (1999). Chinese Americans: From exclusion to prosperity? In A. G. Dworkin & R. J. Dworkin (Eds.), *The minority report: An introduction to racial, ethnic, and gender relations* (3rd ed., pp. 321–342). Fort Worth, TX: Harcourt Brace.

Locke, D. C. (1998). *Increasing multicultural understanding: A comprehensive model* (2nd ed.). Thousand Oaks, CA: Sage.

Loo, C. M. (1994). Race-related PTSD: The Asian American Vietnam veteran. *Journal of Traumatic Stress, 7,* 637–656.

McWhirter, E. H. (1994). *Counseling for empowerment.* Alexandria, VA: American Counseling Association.

Megbolugbe, I. F., & Simmons, P. A. (1995). *An overview of demographic trends and housing market impacts: 1995–2000* (Research Report, Fannie Mae Office of Housing Research). Washington, DC: Fannie Mae Foundation.

National Center for Education Statistics (NCES). (2004a). *The condition of education, 2004.* Retrieved February 22, 2005, from http://nces.ed.gov/pubsearch/pubsinfo.asp?pubid=2004077

National Center for Education Statistics. (2004b). *Dropout rates in the United States: 2000.* Retrieved February 22, 2005, from http://nces.ed.gov/fastfacts/display.asp?id=16

National Center for Education Statistics. (2004c). *Income of graduates.* Retrieved February 22, 2005, from http://nces.ed.gov/fastfacts/display.asp?id=77

National Center for Education Statistics. (2004d). *Student achievement (national).* Retrieved February 22, 2005, from http://nces.ed.gov/fastfacts/display.asp?id=38

National Urban League. (2005). *State of Black America 2004 report.* Retrieved February 22, 2005, from http://www.nul.org/pdf/sobaexec.pdf

Organista, P. B., Chun, K. M., & Marín, G. (Eds.). (1998). *Readings in ethnic psychology.* New York: Routledge.

Parsons, R. (1991). Empowerment: Purpose and practice in principle in social work. *Social Work in Groups, 14,* 7–21.

Pew Hispanic Center. (2005a). *Hispanic youth dropping out of U.S. schools.* Retrieved February 22, 2005, from http://pewhispanic.org/reports/report.php?ReportID=19

Pew Hispanic Center. (2005b). *The wealth of Hispanic households.* Retrieved February 22, 2005, from http://pewhispanic.org/reports/report.php?ReportID=34

Rappaport, J. (1987). Terms of empowerment/examples of prevention: Toward a theory for community psychology. *American Journal of Community Psychology, 15,* 121–144.

Ridley, C. R. (1995). *Overcoming unintentional racism in counseling and therapy.* Thousand Oaks, CA: Sage.

Rollock, D., & Gordon, E. W. (2000). Racism and mental health into the 21st century: Perspectives and parameters. *American Journal of Orthopsychiatry, 70,* 5–13.

Rury, J. L. (2005). *Education and social change: Themes in the history of American schooling* (2nd ed.). Mahwah, NJ: Lawrence Erlbaum.

Saenz, R. (1999). Mexican Americans. In A. G. Dworkin & R. J. Dworkin (Eds.), *The minority report: An introduction to racial, ethnic, and gender relations* (3rd ed., pp. 209–229). Fort Worth, TX: Harcourt Brace.

Snow, D. R. (1979). *Native American prehistory: A critical bibliography.* Bloomington: Indiana University Press.

Sue, S. (1977). Community mental health services to minority groups: Some optimism, some pessimism. *American Psychologist, 32,* 616–624.

Takaki, R. T. (1979). *Iron cages: Race and culture in 19th-century America.* New York: Knopf.

Toporek, R. L., & Liu, W. M. (2001). Advocacy in counseling: Addressing race, class, and gender oppression. In D. B. Pope-Davis & H. L. K. Coleman (Eds.), *The intersection of race, class, and gender in multicultural counseling* (pp. 385–416). Thousand Oaks, CA: Sage.

Torrecilha, R., Cantú, L., & Nguyen, Q. (1999). Puerto Ricans in the United States. In A. G. Dworkin & R. J. Dworkin (Eds.), *The minority report: An introduction to racial, ethnic, and gender relations* (3rd ed., pp. 230–254). Fort Worth, TX: Harcourt Brace.

Turner, J. H., Singleton, R., Jr., & Musick, D. (1984). *Oppression: A sociohistory of Black-White relations in America.* Chicago: Nelson-Hall.

U.S. Census Bureau. (2000). *Employment status brief.* Retrieved February 22, 2005, from http://www.census.gov/prod/2003pubs/c2kbr- 18.pdf

Van Voorhis, R. M. (1998). Culturally relevant practice: A framework for teaching the psychosocial dynamics of oppression. *Journal of Social Work Education, 34,* 121–133.

Wright, R. (1992). *Stolen continents: The Americas through Indian eyes since 1492.* Boston: Houghton Mifflin.

Young, I. M. (1990). *Justice and the politics of difference.* Princeton, NJ: Princeton University Press.

Zimmerman, M. A. (2000). Empowerment theory: Psychological, organizational, and community levels of analysis. In J. Rappaport & E. Seidman (Eds.), *Handbook of community psychology* (pp. 43–64). New York: Plenum Press.

Part II

Social Justice: A Focus on Professional Issues

Chapter 9

Counseling and Social Justice:
An International Perspective

William A. Borgen

For several years, counseling has been recognized to have at its heart three major foci that center on remedial, preventive, and developmental activities. Remedial and developmental activities tend to offer help to individuals or groups in need of assistance. Remedial activities are often what we think of when we discuss a counselor assisting someone with a personal, educational, career, or social challenge. The goal in this instance is often to help clients develop attitudes or behaviors that will lead to a more effective or satisfying interchange with their personal and social environments. Developmental activities are intended to prepare people for anticipated challenges related to life transitions — preparation for college, marriage, childbirth, and so on. Again, the goal is to assist the individual or group to achieve a better level of adjustment to the situation. The third major focus for counseling, one which is often called preventive, centers on the environment in which people live and the aspects of that environment that may contribute to their experiencing remedial or developmental challenges or problems. The goal here is to effect changes in the workplace, family, school, or other relevant environment where processes or policies are the source of the ineffective interchange between an individual or group and the environment. This is the area of counseling that probably suffers from the most neglect in terms of research, theory, and practice. With a few exceptions (Goodman et al., 2004), counselor education and counseling psychology programs in North America do not give this area much attention. It is, however, an area where there is a natural interface between counseling and issues of social justice, for it puts a clear emphasis on environments of discrimination related to poverty, race, ethnicity, religion, sexual orientation, disabling conditions, and so on (Baluch, Pieterse, & Bolden, 2004; Palmer, 2004; Smith, Baluch, Bernabei, Robohm, & Sheehy, 2003; Watts, 2004). In addition to the goal of creating living environments that are less hostile and more conducive to growth for people, there has often been an intention and an expectation that preventive activities will also have a positive impact on the broader society.

Social Justice and the Beginnings of Guidance and Counseling in North America

Historically, issues related to social justice have been central motivators in the creation of counseling-related services. In North America two of the major foundations of counseling — the mental hygiene and vocational guidance movements — had their roots in issues related to social justice.

The founding of the mental hygiene movement is generally credited to Clifford Beers (Kiselica, 2004), who had the determination of a man who had suffered the indignities accorded to a person who was mentally ill at the beginning of the 20th century. He also had some powerful allies in William James, who wrote the foreword to Beers' book, *A Mind That Found Itself* (1950), and Adolf Meyer, who coined the phrase *mental hygiene*. Beers' stated objective for his book was to "change the attitude of the public toward those who are unfortunate enough to have the stigma of mental incompetency put on them" (1950, p. 218). To promote the changes the book described, Beers founded the first mental hygiene society in Connecticut in 1908 and the National Committee for Mental Hygiene in 1909. The aims of the movement were expanded and modified from reform to cure, and from cure to prevention. The final phase had the greatest implications for guidance in education, for it expanded the area of study to include childhood. Beers (1950) wrote, "No less than half of the enormous toll which mental disease takes from youth can be prevented by the application, largely in childhood, of information and practical resources now available" (p. 248).

Luther E. Woodward, in a supplement to the 1950 edition of Beers' book, noted that after the first wave of attention to the treatment of adults who were mentally ill, the focus turned to prevention through the creation of child guidance and other community clinics. Woodward also pointed out that the first movement in the direction of prevention occurred in the field of delinquency. The very earliest demonstration child guidance clinics were set up specifically to show that they could be a helpful means of preventing a substantial amount of delinquency when it was found that court action alone could not curb delinquency. This led to the involvement of all aspects of community life, especially the school and home, in prevention activities (Beers, 1950).

Frank Parsons usually receives credit for developing and nurturing a model for vocational guidance in the early part of the 20th century (Brewer, 1942). Educated as an engineer and a lawyer, Parsons was very much involved with social reform and civic developments. In pursuing his interests, Parsons became involved in the adult education movement in Boston in 1901 and then in "the problem of adolescent confusion and discouragement caused by difficulty in choosing an appropriate career based on possessed aptitudes and capabilities" (Williamson, 1965, p. 76). He began to elaborate his ideas in a series of lectures that generated such interest he was able to establish an active practice in vocational guidance. In 1907 Parsons organized the Vocations Bureau of Boston, the first such facility in the United States. It was formally opened in 1908.

From the Vocations Bureau, vocational guidance spread rapidly to the schools of Boston and then to other parts of North America. Parsons outlined his model for vocational guidance in *Choosing a Vocation,* which was published posthumously in 1911. He emphasized the need for such guidance in stating, "We guide our boys and girls to some extent through school, then drop them into this complex world to sink or swim as the case may be. Yet there is no part of life where the need for guidance is more emphatic than in the transition from school to work—the choice of a vocation, adequate preparation for it, and the attainment of efficiency and success" (Parsons, 1967, p. 4).

I have taken some time to review the development of these two movements within a North American context over the past 100 years or so because they both had a clear intention not only to help individuals, but also to create awareness in the broader society of issues related to mental health and vocational/career development, for the benefit of the individual and the broader society. The goal was to help individuals achieve a less conflictual and more harmonious interaction with their family, school, or work environments for their personal betterment and that of their environments. These movements challenged the assumption that the individual facing a mental health or vocational challenge was the sole source of the problem by discussing ways in which institutional and societal attitudes and approaches were contributing to the problem.

Over the last century, much of the focus has been on how to enhance or fine tune assessment, intervention, and counseling processes and procedures so that we may better understand the bases for the psychological distress that leads individuals to seek counseling for problems and so we may develop maximally effective approaches for addressing problems related to that distress (Hage, 2003; McClure & Russo, 1996).

The paradigm began to shift through the 1960s and afterward as a growing segment of the population in North America and other parts of the world became aware that the environment was not benign, or normal, for everyone in the same way. That is, awareness and discussion of the systemic discrimination that led to the marginalization of several groups in society increased. With this awareness came the rise of issues related to feminism, multiculturalism, disability, poverty, and sexual orientation. All of these movements led counseling to develop a variety of theoretical and professional orientations and practices for working effectively with diverse populations. They also led to the development of some preventive programs to help raise awareness of issues related to systemic discrimination and marginalization.

Initial work in this area tended to focus on attributes of individuals or groups who were somehow seen as being different from the majority, or the norm. Approaches that recognized difference in terms of diversity set out to level the playing field, so that society could be more inclusive in meeting the needs of, and offering opportunities to, a greater proportion of its population.

The International Context

In the current context of so-called developed and developing countries, examples of discrimination based on ethnicity, religion, ability, or color abound—so there is a continuing need for counseling approaches that take difference as the norm and a need to continue to raise awareness of social justice issues. An overarching force that tends to increase problems for people worldwide, and that may lead them to blame their problems on others who are different from themselves, is the increasing acceleration of change. The rapid pace of change influences all of our lives and challenges our cultural assumptions.

IAC and Social Justice

Like the mental hygiene and vocational guidance movements in North America, the International Association for Counseling (IAC) and its predecessors, the International Roundtable for the Advancement of Counseling (IRTAC) and the International Association for Educational and Vocational Guidance (IAEVG), have at their heart a commitment to social justice. Professor Hans Hoxter, the founder of all three organizations, worked in Britain during World War II with refugee groups and others affected by the conflict.

> At the end of the war he realized that children and adolescents affected by the war were in need of assistance, and worked towards making guidance available to them. In the late 1940s Hans, with the help of UNICEF, organized a meeting that involved people who were interested in helping young people. This led him to create the International Association for Educational and Vocational Guidance in 1951.
>
> In the mid-1950s Hans began to see the needs of young people and adults as being broader than what educational and vocational guidance could offer. He saw the need for an approach that encompassed all areas of life. He also realized that a different process would be needed to offer this broader service, and decided that counselling best embodied the aims and processes that he saw as being necessary. (Borgen, 2003, p. 85)

In 1997, Professor Hoxter initiated the change in name from IRTAC to IAC. IAC is involved in activities designed to be catalytic in influencing the development of counseling worldwide, with the aims of helping people address challenging life issues, of assisting in the development of policies that may help to reduce or ameliorate the problems people face, and of creating developmental programs to assist individuals and organizations anticipate issues and challenges in order to reduce future problems. A strong commitment to social justice is reflected in all of these endeavors.

Specific evidence of this commitment is the requirement that all members of IAC sign a document supporting the United Nations Universal Declaration of Human Rights (1948). The first two points of the preamble are particularly relevant within the context of the promotion of social justice:

> recognition of the inherent dignity and of the equal and inalienable rights of all members of the human family is the foundation of freedom, justice, and peace in the world, . . . disregard and contempt for human rights have resulted in barbarous acts which have outraged the conscience of mankind, and the advent of a world in which human beings shall enjoy freedom of speech and belief and freedom from fear and want has been proclaimed as the highest aspiration of the common people. (United Nations, 1948)

The association has consultative status with several organizations including the United Nations Educational, Social, and Cultural Organization (UNESCO), the World Health Organization (WHO), the International Labour Organization (ILO), and the Council of Europe. IAC is currently involved in several important initiatives with UNESCO, and association representatives are serving on key United Nations committees in Geneva, Vienna, and New York, and with the Council of Europe in Strasbourg. In the work of these bodies, social justice issues are at the forefront. It is also encouraging to note a growing awareness and expectation that counseling can play a key role in increasing the effectiveness of interventions to address many of these issues.

Counseling and Social Justice—International Examples

The relevance of a social justice perspective is seen in examining the topics of the conferences and consultations sponsored by IAC since its inception, and is clearly evident in the themes of the conferences held in the last 5 years. These themes often parallel important social justice issues highlighted by bodies like UNESCO, UNICEF, WHO, and ILO, and focus on ways in which counseling can have a positive influence in addressing them.

In keeping with a social justice perspective, it has been important that IAC conferences operate with an intention to be as inclusive as possible in delegate participation through having a differential registration fee structure and, in some cases, travel subsidies. These policies are attempts to reduce systematic exclusion from conference participation on the basis of financial resources.

The format of IAC conferences reflects the spirit of counseling as Hans Hoxter defined it—as an opportunity for people to come together to discuss life issues. Within that spirit, the heart of IAC conferences is often described as residing in the working groups of the conferences. These groups are arranged around topics that fit within the theme of the conference. They are composed of about 12 to 15 conference participants from 5 to 10 countries who have an interest in the topic and meet for 8 to 12 hours over the course of the conference. Participants may present papers during the course of the meetings, and the ideas from the papers are catalytic to the discussion. At the end of their discussion, each working group develops a report that concludes with recommendations; these are incorporated into the overall report of the conference. These reports often point to social justice issues that are relevant to the issue under discussion. In many cases the reports of IAC conferences are presented to UNESCO or other bodies, with recommendations intended to inform their policy development and suggest directions for interventions that incorporate counseling perspectives. In the following sections of the chapter, I present some of the contexts, issues, and recommendations that have characterized IAC conferences over the past 5 years.

Greece, 2000
The conference held in Thessaloniki, Greece, in 2000 had the theme "Counseling in the New Millennium: Meeting the Challenges of Diversity and Promoting Peace and Social Inclusion." The focus of this conference was on the application of counseling principles and approaches to addressing the needs of diverse groups in society, with the intention of promoting more peaceful and inclusive societies. This conference was held in a region of the world influenced by ethnic and religious violence occurring in the former Yugoslavia. The atrocities committed during that conflict and its aftermath highlighted the crucial importance of the theme of this millennial conference. A meeting I had during that conference with a representative of the United Nations High Commission for Refugees drove home a central point with respect to social justice and the need for counseling. She indicated that in one of the former Soviet republics there were several internally displaced people—people who had had to relocate within their country because of discrimination-based violence. A lot of money had been given to help build schools in the settlement camps, but the people weren't grateful or happy about it. She saw a need for counseling to help these individuals who were grieving the loss of their homes to negotiate their new reality and to find a voice to protect their cultural traditions and civil rights.

India, 2001
In 2001 the conference was held in Mumbai-Lonavla, India, and had the theme "Families in Transition—Counseling in Transition." In the cultural context of India, with its strong tradition of the extended family, and with the current challenges to that tradition, people needed new support structures, and counseling to benefit individuals, and the broader society needed to play a larger role. An excerpt from the conference program highlights some of the main challenges:

> The 2001 world conference of the IAC will focus on families in transition as they respond to the pressures of globalization, technological advances, political destabilization and attacks on democratic processes, religious resurgence and ethnic conflicts. Some of these changes such as increasing mobility within and across nations have no doubt generated new opportunities for

individuals and families, and contributed to an improved quality of life. However, for many more individuals and families it has also generated new risks and created stress, anxiety, and alienation, as it has also created scattered families, loosened family ties, and weakened interpersonal relationships between family members. Sometimes it has forced family restructuring. Counseling is also in transition as it attempts to reorient itself to a changing society and to widen its scope in order to respond to the growing ethnic and cultural diversity among families. Counselors will need to review their ideological and ethical bases, their theoretical approaches, techniques, and skills, and reposition themselves so as to cater more effectively to the changing needs of families as well as the complex challenges of advancing the human rights and well-being of all its members as well as protect and promote the family unit's right with reference to its environment. (IAC, 2001, p. 1)

Kenya and New Zealand, 2002

In 2002 two conferences were held. The first was titled the "African Conference on Guidance and Counseling." It involved discussion and action planning related to a range of personal, educational, and social issues important to countries in sub-Saharan Africa. The purpose of this conference was to develop momentum that would lead to research, policies, and practices to enhance counseling and guidance in the continent of Africa.

Delegates to the conference came from 30 countries in sub-Saharan Africa. The main themes were education for all, cultural diversity, HIV/AIDS, the evolving role of girls and women, and ethics. It was clear that all of these issues were highly complex and were being exacerbated by rapid rates of change, corruption, crime, conflict, poverty, and disease. In some senses delegates looked to more economically developed parts of the world for assistance and in other ways questioned the usefulness of that assistance.

A delegate from Rwanda sat with me at lunch one day during the conference and spoke about a massacre in her area of her country. She said they had a ceremony every year to remember the young people who were killed. Then she said that the setting was a school and that it had been known in the morning that an attack was going to take place. She said, " Bill, all of the foreigners left on their planes and would not take any of the children with them. Bill, they took their dogs on the planes but none of the children. . . . I thought they were supposed to be from civilized countries. How do you explain that?"

Two issues related to social justice stood out for me in this conference. First, the delegates were diverse in their cultural backgrounds, languages, and religions, and they were intensely aware of and committed to making a positive change in their rapidly evolving communal societies. As in India, the traditional support structures, in terms of the extended family and the broader community, were dissolving. The delegates saw counseling as a catalyst for creating new support structures within their societies to counterbalance the lure of crime and corruption for young people and adults. In some ways, some of the concerns of Beers and Parsons were echoed in the statements of these delegates. Second, it was evident in this conference, as it is in all IAC conferences, that the intentions and approaches to counseling are highly culturally specific. Conceptions and attempted solutions need to be tailored to the cultural mores of the situations in which they occur.

The second conference held in 2002 was in Auckland, New Zealand, and had the theme "Counseling in the New Millennium: Facing Differences, Respectful Practice." Taken together, these represent a major challenge to all counseling professionals. The first, facing differences, challenged delegates to confront their personal and cultural assumptions and biases, and to recognize the need not only to tolerate diversity, but also to embrace it and see it as a source of learning and strength in our work and our lives. This is particularly important within the current context of rapid, ongoing economic and social change, when we need a broad range of views in order to be in any way effective in what we do. The second theme, respectful practice, challenged delegates to reexamine what ethical practice means within and across cultures. Of particular note in this conference were issues related to the Maori and Pacific Island peoples, who contributed greatly to the conference by raising awareness of issues of systemic marginalization and discrimination, as well as by offering their cultural perspectives on promoting attitudes of inclusion and respect.

From my perspective, all counseling practice is cross-cultural because we don't know the particular worldview of any of the people who come to us for assistance. The challenge to us is to operate within a context of ethical practice that is guided by basic principles of dignity and respect for ourselves and for others. Again, doing so challenges us to look at the intentions that underlie what we do and at how our actions reflect these intentions.

Switzerland, 2003

The 2003 conference was held in Geneva, Switzerland. The association is fortunate to have a very involved representative to the United Nations and other agencies located in Geneva. The theme of this conference was "A World of Change—A World in Crisis: The Counselor and Social Responsibility." Representatives from several United Nations agencies repeatedly told delegates that there was an expectation that counseling would make a difference to the lives of individuals and also to the quality of society more generally. Several issues stand out in my memory related to counseling and social responsibility and social justice. It was reported that 10% of the population of Botswana are children orphaned by AIDS. In many countries in sub-Saharan Africa, the levels of education are going down as young people see their older brothers and sisters who have a good education being unable to find work. In areas of the world affected by wars and other types of conflict, current approaches to treating posttraumatic stress reactions are not seen to be effective. There is a dire need to provide counseling services to the aid workers who are attempting to assist traumatized people.

Jamaica, 2004

The conference held in Runaway Bay, Jamaica, with the theme "Crossing Boundaries in Counseling: Global Issues—Local Context" is another exemplar of the consideration of issues related to social justice. The issues of focus during the conference were social concerns highlighted by UNESCO relative to the Caribbean. I think these are best captured by the following quote from the application to UNESCO for funding in support of the conference:

> *Poverty.* With the increasing impact of globalization on the economies of small island states, there has been a marked increase in the disparity of income between people at the top and those at the bottom of the socioeconomic scales in the Caribbean. This is leading to social unrest in several territories.

> *Drug Use.* The Caribbean produces marijuana and is a major transshipment point for cocaine. Control of this lucrative trade has contributed significantly to the increase in gun-related violence in the region during the past two decades. Drug use within the region has also risen (particularly use of cocaine), and there is now the need for rehabilitation services in most territories.

> *Violence.* There has been a major escalation in violent crimes with the murder rates in territories such as Jamaica and Trinidad being alarmingly high and continuing to trend upward. This increase is not due only to the effects of the drug trade or to gang

violence. There are also a high percentage of domestic murders and other types of family-related violence. Physical abuse of women and children and sexual abuse of children occurs in many households.

Migration. The movement of people has significantly affected the welfare of children. Parents who go away as migrant workers are usually unable to take their children with them. The children are left behind while the parents are away (often without legal status) in an attempt to improve the socioeconomic status of the family. This has given rise to the phenomenon known as "Barrel Children." These are children who have all the material benefits and more than they need sent by parents who work outside of the region, but who are emotionally deprived due to the lack of an effective parental figure in the home. These children may be cared for by members of the extended family, friends of their parents, or the older children may head sibling households.

HIV/AIDS. The Caribbean is second only to sub-Saharan Africa in the number of cases of HIV/AIDS infection. Counseling is needed to help people infected and affected by this illness as testing is now more readily available and people are becoming more willing to acknowledge their HIV status. Most governments have little financial resources to put into treatment and care, so much of this is left to NGOs.

The Education System. Education in the Caribbean is being greatly affected by the recent recruitment of the better teachers to the USA and England. While guidance counselors and family life education have been a part of the high school system in many territories since the early 1980s, guidance counseling for the primary schools is only recently being introduced in a limited number of territories. Training of helping professionals has been primarily as social workers, and indigenous training of counselors and guidance counselors did not begin until the late 1980s and then only with small programmes. While there has been a recent explosion in the numbers of locally trained psychologists and counselors up to the master's level, systems to monitor and license such persons are nonexistent in most islands. There is a great need for technical assistance to local associations in helping them to establish such systems. This will significantly help in protecting the public. (IAC, 2004, p. 6)

Argentina, 2005

Social issues are also evident in the 2005 conference that was held in Buenos Aires, Argentina, with the theme "Expanding the Counseling Profession Within a Context of Profound and Ongoing Change." As noted in the conference prospectus,

> Ongoing change has an impact on everyone in society. Often economic collapse such as that experienced by Argentina and several other South American countries, along with the accompanying upheaval experienced by core institutions such as schools, severely restricts opportunities for people in those societies. This stands in stark contrast to the recommendations of the World Education Forum held in Dakar in 2001, which suggested that there was a renewed need to view education as a right and that no country that is committed to education for all should be frustrated by lack of resources. With an escalation of social problems propelled by rapid economic and social change, in addition to the concern that society's educational institutions must be more inclusive, there is an increasing concern that these institutions may not even be able to continue with the progress that they have made in this direction. Counseling is a profession that can assist in addressing issues like substance abuse, prostitution, rising numbers of teenage pregnancies, and growing unemployment rates for young people, that make young girls and boys ready victims of drug dealers and other organized criminal groups.

> People in the helping professions in South America deal with many of the issues just cited. These are occurring as a result of the increasing impact of globalization on the region, the economic defaults, the migration of the educated and not educated younger generation resulting from their view that there is no future and there are no jobs in their country, and the challenges faced by the elderly who lose their family due to migration. (IAC, 2005, p. 1)

Salient Social Justice Issues Emerging From Different Parts of the World

When considered from an international perspective, counseling and social justice are inextricably linked. This chapter began with a description of counseling on three levels—remedial, preventive, and developmental. Clearly, counseling approaches may be of assistance in addressing an inexhaustible number of challenges, concerns, problems, and crises worldwide. Also, from the perspective of our disciplinary lens, we know that there are culturally appropriate developmental programs and interventions that can be applied in anticipation of challenges that often accompany life transitions. Finally, as is clearly evident from the summaries of issues and discussions that have been part of IAC conferences, several forces within and across our societies often are large contributing factors to the problems that people encounter.

In North America, social justice issues often have been focused on the need for advocacy and intervention related to populations who have experienced and continue to experience discriminatory attitudes and practices in our societies—with major activity in the areas of feminism, multiculturalism, disability, sexual orientation, and poverty. In North America and in the larger world context, issues that affect almost everyone are often related to the rapid nature of globalization and the increasing rates of change.

Rapid advances in communication technology have led the world to shrink psychologically, socially, and economically. We have an unprecedented opportunity to see ourselves as part of a global community, with differences in perspective as well as with many common attributes, intentions, and behaviors. Within this context of opportunity there is also a continuation of bigotry, territoriality, greed, and unjust practices that facilitate the process of labeling others as the enemy or as being somehow less than ourselves, so they can be marginalized or in some other way exploited or hurt.

I believe that as a beginning, we need to refocus on the issues from the United Nations Declaration of Human Rights, which may sound like a given. However, I was reminded by a colleague from the United States who is of African heritage that the declaration works only if everyone is seen to be equally human. She then related several incidents of racial discrimination that she and other people she knows experience on a daily basis. How can those of us who work in counseling try to ensure that this starting point is recognized and honored?

Reviewing Basic Assumptions About Counseling

As a beginning I think that we need to consider all counseling as being cross-cultural, because we cannot know the microculture in which a person lives without getting to know him or her. Second, we need to see people in the context of all aspects of their interpretation of their personal, social, economic, and cultural existence, not to exacerbate and highlight differences among people but to touch them as human beings. Third, we need to be aware of the rapidly and perhaps chaotically changing environments that we and the people we work with inhabit. There is little we can do to stem the accelerating tide of change, but we can be increasingly aware of the cultural and personal fault lines that change can create. R. D. Laing (1972) stated that there are crazy people and there are normal people in crazy situations. The great majority of the people who come for counseling are there because they can't see a way to live effectively in their "crazy situations," whether they be family, school, work, or social.

Examining Ourselves

Self-examination is a given and, as such, may be overlooked. On an individual level the need for self-examination for biases, blind spots, prejudices, and the like is ongoing. In many areas of the world where counseling is developed, this process is encouraged through the requirement of professional development activities to maintain membership in professional associations. In a few instances, as with the British Association for Counselling and Psychotherapy, there is also a requirement for career-long supervision of counseling work.

Examining Current Policies and Procedures

There is a growing awareness internationally that counseling may have a place in addressing a range of personal and social issues. This has led to several initiatives facilitated by governments, the United Nations, and other agencies and nongovernmental organizations around the world that are examining the role of counseling in addressing personal, educational, and social issues for individuals, institutions, and broader societies. The IAC conferences and those of its predecessors represent a sustained program of such initiatives that has been ongoing and increasing since the early 1950s.

More recently there has been an increase in the range of activities exploring the use of guidance and counseling in areas of the world where it is new or in the initial phases of development. I have been involved in four such initiatives since 2002. In December of 2002 I was asked to make a presentation regarding the role of guidance and counseling in secondary education at a conference in Oman, sponsored by the Ministry of Education and UNESCO and addressing the revitalization of secondary education in the country. Guidance and counseling approaches are seen to have many potential benefits, including helping individuals and the broader societies in the region address the mismatch between occupational opportunities and people seeking employment. In the current situation, foreign workers who send their salaries to their families in their home countries hold many nonprofessional jobs. Also, there is an insufficient demand for professionals in the region to respond to the interest of young people in gaining education and working in these areas.

In 2003 I participated in offering training in basic guidance and counseling strategies for instructors and professors from technical and vocational high schools and colleges from across Nigeria. In this setting UNESCO has worked for several years to create an infrastructure that supports the expanding need in the country for people trained in occupations requiring technical and vocational education and training. The challenge is that most parents want their children to enter preprofessional education, where currently there are reduced labor market opportunities. The social impact of this situation is readily apparent. When my colleagues and I arrived in Nigeria in the early morning, we sat in the car until the sun came up because during the night cars are often stopped and robbed. I was told that young people who have not been able to find work are the main perpetrators of these crimes.

In a related activity, in the fall of 2004 I was invited by UNESCO to participate in a conference that brought together leaders from around the world to discuss technical and vocational education and training for sustainable development. Again, the interest of delegates from developing countries in vastly different parts of the world was in exploring the role of guidance and counseling in promoting sustainable development of individuals and societies.

In 2004, I was invited to Bhutan to consult with government and school officials, teachers, and secondary school students regarding ways to further develop guidance and counseling in secondary schools. The challenge in this situation again was the hope and expectation that young people with suitable abilities and interests would be able to progress from high school to college or university and enter a professional occupation. With 45% of the population of the country being age 15 or younger, it is unlikely that this expectation can be met. Again guidance and counseling can offer approaches and orientations that can assist individuals and institutions in addressing issues that challenge fairly basic assumptions within that societal context.

Offering Counseling Services in a Way That Respects Cultural Context

The concluding discussion of the training workshop in Nigeria centered on what participants found of value and what they would suggest for future workshops. An astute participant summarized what she would be taking away in the following words: "What I have learned is that if you want people to listen to you, first you have to listen to them." This phrase is a core piece of what counseling is about. Research has shown that it is a key in building a counseling relationship. It is also central in learning about what is important to our clients and to those in their family, work, and community cultures. Finally, it is the foundation for gaining the knowledge needed to adapt services so that they are relevant and effective across and within cultural settings. This is probably the hardest work that we do as counselors, because it demands that we listen as much as possible in full awareness of our own cultural filters and biases.

Challenging and Assisting the System

We are valued as counselors because we assist individuals to consider new perspectives that shake up their personal belief systems and attitudes. In terms of social justice, we need to do the same with larger institutional, community, and societal systems as well. To do this we need to use our counseling skills and approaches with the systems in which we work, listening to its members, helping them consider new approaches, and assisting with new action plans based on the awareness of new approaches. In order to do this, counselors need to consider whatever cultural organization or system they want to influence as their client.

Marketing Ourselves and Our Results

It has been my experience in North America as well as in other parts of the world that most counselors lack either the confidence or interest to promote the use of counseling services to address the needs of the broader society. We often focus on making our gains one client at a time. This has resulted in a great deal of assistance that has rippled through family, school, and work environments. Within a social justice perspective, this work needs to continue, and we need to add a lens that clearly centers on the attitudes of institutions and other structures that marginalize individuals and groups. We know the cost to individuals of these practices, and we have the communication skills to express our concerns and suggestions effectively. So why is this advocacy not a major part of what counselors do across the settings in which counseling occurs?

What Is Needed?

At its core counseling is about developing and implementing intentional communication processes to facilitate interaction with people and systems. The desired outcome is most often a change in behavior or attitude toward an issue. Counselor education programs usually focus much attention on the development of competence in helping individuals and groups resolve remedial and developmental issues. Over the past several years there has been increasing sensitivity and direct instruction regarding issues related to diversity, inclusion, and ethics as the primary lenses for all counseling work.

What has been less developed in counselor education is a similar level of attention and development in the education of counselors to see systems as their clients. With this focus counselors would be much better equipped to assess the needs of the institutions with which they work, to develop approaches for developing relationships within their power structures, and to mount credible and informed challenges to their policies and systems of operation in order to help institutions become more inclusive in their approaches to issues and people.

Those involved in the activities of the IAC hope and expect that counseling will expand opportunities for all peoples and their societies through affecting both the individual and the systemic or policy levels. Those of us in parts of the world where counseling has a long history should remember that this was also the expectation of those who first developed counseling approaches, and that the need to have a social impact has not diminished. Indeed, in the preventive area of counseling the playing field is level: Some countries have addressed issues in more formal ways but some of the attitudes that fuel discriminatory practices appear to be present in all of our societies. The question that remains to be answered is the extent to which the discipline of counseling will put its attention to making this form of intervention a priority in training, practice, and research.

References

Baluch, S., Pieterse, A. L., & Bolden, M. A. (2004). Counseling psychology and social justice: Houston . . . we have a problem. *The Counseling Psychologist, 32,* 89–98.

Beers, C. (1950). *A mind that found itself.* New York: Doubleday.

Borgen, W. A. (2003). Remembering Hans: His ongoing legacy for guidance and counselling. *International Journal for the Advancement of Counselling, 25,* 83–89.

Brewer, J. M. (1942). *History of vocational guidance.* New York: Harper.

Goodman, L. A., Laing, B., Helms, J. E., Latta, R. E., Sparks, E., & Weintraub, S. R. (2004). Training counseling psychologists as social justice agents: Feminist and multicultural principles in action. *The Counseling Psychologist, 32,* 793–837.

Hage S. M. (2003). Reaffirming the unique identity of counseling psychology: Opting for the "road less traveled." *The Counseling Psychologist, 31,* 555–563.

International Association for Counseling. (2001). *Families in transition—Counselling in transition.* Vancouver, BC, Canada: Author.

International Association for Counseling. (2004). *Participation programme, 2004–05: Form for submission of a request.* Vancouver, BC, Canada: Author.

International Association for Counselors. (2005). *Expanding the counselling profession within the context of profound and ongoing change.* Vancouver, BC, Canada: Author.

Kiselica, M. S. (2004). When duty calls: The implications of social justice work for policy, education, and practice in the mental health professions. *The Counseling Psychologist, 32,* 838–854.

Laing, R. D. (1972). *The politics of experience and the bird of paradise.* Baltimore: Penguin.

McClure, B. A., & Russo (1996). The politics of counseling: Looking back and forward, *Counseling and Values, 40,* 162–174.

Palmer, L. K. (2004). The call to social justice: A multidiscipline agenda, *The Counseling Psychologist, 32,* 879–885.

Parsons, F. (1967). *Choosing a vocation.* New York: Agathon Press.

Smith, L., Baluch, S., Bernabei, S., Robohm, J., & Sheehy, J. (2003). Applying a social justice framework to college counseling center practice. *Journal of College Counseling, 6,* 3 -13.

United Nations. (1948). *Universal declaration of human rights.* San Francisco: Author. Available from http://www.un.htmlorg/ Overview/rights

Watts, R. J. (2004). Integrating social justice and psychology, *The Counseling Psychologist, 32,* 855–865.

Williamson, E. G. (1965). *Vocational counseling.* New York: McGraw-Hill.

Chapter 10

Social Justice and Counseling Ethics

Barbara Richter Herlihy and Zarus E. P. Watson

The movement for social justice in counseling has evolved from a concern that the problems many clients bring to counseling are exacerbated, if not caused, by continuing social inequities in the United States, such as poverty, lack of adequate health care, unsafe housing, exposure to violence, and substandard schooling. The goal of counseling for social justice is to foster the empowerment of people who have been and often continue to be marginalized and oppressed in our society. Counselors who espouse this goal are committed to using their knowledge and skills in advocacy to promote constructive change in the systems (families, schools, workplaces, and communities) in which their clients live and in society as a whole (D'Andrea & Daniels, 2005). In order to effect social change, many counselors will need to reconceptualize how they traditionally have perceived the counseling process. They will no longer be able to view counseling as a one-on-one, in-the-office encounter, nor will they be able to assume that the problems a client brings to counseling originate within him or her. In other words, counseling for social justice requires a paradigm shift.

We believe that the social justice perspective requires a paradigm shift in how counselors think about ethics as well. When counselors attempt to resolve ethical issues, it is only natural for them to rely on the traditional approaches they have been taught. Yet, because these approaches are not based on a social justice perspective, they may lead to outcomes or ethical decisions that are incongruent with this perspective. In this chapter, we suggest an alternative approach to ethical decision making that we believe may enhance ethical counseling practice and promote social justice.

Multicultural Competence

Multicultural competence lies at the core of counseling for social justice and is equally essential to ethical counseling practice. The literature has clearly established that it is unethical for a counselor to provide counseling services to a client from a different culture unless the counselor is competent to work effectively with that client (Corey, Corey, & Callanan, 2003; Herlihy & Watson, 2003; Lee & Kurilla, 1997; Pedersen, Draguns, Lonner, & Trimble, 2002; Ponterotto & Casas; 1991; Remley & Herlihy, 2005; Robinson & Howard-Hamilton, 2000; Vontress, 2002). The *ACA Code of Ethics* (2005) also makes it clear that counselors have an ethical obligation to be multiculturally competent.

The current *ACA Code of Ethics,* adopted in July 2005, represents an extensive revision of the previous (1995) code. The revision process was spearheaded by the Ethics Code Revision Taskforce, formed in 2002 at the direction of then ACA President David Kaplan, and charged with focusing on more clearly articulating the profession's commitment to multiculturalism and diversity. The 2005 *Code* requires counselors to gain knowledge, personal awareness, and skills pertinent to working with a diverse client population (Standard C.2.a). Counselors' ethical duties with respect to the three components of multicultural competence identified by Sue and Sue (1990)—namely, awareness of self and others, knowledge, and skills—are reiterated throughout the *Code.*

The first component—the ethical responsibility to gain self-awareness—is addressed in the introduction to Section A ("The Counseling Relationship") in the statement that counselors are expected to learn how their own cultural identities influence their values and beliefs about the counseling process. The *Code* further requires counselors to be aware of their own values, attitudes, beliefs, and behaviors; to avoid imposing their values on clients; and to respect the diversity of clients (Standard A.4.b). The second component—knowledge and understanding of the worldviews of diverse clients—is addressed in the statement that counselors must actively attempt to understand the diverse cultural backgrounds of their clients (introduction to Section A). The skills component can be found in the obligations of counselors to maintain competence in their skills, to keep current with the diverse populations they serve (Standard C.2.f), and to expand their boundaries of competence by gaining knowledge and skills for working with diverse client populations (Standard C.2.a). Additional standards related to nondiscrimination and respect for diversity are found throughout all sections of the *Code.*

A content analysis of the *ACA Code of Ethics* seems to support a conclusion that the counseling profession has embraced multicultural competence as an ethical mandate. However, as Sue (1996) cautioned, written words will ring hollow unless they are translated into meaningful action. Although the *ACA Code of Ethics* is a useful and valuable source of guidance, it answers only the *what* questions regarding multicultural competence as an ethical responsibility. The *Code* does not address the question of *how* counselors can acquire the multicultural counseling competencies needed to translate the standards into action.

Traditional Approaches to Ethical Decision Making

Ethical decision making is a complex process that requires counselors to apply critical reflection and creative problem-solving skills (Pope & Vasquez, 1998; Ridley, Liddle, Hill, & Li, 2001). Thus, fostering the aims of social justice requires an ethical decision-making model that puts multicultural competence at the core of the ethical reasoning process. Numerous models are available in the literature, but they tend to ignore multicultural considerations, as we describe in this section.

Principle Ethics

Most of the models that have been offered to assist counselors in confronting ethical issues are based in *principle ethics*. Principle ethics, the dominant model in medicine and bioethics (Cottone & Tarvydas, 2003), also has been espoused historically by the counseling profession. This approach is grounded in certain moral principles, or generally accepted assumptions or values in society, that are seen as prima facie binding. Therefore, they must always be considered when attempting to resolve an ethical dilemma.

Five moral principles generally are seen as being essential to counseling practice. These are autonomy (foster self-determination), nonmaleficence (do no harm), beneficence (do good, or promote mental health), justice (be fair), and fidelity (be faithful, or keep promises). Counselors apply principle ethics by objectively, rationally, and universally applying a system of ethical rules and principles to determine the right course of action (Cottone & Tarvydas, 2003; Pedersen, 1997).

Although principle ethics has a legitimate place in counselors' ethical decision making, there are problems with this approach from a social justice perspective. A fundamental issue often overlooked when attempting to apply a principle- or rule-driven model is the question of who made the rules in the first place. Because principle ethics evolved from a Western, White, individualistic tradition (DuBose, Hamel, & O'Connell, 1994; Meara, Schmidt, & Day, 1996), this approach may not be appropriate when working with culturally diverse clients. Counselors who assume that the goals of client autonomy and self-determination are universally applicable may fail to recognize that many clients make choices and decisions in the context of family, group, or community. When counselors are not sensitive to their dominant power position in the counseling relationship and assume that they should decide what is good for the client, the principles of client autonomy and beneficence are violated (Herlihy & Watson, 2003). Counselors who are not multiculturally competent can easily violate the principle of nonmaleficence when they are unaware of their own cultural biases and thus impose them on clients (Meara et al., 1996; Tsiu & Schultz, 1988). Counselors can easily misapply the principles of beneficence and justice in working with clients whose problems arise from discrimination and oppression. Justice demands equality, and client welfare in these instances might best be promoted by challenging predominant social institutions in order to further the rights of culturally different individuals and groups, rather than by assuming that the problem lies within the individual client (Herlihy & Watson 2003).

Ethical Decision-Making Models

Kitchener (1984) developed one of the first well-known models of ethical decision making for counselors and counseling psychologists. She created a principle ethics–based model that drew on the moral principles of biomedical ethics described earlier by Beauchamp and Childress (1979). Cottone and Claus (2000) reviewed the literature and found nine practice-based ethical decision-making models that had appeared between Kitchener's 1984 publication and 1998. According to these authors' analysis, most of these models followed Kitchener's lead and relied heavily on principle ethics as a primary basis for determining ethical actions.

All nine models reviewed by Cottone and Claus (2000) offered a series of steps that counselors could follow to arrive at ethical decisions. Although no two were identical, many had in common the recommended steps of identifying the problem, examining codes of ethics, consulting with experts or peers, considering the consequences of any actions, and choosing an action. When we examined these steps, what stood out for us was that these models seemed to share three assumptions: (1) that ethical decision making entails gathering information from resources that are external to the personhood of the counselor (resources such as codes of ethics, peers or supervisors as consultants, and relevant literature); (2) that ethical decision making is a rational, dispassionate, logical process in which emotions play no part; and (3) that the counselor makes the final decision regarding the ethical course of action in isolation rather than in dialogue and discussion with the client or clients involved.

Our proposed model for ethical decision making challenges each of these assumptions. We agree that external resources such as codes of ethics, experts and colleagues, and the ethics literature are valuable and necessary elements of the ethical deliberation process. We also believe, however, that the aims of social justice will be better served if counselors begin their ethical reasoning process by focusing inward and engaging in self-reflection.

A Proposed Ethical Paradigm

We propose a foundation for ethical decision making based on three key assumptions: (a) that *virtue ethics* (an approach that is quite different from principle ethics) holds significant promise for promoting social justice; (b) that *cultural identity development,* a concept that is largely overlooked in most discussions of ethical reasoning, is an essential consideration in ethical practice; and (c) that ethical decision making is a *collaborative process* in which clients are actively involved and thus are empowered.

Virtue Ethics

Virtue ethics, which evolved in response to the limitations of rule-based models (Teehan, 1995), presents counselors with an alternative approach to principle ethics. A number of ethics scholars have asserted that virtue ethics can provide a more informed and more culturally sensitive approach than can principle ethics alone (Cottone & Tarvydas, 2003; Ibrahim, 1996; Remley & Herlihy, 2005).

Virtue ethics starts from the premise that professional ethics involve more than moral actions; they also involve traits of character or virtue (Jordan & Meara, 1991; Meara et al., 1996). In contrast to principle ethics, the virtue ethics perspective focuses on the *actor* rather than the *action*. The question for counselors to ask themselves when confronted with an ethical dilemma becomes "Who should I be?" rather than "What should I do?" (Vasquez, 1996).

The goals of virtue ethics are to achieve and maintain professional competence and to work for the common good by cultivating virtues such as discernment, respectfulness, recognition of the role of emotion in judging ethical conduct, self-awareness or self-understanding, and connectedness with one's community (Meara et al., 1996). The exercise of each of these virtues can further the aims of social justice counseling.

Discernment (sometimes called prudence) has been described as a foundational virtue that provides a thoughtful approach to cross-cultural encounters (Meara et al., 1996). Discernment allows counselors to be aware that, in a multicultural milieu, another's definition of the situation is not necessarily the same as their own (Vasquez, 1996). Because discernment includes a tolerance for ambiguity, its application can be crucial when counselors are faced with ethical dilemmas, which tend to be fraught with ambiguities. Discerning counselors approach ethical quandaries with appropriate caution, deliberate reflection, and a realization of what they do not know.

Respectfulness encompasses much more than respect for autonomy, which is a highly individualistic concept. This virtue is crucial in a multicultural society because it requires counselors to "respect individuals or communities on and in the terms they themselves [not the counselor] define. The critical question is how others wish to be respected" (Meara et al., 1996, p. 44).

A third characteristic of virtue ethics is its acknowledgement of the place of emotions in the ethical decision-making process. Feminist ethics scholars, in particular, have been critical of rule-based approaches that reflect a rational, logical, objective, linear, dispassionate, and abstract "male" model. They believe ethical reasoning can also be intuitive, subjective, holistic, compassionate, and contextual, and that such an approach might be more inclusive of other processing styles and more culturally appropriate (Glosoff, Stadler, & Herlihy, 1997; Rave & Larsen, 1995). Although virtue ethicists do not discount the value of systematic deliberation and logic in deliberating ethical issues, they caution counselors against assuming that emotion clouds reason. Instead, they believe that emotion can inform reason. They emphasize the importance of compassion, which includes a regard for the welfare of others, sensitivity to and sympathy for their suffering, and action to reduce or alleviate their pain—also hallmarks of counseling for social justice. Meara et al. (1996) have argued that emotion plays a vital role in developing both traits of virtue and virtuous action, as "our sense of outrage at injustice not only provides us with information that something needs to be done but also with a motivation to do it" (p. 30).

The counselor's search for an answer to the question of "Who should I be in my relationships with my clients?" begins with self-understanding. Self-knowledge requires that counselors know their own assumptions and biases and how these may affect their relationships with others. This awareness is a prerequisite for effective cross-cultural understanding (Meara et al., 1996). Virtue ethicists consistently have acknowledged that values are culturally shaped and have defined counseling as a healing process that takes place within a cultural context (Spohn, 1992). Thus, for counselors in our culturally diverse society, understanding their own cultural identities is a crucial component of self-knowledge (a point on which we will elaborate in the next section).

Finally, the community is of primary importance in virtue ethics (Freeman, 2000). "Virtue ethics is rooted in community and relies on a community's wisdom and its moral sense" (Meara et al., 1996, p. 12). Virtue ethicists believe that counselors must connect with and understand the norms and values of their communities as well as the importance of community in ethical decision making. They contend that the values of the counseling profession must be integrated with the goals, assumptions, and understandings of the communities that support those values and that the counseling profession seeks to serve. Being grounded in a particular community's wisdom and moral sense enhances counselors' ethical practice in multicultural contexts (Ibrahim, 1996). Virtuous counselors are interdependent with their community and comprehend the community's ideals, expectations, mores, and sensibilities.

Although some have argued that virtue ethics and principle ethics stand in conflict with each other, others have suggested that they are complementary rather than competitive models (Freeman, 2000; Meara et al., 1996; Remley & Herlihy, 2005). Both approaches are important and useful. We believe, however, that the foundation for ethical decision making lies in the careful consideration and inclusion of virtue ethics. Virtue ethics opens new worlds of possibilities for counseling for social justice—new possibilities for effective counseling practice that are not available in the traditional medical model, which assumes that clients' concerns have an intrapsychic origin. The emphasis in virtue ethics on community connectedness reminds counselors to consider that the client's problems may originate not in the client, but in the oppressive environment in which the client lives. The focus in virtue ethics on the counselor's motives, intentions, character, and ethical consciousness reminds counselors to consider that problems in the counseling relationship may reside not in the client, but in fact in the practitioner.

Cultural Identity Development

Culture is a pervasive force in our lives that fundamentally shapes how we see ourselves and the world. All individuals develop a cultural identity that is partly conscious but largely unconscious and includes their self-perceptions as well as values, attitudes, beliefs, and worldviews (Hoare, 1991). Counselors, like everyone else, have multiple cultural identities (including ones based on race or ethnicity, gender, socioeconomic status, sexual orientation, religion, and disability status) that have been shaped by their experiences and memberships in both dominant and nondominant societal groups.

Cultural identity development has come to be recognized as a crucial variable in counseling processes and outcomes (Atkinson, Morten, & Sue, 1993). It is essential that counselors have done their own personal work and have attended to their own cultural identity development before they attempt to work with clients who are culturally different from themselves. If counselors are unaware of their cultural conditioning and resultant biases, they will bring these biases into their counseling relationships. The counseling relationships will then, in turn, mirror the prejudices and stereotyping with which their clients are struggling in their daily lives.

Numerous cultural identity development models are available to help counselors develop and strengthen their cultural self-understanding. The earliest cultural identity development models (Cross, 1971; Jackson, 1975) were created to describe the transformation that Blacks experienced in becoming aware of themselves as racial beings. Cross' four-stage model described a process through which the individual progresses from a state of self-denigration and unreasoning dominant-group affiliation to a state of internalized self-regard.

These pioneering efforts were followed by a proliferation of cultural identity development models. In addition to the continued development of Black racial identity theories (e.g., Helms, 1984), models described identity development among members of other racial and ethnic groups, including Chicanos/Latinos (Ruiz, 1990), Asian Americans (Ibrahim & Ohnishi, 1997), Filipino Americans (Nadal, 2004), and biracial individuals (Kerwin & Ponterotto, 1995; Poston, 1990). Dimensions other than race and ethnicity were addressed in models based on gender (e.g., Downing & Roush, 1985) and sexual orientation (e.g., Cass, 1984; Coleman, 1982).

More inclusive models include Sue and Sue's schema (1990) of racial and cultural identity development (R/CID); Helms and Cook's (1999) extension of their Black racial identity development model to include all people of color; Atkinson, Morten, and Sue's (1983) minority development model (MID); and the optimal theory applied to identity development (OTAID) of Myers and colleagues (1991), which offers a pluralistic framework applicable across a range of groups. Once it was recognized that all individuals, including members of dominant societal groups, have cultural identities, theories appeared that described the identity development of Whites (Helms, 1990), heterosexuals (Mohr,

2002; Worthington & Mohr, 2002; Worthington, Savoy, Dillon, & Vernaglia, 2002), and White males (Scott & Robinson, 2001).

Clearly, there are a plethora of models of cultural identity development, and we have provided nowhere near an inclusive list. Even though they use differing terminology and posit different numbers of stages or statuses, almost all the models describe a similar process. In general, individuals are seen as progressing though a series of socialized phases. The initial phase is characterized by lack of awareness and obliviousness to societal inequities. In successive phases, individuals progress to a time of reexamination, often triggered by a conflict or crisis, through an appreciation of and identification with their own cultural group, to a final phase, or status, that has been given various labels, including "integrative awareness" (Helms & Cook, 1999) or "active commitment" (Downing & Roush, 1985). This final phase is characterized by a change in worldview that entails "a holistic understanding of the common struggles of all people" (Scott & Robinson, 2001, p. 420). A more sophisticated understanding leads to a commitment to work to eliminate all forms of oppression through involvement in activities to effect social change. It is at this last phase of identity development, and only at this phase, that action to promote social justice becomes possible.

If counselors are to empower clients to progress through these phases, they must first attend to their own processes of cultural identity development. Counselors cannot guide their clients to a level of awareness that they themselves have not reached. Helms (1990) has described how the counselor's and client's cultural identity development interact to directly affect the counseling outcome. She has used the term *progressive interactions* to describe the type of counseling relationships that are most effective in facilitating client growth and change. In progressive relationships, counselors act in a manner that is more sophisticated with respect to cultural identity development than where their clients are, and therefore, they are able to educate and assist clients to progress in their own development.

Process and Outcomes

It may seem paradoxical that our suggested approach to ethical decision making—which aims to foster the broad goal of societal change—begins with the suggestion that counselors engage in self-reflection. We believe, however, that counselors cannot wait to develop ethical reasoning skills until they are confronted with an ethical issue in their practice. We contend, rather, that counselors who have given careful consideration to the question of "Who shall I be?" as virtuous agents and who have worked to develop their cultural identities to the highest stages of functioning will be better prepared to deal with the ethical quandaries that inevitably will arise in their work. We offer a simple case example to illustrate how the counseling process might unfold when a counselor brings this level of preparedness to the therapeutic endeavor.

> Walter is a counselor who has had three counseling sessions with Yusef, a client from a different culture than himself. Yusef has sought counseling because he is unhappy and frustrated in his work environment. Some of Yusef's behaviors during the sessions are making Walter feel a bit uncomfortable. Twice, Yusef has brought Walter token gifts as a way of expressing his appreciation for the counseling services. Additionally, although Walter has attempted to keep the focus of sessions on Yusef's work-related problems, Yusef frequently changes the focus by asking Walter "personal" questions about his values and his life outside the counseling sessions.

A counselor operating from a traditional conceptualization of Yusef's behaviors might conclude that Yusef has a problem with understanding and respecting the boundaries of the counseling relationship. A principle- or rule-based orientation might lead the counselor to be concerned about whether he might be committing a violation of ethical standards if he continues to accept even token gifts. His strategy for dealing with Yusef's intrusive questions might be to redirect the conversation back to Yusef and his presenting concerns.

We are assuming, though, that Walter is a culturally competent counselor whose goal in working with Yusef is to act as a virtuous agent. Using discernment (or prudence), Walter will not be likely to jump to conclusions based on an assumption that Yusef's problems have an intrapsychic origin. Rather than conceptualizing the gift giving as an ethical issue, or conceptualizing Yusef's asking of personal questions as "avoidance" of his own work, Walter will be tolerant of the complexities and ambiguities involved in searching for a broader explanation of the meaning of the gifts and the questions within the context of Yusef's cultural values.

Being aware of his own emotional discomfort with being offered gifts and being asked personal questions, Walter will respond immediately by appropriately self-disclosing his emotional reactions. Walter will respectfully engage in a dialogue with the client to understand, in Yusef's own terms, the meanings of the behaviors.

Through this approach, Walter will learn that gift giving has a cultural meaning for Yusef of which Walter was not aware and that the questioning arises out of Yusef's own uncertaintics about the therapeutic relationship. Taking his cue from Walter's focus on the emotional dynamics of the relationship, Yusef may reveal that he is questioning whether someone like Walter, who is so culturally different from him, will be capable of understanding him.

Once the interpersonal dynamics between counselor and client have been explored, the focus of the counseling process can shift to addressing Yusef's presenting concerns about his work situation. The foundation now exists for Yusef to discuss his experiences with prejudice and discrimination at work, which he sees as stemming from his Middle Eastern origin. Together, Walter and Yusef can begin to explore strategies for effecting change in the work situation and, eventually, to explore ways to advocate for the many people of Middle Eastern origin who encounter prejudice and mistreatment in the current climate of our society.

It is important to emphasize that in the case example just described, the client defined the meanings of his behaviors and was an active partner in the counseling process. This brings us to the last of the three assumptions on which our proposed model is based: that ethical decision making is a *collaborative process* in which the client is actively involved.

Shared Decision Making

The idea that clients are active partners in the counseling process is certainly not new. A number of theories of counseling—notably the social constructivist (Cottone, 2001), multicultural, and feminist approaches—hold this as a fundamental value. However, this value rarely seems to be applied to ethical decisions. As we noted earlier in the chapter, Cottone and Claus (2000) found that existing models for ethical decision making provide a series of steps, the last of which is that the *counselor* decides on the best course of action and implements the decision. We are concerned that there is an underlying paternalism in the assumption that the counselor is the one who must decide.

Walden (1996), basing her work on feminist theory, argued persuasively that clients are robbed of their power in the counseling relationship when counselors make decisions *for* them rather than *with* them. Conversely, when a partnership is created, the client is empowered. Walden cautioned that "inclusion of the client in ethical considerations is not an attempt to 'victim blame' or to shift the responsibility for ethical practice onto the client" (p. 40), and that the counselor always bears the burden of maintaining professionalism. Yet, inclusion of the client can provide a valuable resource to the counselor and can be a source of empowerment for the client.

We can think of very few ethical questions that might arise in a counseling relationship that could not be discussed with clients. We would see such a dialogue as being contraindicated only when such a discussion would be initiated to meet the counselor's needs at the potential expense of the client (for instance, a counselor disclosing a sexual attraction to a client) or in an emergency situation when the client's condition poses an imminent danger of serious harm to self or others.

In the vast majority of circumstances, a collaborative decision-making process is not only possible but has the benefit of empowering the client. This is the outcome that situates our proposed paradigm for ethical practice within the context of social justice. If a primary goal of counseling for social justice is to empower clients who have been disempowered in the larger society, then this empowerment must be modeled within the counseling relationship.

Merging the Proposed and Traditional Models

Our proposed alternative model for ethical decision making is not intended to replace traditional models, which have much to offer. Rather, we see the internal, self-reflective process we have described as providing a *foundation* for sound, ethical counseling practice. Counselors who have engaged in this self-reflection can make thoughtful applications of the external resources suggested by the more traditional models in a collaborative decision-making process with their clients.

The *ACA Code of Ethics* (2005) is perhaps the primary external resource for counselors (and clients) to consult when they have ethical questions. As we noted earlier, the revised *Code* puts considerations of cultural diversity strongly at the forefront. Yet, in applying the *Code*, it is important for counselors to keep in mind that codes of ethics represent the consensus of a profession's thinking about ethical issues at the time the standards are written. Thus, they are reactive rather than proactive (Corey, Corey, & Callanan, 2003) and tend to lag behind social changes. They can quickly become out of step with trends in society or in the profession (Mabe & Rollin, 1986). For example, outside of the community of multicultural scholars, *counseling for social justice* is relatively recent terminology. Although scholars have long promoted client advocacy as a role for counselors (e.g., Atkinson et al., 1993; Helms & Cook, 1999; Lee & Richardson, 1991), in the counseling for social justice movement the advocate role has assumed a central, defining position. Advocacy is addressed for the first time in ACA's 2005 ethical standards (A.6.a and b), but the *Code* makes no mention of the term *social justice*. Codes of ethics typically are revised every 7 to 10 years. Yet, the counseling profession's knowledge base and awareness of emerging ethical issues are continually expanding. Therefore, as time passes, counselors increasingly will need to use discernment to interpret the *Code*.

Consultation with experts and colleagues is another valuable strategy often suggested in traditional models. We agree that decisions made in isolation are rarely as sound as decisions made in consultation. However, consulting with experts and peers makes use only of the external resources available in the counselor's *professional* community. Culturally competent counselors acting from a virtue ethics perspective recognize that the counseling relationship is situated in a *shared* community that includes clients, their social support systems, and a variety of resources that might be enlisted in removing systemic barriers to client growth. In resolving ethical issues, culturally competent counselors will enlist the aid of these community resources.

Reading the relevant literature is a third strategy recommended in many of the traditional approaches. Culturally competent counselors acting as virtuous agents will consult the literature together with their clients, in a collaborative search for guidance in resolving their questions.

To return to our case example, Walter and Yusef might review the *ACA Code of Ethics* together, as a means of understanding the ethical considerations involved in accepting gifts (Standard A.10.e). They might look at some of the literature that argues that, in some circumstances, accepting gifts may be culturally appropriate and beneficial to clients (e.g., Herlihy & Corey, 1997; Lazarus & Zur, 2002). As Walter and Yusef work to develop strategies to counteract the prejudice that Yusef is encountering at work, they might enlist the assistance of community agencies that exist to deal with discrimination in the workplace. Social support systems in the community might be another resource that they could tap into, to help Yusef to feel less isolated in his situation.

Conclusion

In conclusion, we hope that counselors will be able to use this proposed approach to strengthen and enrich their ethical reasoning abilities, and thus to enhance ethical counseling practice from a social justice perspective. This approach merges the concepts of multicultural competence, virtue ethics, and cultural identity development from parallel paths to create a collaborative model for ethical counseling practice.

A challenge for the future will be to expand our holistic vision to encompass the understanding that individual counseling and societal change are not separate and discrete processes. Rather, they are a collaborative means to an end. By providing individuals with culturally competent, effective counseling services that emphasize advocacy and client empowerment, counselors help to effect social change.

References

American Counseling Association. (2005). *ACA code of ethics.* Alexandria, VA: Author.

Atkinson, D. R., Morten, G., & Sue, D. W. (1983). *Counseling American minorities: A cross-cultural perspective* (2nd ed.). Dubuque, IA: Wm. C. Brown.

Atkinson, D. R., Morten, G., & Sue, D. W. (1993). *Counseling American minorities: A cross-cultural perspective*(4th ed.). Madison, WI: Brown & Benchmark.

Beauchamp, T. L., & Childress, J. F. (1979). *Principles of biomedical ethics* (3rd ed.). Oxford, UK: Oxford University Press.

Cass, V. C. (1984). Homosexual identity formation: Testing a theoretical model. *Journal of Sex Research, 20,* 143–167.

Coleman, E. (1982). Developmental stages of the coming-out process. *American Behavioral Scientist, 25,* 469–482.

Corey, G., Corey, M. S., & Callanan, P. (2003). *Issues and ethics in the helping professions* (6th ed.). Pacific Grove, CA: Brooks/Cole.

Cottone, R. R. (2001). A social constructivism model of ethical decision making in counseling. *Journal of Counseling & Development, 79,* 39–45.

Cottone, R. R., & Claus, R. E. (2000). Ethical decision-making models: A review of the literature. *Journal of Counseling & Development, 78,* 276–283.

Cottone, R. R., & Tarvydas, V. M. (2003*). Ethical and professional issues in counseling* (2nd ed.). Upper Saddle River, NJ: Merrill Prentice Hall.

Cross, W. E., Jr. (1971). The Negro-to-Black conversion experience: Toward a psychology of Black liberation. *Black World, 20*(9), 13–27.

D'Andrea, M., & Daniels, J. (2005, January). Promoting multiculturalism and social justice: A New Year's resolution. *Counseling Today,* pp. 32–34.

Downing, N. E., & Roush, K. L. (1985). From passive acceptance to active commitment: A model of feminist identity development for women. *The Counseling Psychologist, 13,* 695–709.

DuBose, E. R., Hamel, R. P., & O'Connell, L. J. (Eds.). (1994). *A matter of principles? Ferment in U.S. bioethics.* Valley Forge, PA: Trinity Press International.

Freeman, S. J. (2000). *Ethics: An introduction to philosophy and practice.* Belmont, CA: Wadsworth.

Glosoff, H. L., Stadler, H. A., & Herlihy, B. (1997, April). *Relational ethics in counseling: Bringing different voices to old models.* Paper presented at the American Counseling Association World Conference, Orlando, FL.

Helms, J. E. (1984). Toward a theoretical explanation of the effects of race on counseling: A Black and White model. *The Counseling Psychologist, 12,* 153–165.

Helms, J. E. (Ed.). (1990). *Black and White racial identity: Theory, research, and practice.* Westport, CT: Greenwood Press.

Helms, J. E., & Cook, D. A. (1999). *Using race and culture in counseling and psychotherapy: Theory and process.* Needham Heights, MA: Allyn & Bacon.

Herlihy, B., & Corey, G. (1997). *Boundary issues in counseling: Multiple roles and responsibilities.* Alexandria, VA: American Counseling Association.

Herlihy, B., & Watson, Z. E. (2003). Ethical issues and multicultural competence in counseling. In F. D. Harper & J. McFadden (Eds.), *Culture and counseling: New approaches* (pp. 363–378). Boston: Allyn & Bacon.

Hoare, C. H. (1991). Psychosocial identity development and cultural others. *Journal of Counseling & Development, 70,* 45–53.

Ibrahim, F. A. (1996). A multicultural perspective on principle and virtue ethics. *The Counseling Psychologist, 24,* 78–85.

Ibrahim, F. A., & Ohnishi, H. (1997). Asian American identity development: A culture-specific model for South Asian Americans. *Journal of Multicultural Counseling and Development, 25,* 34–51.

Jackson, B. (1975). Black identity development. *MEFORM: Journal of Educational Diversity and Innovation, 2,* 19–25.

Jordan, A. E., & Meara, N. M. (1991). The role of virtues and principles in moral collapse: A response to Miller. *Professional Psychology: Research and Practice, 22,* 107–109.

Kerwin, C., & Ponterotto, J. G. (1995). Biracial identity development: Research and practice. In J. Ponterotto, M. Casas, L. Suzuki, & C. Alexander (Eds.), *Handbook of multicultural counseling* (pp. 199–217). Newbury Park, CA: Sage.

Kitchener, K. S. (1984). Intuition, critical evaluation, and ethical principles: The foundation for ethical decisions in counseling psychology. *The Counseling Psychologist, 12,* 43–55.

Lazarus, A. L., & Zur, O. (Eds.) (2002). *Dual relationships and psychotherapy.* New York: Springer.

Lee, C. C., & Kurilla, V. (1997). Ethics and multiculturalism: The challenge of diversity. In *Hatherleigh guide to ethics in therapy* (pp. 235–248). New York: Hatherleigh.

Lee, C. C., & Richardson, B. L. (1991). *Multicultural issues in counseling: New approaches to diversity.* Alexandria, VA: American Association for Counseling and Development.

Mabe, A. R., & Rollin, S. A. (1986). The role of a code of ethical standards in counseling. *Journal of Counseling and Development, 64,* 294–297.

Meara, N. M., Schmidt, L. D., & Day, J. D. (1996). Principles and virtues: A foundation for ethical decisions, policies, and character. *The Counseling Psychologist, 24,* 4–77.

Mohr, J. J. (2002). Heterosexual identity and the heterosexual therapist: Using identity as a framework for understanding sexual orientation issues in psychotherapy. *The Counseling Psychologist, 30,* 532–566.

Myers, L. J., Speight, S. L., Highlen, P. S., Cox, C. I., Reynolds, A. L., Adams, E. M., et al. (1991). Identity development and worldview: Toward an optimal conceptualization. *Journal of Counseling & Development, 70,* 54–63.

Nadal, K. L. (2004). Pilipino American identity development model. *Journal of Multicultural Counseling and Development, 32,* 45–62.

Pedersen, P. B. (1997). The cultural context of the American Counseling Association Code of Ethics. *Journal of Counseling & Development, 76,* 23–29.

Pedersen, P. B., Draguns, J. G., Lonner, W. J., & Trimble, J. E. (Eds.). (2002). *Counseling across cultures* (5th ed.). Thousand Oaks, CA: Sage.

Ponterotto, J. G., & Casas, J. M. (1991). *Handbook of multicultural counseling research.* Springfield, IL: Charles C Thomas.

Pope, K. S., & Vasquez, M. J. T. (1998). *Ethics in psychotherapy and counseling: A practical guide for psychologists* (2nd ed.). San Francisco: Jossey-Bass.

Poston, W. S. C. (1990). The biracial identity development model: A needed addition. *Journal of Counseling & Development, 69,* 152–155.

Rave, E. J., & Larsen, C. C. (1995). *Ethical decision making in therapy: Feminist perspectives.* New York: Guilford Press.

Remley, T. P., & Herlihy, B. (2005). *Ethical, legal, and professional issues in counseling* (2nd ed.). Upper Saddle River, NJ: Merrill Prentice Hall.

Ridley, C. R., Liddle, M. C., Hill, C. L., & Li, L. C. (2001). Ethical decision making in multicultural counseling. In J. C. Ponterotto, J. M. Casas, L. A. Suzuki, & C. M. Alexander (Eds.), *Handbook of multicultural counseling* (2nd ed., pp. 165–188). Thousand Oaks, CA: Sage.

Robinson, T. L., & Howard-Hamilton, M. F. (2000). *The convergence of race, ethnicity, and gender: Multiple identities in counseling.* Upper Saddle River, NJ: Merrill Prentice Hall.

Ruiz, A. S. (1990). Ethnic identity: Crisis and resolution. *Journal of Multicultural Counseling and Development, 18,* 29–40.

Scott, D. A., & Robinson, T. L. (2001). White male identity development: The key model. *Journal of Counseling & Development, 79,* 415–421.

Spohn, S. (1992). Notes on moral theology. *Theological Studies, 53,* 60–74.

Sue, D. W. (1996). Ethical issues in multicultural counseling. In B. Herlihy & G. Corey (Eds.), *ACA ethical standards casebook* (5th ed., pp. 193–197). Alexandria, VA: American Counseling Association.

Sue, D. W., & Sue, D. (1990). *Counseling the culturally different: Theory and practice* (2nd ed.). New York: Wiley.

Teehan, J. (1995). Character, integrity and Dewey's virtue ethics. *Translations of the Charles S. Pierce Society, 31,* 841–863.

Tsiu, P., & Schultz, G. L. (1988). Ethnic factors in group process: Cultural dynamics in multiethnic therapy groups. *American Journal of Orthopsychiatry, 58,* 136–142.

Vasquez, M. J. T. (1996). Will virtue ethics improve ethical conduct in multicultural settings and interactions? *The Counseling Psychologist, 24,* 98–104.

Vontress, C. E. (2002). Introduction: Multicultural awareness as a generic competence for counseling. In P. B. Pedersen, J. G. Draguns, W. J. Lonner, & J. E. Trimble (Eds.), *Counseling across cultures* (5th ed., pp. xiii–xix). Thousand Oaks, CA: Sage.

Walden, S. L. (1996). Inclusion of the client perspective in ethical practice. In B. Herlihy & G. Corey, *Boundary issues in counseling* (pp. 40–47). Alexandria, VA: American Counseling Association.

Worthington, R. L., & Mohr, J. J. (2002). Theorizing heterosexual identity development. *The Counseling Psychologist, 30,* 491–495.

Worthington, R. L., Savoy, H. B., Dillon, F. R., & Vernaglia, E. R. (2002). Heterosexual identity development: A multidimensional model of individual and group identity. *The Counseling Psychologist, 30,* 496–531.

Chapter 11

Fair Access to and Use of Assessment in Counseling

Larry C. Loesch

An underlying theme of this book is that professional counselors (used here to mean certified or licensed counselors who have received at least a master's degree from an accredited counselor preparation program or students in such a program who aspire to become certified or licensed counselors) should be engaged in applied social justice. That is, professional counselors must do more than just espouse a belief in social justice; they must act upon that belief. Basically, this means that their belief in social justice should pervade all of their professional being and be evident throughout their professional behaviors. Involvement with assessment has long been, and remains, an integral part of a professional counselor's functioning. How can professional counselors manifest a belief in social justice in their professional work as it relates to assessment? More specifically, how can and should professional counselors be both socially responsive and socially responsible in regard to assessment?

Responding to these important questions is by no means simple, nor is any particular framework for responding clearly better than others; it is simply a matter of choice. Clearly, being socially responsive and demonstrating social responsibility in regard to assessment are integrally related, and in fact inseparable. However, for clarity of presentation, they can be discussed separately. Thus, I address socially responsive assessment and socially responsible assessment as separate but related topics. Note that both socially responsive and socially responsible assessment include not only considerations for the professional counselor as a member of the counseling profession (i.e., a collective response) but also as a part of her or his professional practice (i.e., an individual response).

Socially Responsive Assessment

Clearly the demography of the United States is changing, and changing rapidly. For example, Garcia and Marotta (1997) wrote

> Projections for comparative population growth rates indicate that the Latino population will increase at a rate three to five times faster than the general population. . . . This means that the Latino population is the fastest growing group in the United States and will be the largest minority group. . . . By 2020 it is expected that Latinos will be about 15% of the total U.S. population. (p. 5)

Rodriguez (2002) noted that this will have substantial implications for American society. Similarly, Atkinson (2004), citing Schmidley (2001), noted that

> although the largest number of immigrants (8.8 million) entered the United States in the decade between 1901 and 1910, the steadily increasing influx of immigrants since 1970 has resulted in more foreign-born residents in the year 2000 (28.4 million) than at any other time in our nation's history. (p. 3)

Changing demography means a changing society, and a changing society means that professional counselors must be socially responsive in new, comprehensive, innovative, and thoughtful ways. Dana (1993) noted,

> Mental health services in the United States were originally designed by middle-class Anglo-Americans for clients who were similar to themselves. Populations from other cultures were provided services on the basis of the belief that these clients either were highly similar to Anglo-Americans or would inevitably become more similar over time. . . . As a result these services were underutilized because they were often perceived by potential consumers as inappropriate and/or ineffective. (p. 2)

Atkinson (2004) captured the task with which professional counselors are confronted succinctly when he wrote "it is essential that mental health practitioners become sensitive to the needs, values, and beliefs of the many groups who currently reside in the United States" (p. 3). The charge to professional counselors is easy enough to understand, but fulfilling the charge will require substantial thought and action.

In order to be socially responsive in regard to assessment, professional counselors need to establish a clear direction for how assessment practices can be socially responsive in general and in particular as they relate to diverse or minority populations. Historically, social responsiveness in regard to assessment appears to have been focused upon the so-called majority (i.e., Caucasian) population in the United States. Actions from this perspective have been somewhat successful for all Americans (e.g., in favorably altering some educational practices). There remains however a great need for revision, updating, and improvement of existing practices, even those that heretofore have given the pretense of being socially responsive. In addition, professional counselors' uses of and responses to assessment in serving diverse groups need to be especially well defined and well understood. For example, professional counselors need to be educated in how clients' respective social environments and contexts affect assessment practices because successful assessment does not take place in isolation. Rather, it is linked with knowledge of, and even contingent upon, cultural context.

Effective solutions to the challenges posed by the need for assessments for an increasingly ethnically and culturally diverse population, and a proportionately diminishing majority population, will not be found simply in new tests or through revisions of present tests. As Anastasi (1997) adroitly indicated, "No single test can be universally applicable or equally 'fair' to all cultures. . . . It is unlikely, moreover, that any test can be equally 'fair' to more than one cultural group" (p. 345). Rather, what professional counselors and other mental health professionals need are better assessment practices. Some substantive progress in this regard has been made. For example, the most recent version of the *Standards for Educational and Psychological Testing* (American Educational Research Association [AERA], American Psychological Association [APA], and National Council of Measurement and Evaluation [NCME], 1999) evidences a change in the nature of the conceptualization of validity (the fundamental and most important quality of a measurement) from being a characteristic of the assessment itself to being a characteristic of the uses of the assessment results, including consideration of all factors pertinent to effective interpretation of the results (Goodwin & Leech, 2003). Linn and Miller (2005) put it succinctly: "Validity is an evaluation of the adequacy and appropriateness of the interpretation and uses of assessment results" (p. 68). This perspective casts validity as a context-specific construct, which means that, by definition and intention, both the context of the assessment process and the characteristics of the assessment respondent must be taken into consideration. Clearly, this is the most appropriate and equitable way to evaluate the validity of an assessment given that any assessment can be used with a wide variety of people.

Changing the technical practices for assessment is important but is only part of effective social responsiveness. Effective solutions are possible only through recognition of the larger problem, with the critical issue being the quality and effectiveness of professional services to all clients in all social environments and contexts. Professional counselors need to examine the quality and usefulness of available assessment activities relative to how such assessments may negatively affect clients, no matter the population group to which they may belong. Needed is a reorientation of assessment practices to promote the development of human talent and resources for all who are assessed.

Fair Access to Assessment Instruments

Regrettably, some professional counselors perceive assessment (testing) as a potpourri of activities not integrally linked to their scope of practice. Such a perspective is indeed naïve and in effect diminishes the true meaning of being a professional counselor. Therefore, assessment needs a clearer identity within counseling so that the harmful effects on both clients and counselors of limitations on professional counselors' access to assessment instruments can be minimized. To achieve this goal, professional counselors need to commit themselves to a clear conceptualization of the purposes of assessment in counseling, particularly as it relates to effective treatment methods for all who are served (Dana, 1993).

Critical to professional counselors' appropriate conceptualization of assessment is legitimate and fair access to selecting, administering, scoring, and interpreting assessment instruments. Among numerous issues surrounding fair access, one of the most important is the core assumption that professional counselors are qualified and able to do assessment, including that master's-level counselors are fully functioning mental-health service providers able to select, administer, score, and interpret tests and assessments. This core assumption is, for example, fundamental to the viability of the American Counseling Association, in which fair access to assessment instruments and the use of assessment in counseling help to define the scope of practice for professional counselors. Although this issue may be viewed as self-serving for professional counselors because it addresses a seemingly personalized professional concern, it clearly speaks to the broad social issue of the availability of clinical services and thus affects client well-being. Professional counselors must have broad access to assessment instruments if counseling is to continue as a profession.

External Events Affecting Professional Counselors' Fair Access to Assessments

Most professional counselors are aware of initiatives by some state regulatory agencies and state psychological associations to limit (master's-level) professional counselors' access to educational and psychological tests. For example, professional counselors' use of assessments in general was challenged in the state of Louisiana through the *Louisiana State Board of Examiners of Psychologists of the Department of Health and Human Services V. Boyd J. Attenberry* (1995). The California Board of Psychology, during hearings, discussed qualifications for use of the Strong Interests Inventory and the Myers-Briggs Type Indicator by mental health service providers other than psychologists. And finally, in Indiana, the Indiana state legislature passed a bill that would have restricted the use of 318 specific, named tests (including, for example, the Connors' Rating Scale for Parents, Kaufman Brief Intelligence Test, Sixteen Personality Factor Questionnaire, and Seashore Tests of Musical Talent) to licensed psychologists (Fair Access Coalition on Testing [FACT], 2000b). Fortunately, this bill was not signed by the governor of Indiana and did not become law. All of these efforts were intended to limit professional counselors' use of tests. Had any of these or similar efforts been successful in restricting the assessments that professional counselors can use, the scope of practice for professional counselors would have been severely limited. Thus, the issue of test-user qualifications has significant implications for the counseling profession.

In summing up their research on test-user qualifications, Moreland, Eyde, Robertson, Primoff, and Most (1995) reported that educational efforts are more effective in promoting good testing practices than is limiting the use of tests. Their report is a product of the Joint Committee on Testing Practices, which is composed of representatives from the ACA, the American Psychological Association (APA), the National Council of Measurement and Evaluation (NCME), the National Association of School Psychologists (NASP), and the American Speech-Language-Hearing Association (ASHA). Thus professional counselors, individually and collectively, should work to educate the numerous stakeholders for the counseling profession about what good assessment is, how it is integral to and integrated into the work of professional counselors, how professional counselors are competent in regard to assessment, and how the public will be the ultimate beneficiary of professional counselors' appropriate and good assessment activities.

The American Psychological Association established a committee charged with describing the knowledge and skills necessary for mental health professionals to administer, score, and interpret assessment instruments in a "competent and responsible manner." This committee addressed the issues of (a) informing psychologists and other health service providers of the skills and knowledge required in the responsible conduct of assessment; (b) influencing the curriculum of graduate training programs toward the identified knowledge and skills; (c) assisting test publishers in determining appropriate qualifications for test uses and users; (d) informing the public about appropriate test-user qualifications; and (e) informing regulatory, disciplinary, accrediting, and credentialing bodies about test-user qualifications in order to assist in their development of standards, regulations, or guidelines. Clearly, the American Psychological Association, with its long history of test usage, is having an influential effect on and is a strong force in addressing access to assessment instruments.

Professional counselors need to take similar actions, most likely through the Association for Assessment in Counseling and Education (AACE) and similarly oriented professional organizations. Myers and Sweeney (2004) reported that current and recent AACE leaders highly value professional advocacy on behalf of both clients and the counseling profession itself. Some progress has been made in, for example, AACE's development of documents such as the *Responsibilities of Users of Standardized Tests, Standards for Multicultural Assessment, Standards for Qualifications of Test Users,* and *Test Takers Rights and Responsibilities.* Unfortunately, however, although counseling profession advocacy is valued and has been initiated to some extent, assessment-related issues have not been readily apparent among the efforts. This situation must change if professional counselors are to achieve their rightful place among respected mental health service providers.

Events seemingly external to the profession that create more regulation through state statutes, more restrictions through scope-of-practice limitations, and more control by noncounseling professional organizations also should be of concern to professional counselors. Curiously, some of these external events are aided by so-called civil rights advocacy groups and antitest groups that are not interested in scope-of-practice issues. Rather, they are seeking a mechanism by which to assert control over assessment and its consequences (e.g., placement;

labeling; and restricted access to colleges, universities, professions, and employment).

Whiston (2005) wrote, "Numerous research studies indicate that counselors in a variety of settings (e.g., schools, community agencies, mental health facilities) view formal assessment strategies as a significant aspect of their work" (p. 6); that much is well known among professional counselors. Perhaps less well known is the extent to which assessments are used in our society. Standardized tests were reportedly administered annually to more than 40 million individuals (Camara, 1988) in the 1980s, and certainly that number has increased since then. Cohen and Swerdlik (2005) suggested that as many as 20,000 new tests are developed each year; clearly, there is both a need and a market for assessment.

These tests are used for a multitude of purposes and thus greatly affect the general public; in response, some segments of the public seek to assert significant control over assessment and its consequences. For example, the National Center for Fair and Open Testing (FairTest)

> works to end the misuses and flaws of standardized testing and to ensure that evaluation of students, teachers, and schools is fair, open, valid, and educationally beneficial. We place special emphasis on eliminating the racial, class, gender, and cultural barriers to equal opportunity posed by standardized tests, and preventing their damage to the quality of education. (2004)

Although the stated purpose of FairTest at first glance seems compatible with the orientation of professional counselors, FairTest is in fact essentially opposed to testing in general. At a minimum, professional counselors should be cognizant of factors in the public sector that have the potential to influence their work and their profession, and more important, should be active in responding to potential limitations on professional practice that emerge from the public sector.

Unfortunately, the current state of affairs concerning selection, administration, scoring, and interpretation of assessments, as well as test-users' qualifications, is ambiguous. Consider the *Standards for Educational and Psychological Testing* (AERA, APA, & NCME, 1999), which represents the expert opinion of the American Psychological Association, the American Educational Research Association, and the National Council of Measurement and Evaluation, and which is frequently viewed as "the authoritative document on test development and use" (e.g., Cohen & Swerdlik, 2005). This document does not address assessment user qualifications other than to state that responsibility for test use should be assumed only by those who are properly trained, and that test manuals should specify the qualifications required to administer and interpret a given test. Because some test publishers will not permit professional counselors to purchase their assessment instruments, however, test-user qualifications are an issue that should be addressed long before getting to the test manual. That is, professional counselors need to inform test publishers of their skills, knowledge, and responsible conduct in using assessment instruments. Test publishers should not make decisions about access to assessment instruments in a vacuum. Again, decisions about assessment should be influenced to a large extent by professional policies of the counseling profession rather than being left to the discretion of those outside the counseling profession.

Actions to Ensure Fair Access

The American Psychological Association, American Educational Research Association, and National Council of Measurement and Evaluation are not alone in addressing the issue of test-user qualifications and in defining who may select, administer, score, and interpret assessment instruments. The ACA and the National Board for Certified Counselors (NBCC) have mobilized themselves to inform the general public, counselors, and other professionals about the relevant issues. They are also taking steps to prevent restrictions on professional counselors' access to assessment instruments. The Fair Access Coalition on Testing, a group formed to protect professional counselors (among others) from loss or restriction of access to assessment instruments, is a coalition of professional groups consisting primarily of professional counselors but also including other professionals whose entry-level preparation is the master's degree, such as speech-language and hearing therapists (FACT, 2000a). FACT has prepared a policy statement in which it seeks fairness in any restrictions on the access to and use of tests. The highest priority of FACT is to address the issues of access to and use of tests by professional counselors. FACT's goals include (a) developing model legislation regarding access to and use of tests by professional counselors and serving as a clearinghouse for this legislation, (b) developing standards of practice for mental health assessment and persuading managed health care firms to reimburse qualified providers, (c) obtaining a legal definition of *psychological activities* in every state, (d) working with test publishers to clarify qualifications in test manuals for each test user, and (e) establishing core statements about informing other professionals about the use of tests. These goals will involve FACT in both the professional and public sectors and will include attention to professional ethics, test publishers' policies and practices, and scope-of-practice sections of state regulations and statutes.

Many important events and philosophical movements have shaped counseling as we know it today, but much remains to be done to answer the questions concerning professional counselors' fair access to assessment instruments, questions that are currently being debated among professional groups. These questions undoubtedly will lead to significant court cases, legislation, and public policy decisions mandating certain practices. Practicing psychologists and other doctoral-level mental health service providers who traditionally have had the privilege of independent practice are understandably concerned over the increase in the independent status and vendorship of master's-level (professional) counseling practitioners. For example, these providers typically view master's-level professional counselors as contributing to the lower fees offered by managed care organizations. Assessment is clearly a critical issue in the turf war, but it need not be. Professional counselors must work to maintain their rights of access to assessments, but should do so in ways that are collaborative with other mental health service providers. Any significant limitations on access to and use of assessments would necessarily restrict the comprehensiveness of mental health service provision. Ultimately, all potential mental health service recipients would suffer from such limitations.

Principles of Socially Responsive Assessment

One of the hallmarks of effective mental health service provision (i.e., treatment) is the necessity to make a diagnosis through assessing a client's mental status. Thus, assessment is not only integral to diagnosis but also is a critical component of the counseling process (Vacc & Loesch, 2000). Assessment allows professional counselors to make relevant, appropriate, and valid decisions about interventions through diagnosing the status of the client's well-being.

The single best axiom for professional counselors and other professionals to follow when involved in assessment is to assume that all tests are biased in some contexts. Therefore, provisions should be made to try to eliminate, or at least reduce, the effects of bias in any particular assessment application. Thorndike (2005) noted that "the issue of bias in testing has probably been the most hotly debated topic relating to educational and psychological measurement during the last few decades" (p. 432). Cohen and Swerdlik (2005) defined test bias as "a factor inherent within a test that systematically prevents accurate, impartial measurement" (p. i-3). Unfortunately, *test bias* is a term not easily defined nor understood, and a variety of ways for considering the concept of test bias exist. For example, couching test bias under the broader rubric of test fairness, Linn and Miller (2005) wrote, "The issue of fairness to racial and ethnic minorities is a critical issue for any assessment program" (p. 17). They described four types of fairness related to testing: (a) absence of bias (e.g., in the actual composition of the test), (b) procedural fairness (i.e., equitable application and administration of tests), (c) opportunity to learn (i.e., equitable preparation to perform effectively on a test), and (d) equality of results (i.e., achievement of equal group results when there is no reason to expect differential results). Regardless of the definition of bias used, however, the concepts of fairness and social equity are of primary importance. Anastasi (1997) noted that test bias is still being examined, and with the present state of knowledge, there exists an insufficient basis for correcting all inequities. Yet professional counselors need to examine the degree of bias that exists. The question is how?

Rollock and Terrell (1996) listed six points of comparison by which (historically) traditional assessment may be differentiated from a multicultural approach to assessment:

1. *Standards versus relativism.* Traditional assessment perspectives emphasize universal standards, whereas multicultural assessment attends to differences between groups as a function of cultural experience.

2. *Focused interaction versus sociopolitical orientation.* In traditional assessment the examiner typically has minimal obligations to the examinee, whereas the sociopolitical view holds that the examiner must give substantive consideration to and involvement with the context in which the assessment, its results, and its interpretations occur.

3. *Reductionism versus ecological/systems sensitivity.* Reductionism assumes that behavior is (best) measured through finding small units of behavior that can be identified within reproducible conditions, whereas an ecological/systems perspective assumes evident human behavior is shaped by immediate and past experiences.

4. *Investigation focus versus participant focus.* Traditional assessment involves evaluating behavior relative to existing social norms (usually those of the majority

culture), whereas participant-focused assessment emphasizes the subjective meanings of behaviors as they relate to the situations that confront individuals.

5. *Classification versus description.* Traditional assessment is focused on classifying behavior as it relates to standards or norms, whereas multicultural assessment recognizes the need to understand the precipitants and contexts of behavior before it can be judged.

6. *Prediction versus prescription.* The multicultural approach to assessment recognizes both the benefits and limits of prediction, and adds emphasis on implications and on designing effective treatment plans that maximize human potential.

In general then, multicultural assessment, be it for members of the majority or minority groups, is much akin to the new perspective on validity presented previously. That is, in the assessment of human behavior, characteristics, or traits, effective multicultural assessment places great emphasis on taking into account contextual factors that influence the assessment process itself, its results, and interpretations of the results.

Perceptual and conceptual frameworks such as that proposed by Rollock and Terrell help to clarify how assessment can be multiculturally sensitive and appropriate and thereby reduce bias in assessment. Paniagua (1994) provided even more specific guidelines to reduce bias in assessment, including

- examining our own biases and prejudices;
- becoming aware of the potential effects of racism on the diagnosis of mental disorders;
- considering carefully socioeconomic factors and variables;
- reducing the sociocultural gap between the client and therapist;
- considering culture-related syndromes;
- asking culturally appropriate questions;
- using the least biased assessment strategies first, including physiological measures, direct behavioral observations, self-monitoring, behavioral self-report rating scales, clinical interviews, trait measures, and self-report psychopathology measures;

- consulting paraprofessionals within the respective racial/ethnic group;
- avoiding impersonal (i.e., not culturally and context sensitive) mental status examination procedures; and
- using a multicultural assessment model (e.g., Dana, 1993), which includes consideration of acculturation, provision of culturally specific services, use of the client's native or preferred language, use of the emic perspective on assessment, and provision of the findings to clients using a culturally specific strategy.

All professional counselors work cross-culturally, and therefore they need to highlight the role of culture in assessment. This perspective requires professional counselors to reconsider some of the basic assumptions underlying their past assessment practices and to challenge existing "professional wisdom." Professional counselors have to make some fundamental changes in assessment practices because the cultural experiences of a diverse public influence what is seen and what eludes attention. Assessment issues needing professional counselors' further attention and consideration in our increasingly diverse society include (a) appropriate skills needed to work in a socially responsive, responsible, and effective manner with various populations; (b) appropriate place of standardized assessment with individuals of culturally different backgrounds; (c) implications of acculturation and language differences when assessing human behavior or characteristics; and (d) research questions concerning assessment that professional counselors need to ask in order to understand our diverse society.

Socially Responsible Assessment

Socially responsible assessment is the practical application of the principles of socially responsive assessment. This means that professional counselors should have a contextual understanding of the place of assessment as it speaks to the broad social issues that affect client well-being. A contextual understanding of assessment encompasses an understanding of the counseling process, particularly as it relates to diagnosis and treatment. Whiston (2005, p. 5) presented a very general model of the counseling process as involving four functions: (a) assessing the client's problem or problems, (b) conceptualizing and defining the client's problem or problems, (c) selecting and implementing effective treatments, and (d) evaluating the counseling. Although assessment can rightfully be used in any of these four functions, most frequently it is used in fulfilling the first. Thus, effective assessment is essential to starting the counseling process correctly, and even more importantly here, both assessment and counseling must be sensitive and responsive to contextual considerations from the very beginning if counseling is to have even a remote chance of being successful.

Confusion exists about some of the semantics concerning assessment, some of which can be alleviated by making a distinction between *assessment* and *measurement*. Assessment, which can be considered the total data-gathering process in counseling (Vacc, 1991; Vacc & Loesch, 2000), subsumes measurement, which is strictly the assignment of numerical or categorical values to human attributes according to rules (Cohen & Swerdlik, 2005; Thorndike, 2005). Accordingly, assessment is broader in scope than measurement and requires the counselor to understand, among other things, the types and purposes of the various assessment procedures. A distinction also can be made between *assessment* and *testing*, with testing being a systematic procedure for obtaining data from which to compare (a sample of the) behavior of two or more persons (Whiston, 2005). Professional counselors do not just administer tests; they perform socially responsible assessment.

Evaluation subsumes assessment and is considered to be the (composite) of the interpretation, application, and assignment of values to assessment data. Unfortunately, testing has been used as a synonym for assessment, for measurement, and for evaluation (Vacc & Loesch, 2000). It is important to understand that the term *assessment* implies ways of gathering information about an individual and determining differences, whereas testing is only one way of gathering data using procedures such as structured interviews, observations of behavior in natural or structured settings, recording of various physiological functions, or use of paper-and-pencil or computer-based instruments. Information gathered from procedures such as these can best be understood through an assessment model that is a conceptual framework for socially responsible assessment and through effective evaluation of the resultant information.

Current Assessment Practices

Because there is some disagreement concerning the use of assessment in counseling, perhaps what is needed at this time is not specific guidelines concerning the content of assessment in counseling, but rather a focus on identifying what counselors are expected to do in their work. Such specific information related to work behaviors provides the basis for classifying the importance of assessment practices.

For the National Board for Certified Counselors (1993), Loesch and Vacc conducted an empirical occupational analysis of counselors to determine the actual tasks professional counselors perform routinely. This study investigated the types, frequencies, and relative importance of various professional counselor activities. Unique to this study was that the focus was shifted from what authorities and experts think professional counselors ought to be doing to a focus on the actual activities performed by professional counselors in their day-to-day professional roles. We identified 151 specific work behaviors through a review of the literature and critical review by experts in the counseling profession, using three levels of item refinement. The relative frequency of professional counselors' involvement with each specific work behavior was based on responses from a nationally representative sample of 722 professional counselors holding the NBCC's National Certified Counselor credential. Of the 10% of work behaviors used most frequently, almost half were assessment activities: evaluating existing precounseling data, assessing psychosocial status, assessing the potential for a client to harm self or others, self-evaluating counseling effectiveness, evaluating need for client referral, and evaluating clients' movement toward counseling goals. This work-behavior investigation documented clearly that assessment is integral to professional counselors' work and to the counseling process; that is, assessment in counseling is important.

Unfortunately, it is difficult to characterize a universal relationship between counseling and assessment because of the diverse theoretical counseling approaches employed within the profession. Further, Daniels and Altekruse (1982) reported that the relationship between counseling and assessment has not received clear, concise, or adequate coverage in the literature. This situation does not appear to have changed in the almost two decades since they made that conclusion; different professional counselors place different emphases on the importance of or need for assessment in these approaches. An inclusive model of assessment that moves counseling closer to scientific practice could overcome these discrepancies.

A Proposed Model for Socially Responsible Assessment in Counseling

Clearly, an approach to assessment in counseling that is sensitive both to variations in theoretical frameworks and to clients from diverse cultural groups and life circumstances (i.e., contexts) is needed. Such a model should be designed to help professional counselors conceptualize assessment in a socially responsible manner intended to improve counseling effectiveness, accommodate diagnosis, and use good integration of science and practice. Note that *diagnosis* as I use it here encompasses the more general interpretation of gathering information about a client as well as the more specific interpretation of deciding upon a formal, clinical label of psychological distress. Following is a general beginning to such a model, the empirical counseling perspective as proposed previously by Vacc and Loesch (2000) and as loosely derived from the scientist-practitioner conceptualization of professional functioning (Barlow, Hayes, & Nelson, 1984) as applied to the work of professional counselors.

At the foundation of mental health services in general, and managed care in particular, is the necessity of problem conceptualization and treatment planning based on valid diagnoses. Certainly not all settings where professional counselors work require establishment of formal diagnoses, and some counselors are uncomfortable assigning a label. Yet conceptualizing assessment and diagnosis (interpreted in the broad or limited sense) as integral to the counseling process is helpful in defining a professional counselor's scope of practice and in promoting client change.

Assessment is viewed within the empirical counseling perspective as gathering information from which to formulate the focus of or purpose for counseling (Vacc & Loesch, 2000). Inherent in the empirical counseling perspective are interviewing the client and determining and specifying the purpose of counseling, all of which are done with careful consideration to culturally specific factors associated with the client's situation. For example, Fouad and Chan (1999) noted that effective test use and interpretation (i.e., assessment) must take into account psychometric considerations (e.g., test content, conceptual and functional equivalence and content, internal structure, and predictive bias), client considerations (e.g., race, gender, socioeconomic status, level of acculturation, and test-taking attitude), and counselor considerations (e.g., level of racial identity development and perception of gender and ethnicity). In order to address these considerations effectively and successfully, the professional counselor can be viewed as a scientist who is continually assessing and reconceptualizing the counseling relationship based on information obtained, cultural and ethnic context of the client, counseling goals, and counseling strategies.

Assessment within the empirical counseling context includes activities that focus on the selection of information obtained for counseling purposes. By beginning the counseling process with assessment, the counselor identifies the purpose for counseling as it relates to the client's situational, social, and psychological factors and the goals of intervention, *all within the context of the client's cultural background or situation*. Therefore, establishing the purpose of counseling is not an end unto itself, but rather a method for delineating (change) goals, determining and implementing intervention strategies, and constructing a framework for the continuous assessment of progress within the context of the client's social framework.

Establishing the purpose of counseling within the context of the client's cultural and ethnic background is at the heart of empirical counseling because, among other reasons, without defining the purpose for counseling effectively, the outcomes of counseling cannot be assessed effectively. Counseling, by definition, suggests some type of ultimate client action (i.e., has an action-oriented, behavior-change purpose). The professional counselor, however, must be able to identify the specific nature of the purposeful action within the client's situational and social contexts. Therefore, the purpose of counseling should be defined in ways that make it as specific (i.e., concrete) and observable as possible, in order to permit measurement of progress and change. All too often, professional counselors focus only on the client's psychological state of being (e.g., having a good self-concept). Such a perspective is laudable but difficult to turn into specific, highly focused counseling interventions. In the empirical perspective, the focus is on client actions (i.e., behaviors) that reflect the client's psychological state of being.

Ideally, the purpose and goals for counseling should be specific, observable, and potentially measurable by more than one person. Some (behavioral) purposes and goals for counseling are not easily specified, but empirical counseling still strives to produce measurable data. For example, although a self-report method of assessment will not suffice as a sole criterion for evaluation of outcome within the context of empirical counseling, it can be a useful activity in regard to establishing goals and purposes. Careful and prudent assessment, which necessarily includes measurable outcomes, also is important for communication with other professionals and to meet the requirements for payment by some regulatory groups. The latter requirements typically involve the use of the *Diagnostic and Statistical Manual of Mental Disorders* (fourth edition, text revision [*DSM-IV-TR*]; American Psychiatric Association, 2000).

Professional counselors use the *DSM-IV-TR* for psychodiagnosis and treatment planning, insurance reimbursement, and communication with other helping professionals. The *DSM-IV-TR* conceptualizes behaviors as a pattern, or syndrome, associated with a present distress (i.e., symptom), with a disability (i.e., impairment in one or more areas of functioning), or with a significantly increased risk of suffering. The *DSM-IV-TR* contains specific diagnostic criteria, a clinical sketch of each disorder, diagnostic considerations, information about the onset and nature of a problem, and any known predisposing factors. Diagnostic classifications in the *DSM-IV-TR* are viewed as mental disorders rather than as expected responses to particular events. The language and tone of the *DSM-IV-TR* is reflective of the medical profession's view of human behavior as being either free from symptoms or free from illness in a medical sense, which is not appealing to some in the counseling profession. However, although some professional counselors may disdain use of the *DSM-IV-TR*, it is clearly the best resource, and perhaps best model, for viewing psychological states of being in behavioral terms.

It is common for some clients, especially initially, to express concern about a facet of their lives without being able to indicate what they might want to do differently. Thus the counseling process often involves confounding information, and it is the dilemma of the professional counselor to help identify realistic, specific, and observable goals. The goals of counseling are the desirable (behavioral) changes the client and the counselor seek to obtain; for obvious reasons, they are highly related to the purpose of the counseling. Establishing behavioral goals permits the professional counselor to determine, ultimately, whether the purpose for counseling has been achieved. Stating counseling goals in a positive orientation is recommended because this focuses attention on the positive aspects and potentials of intervention and suggests what the future could be if the present negative situation could be minimized or eliminated.

At an early point in the counseling process, the professional counselor needs to determine a course of action, which means that waiting to find out and know everything there is to know about the purpose for counseling is not always, or even usually, possible. So, based on the various assessment information obtained, professional counselors determine, often in conjunction with their clients, an initial framework for action; that is, an intervention strategy. When deciding upon an intervention strategy, professional counselors judge the probability of the success of their actions based on already acquired data, which should include knowledge of the experience (i.e., past history) and personality attributes of the client. Specific intervention strategies selected depend on the counseling orientation of the professional counselor. Strategies, however, may change over the course of counseling because the client's presenting purpose for counseling often is not the real purpose for which counseling was sought.

The entire process of empirical counseling is built on specification, which is a tangible and focal orientation to the purpose of counseling and enables counseling to be conducted with specific techniques and purposes. Up to this point, the professional counselor has had only data on which to decide on a strategy; a focus for the counseling process exists but not the means to determine the effectiveness of the strategy. The professional counselor has, in a heuristic manner, planned for the sequencing of intervention activities. Subsequently, the professional counselor engages in the intervention. In a very real sense, the professional counselor is now engaged in a scientific method in order to determine the purpose and goals of counseling, make a hypothesis about likely outcome(s), implement and test the strategy, and then make changes in the process based on the results and conclusions as new data become available.

When new purposes for counseling are determined or treatment strategies fail as the counseling process continues, the professional counselor returns to the first phase of the empirical counseling approach. Assessment, therefore, is a continuous process. Once the strategy has been implemented, the goal(s) and objectives of the strategy may need to be changed or reformulated based on continuous assessment to address the question, "Has there been progress?" If no progress has been made, the professional counselor must decide whether to change the goals and objectives. He or she may decide not to change the goals, but instead to review and possibly redefine the strategy, and counseling continues. If the professional counselor decides to change the goals, he or she will formulate new goals based on continuous assessment.

The empirical counseling process ends with assessment of achievement of desired outcomes. This assessment process seeks to determine whether the client is, in fact, engaging in desired behaviors. Presumably, the desired behaviors are related to desired psychological states of being. In empirical counseling, however, loosely assessed (e.g., client self-reported) change in psychological states of being is far less important than evidence of effectiveness from indicators of (positive) behavior change.

Conclusion

Research has revealed that situational contexts play a critical role in behavior (Miller-Jones, 1989), and that people of different backgrounds are indeed exposed to different experiences that can affect assessment results (Dana, 1993; Rollock & Terrell, 1996). Further, Lee (2001) noted that personal dynamics such as language, kinship, religion/spirituality, roles and status, sex role socialization, learning style, and attitudinal orientation are important considerations in effective assessment, concluding that "failure to take such dynamics into consideration could affect not only the assessment process but also the interpretation of assessment information as well" (p. 118).

Although the populations that participate in assessment are multicultural and diverse, the models typically used in counseling are monocultural, meaning that they are based on principles specifically applicable only or at least primarily to Whites (Dana, 1993). Use of monocultural assessment with clients of diverse cultural backgrounds may result in obtaining inaccurate information and subsequently making unfair predictions, assumptions, or decisions. Therefore, professional counselors should strive to use culture-fair assessments and must be aware of and sensitive to different values, languages, expectations, and customs that affect assessment.

Assessment within counseling should be a multidimensional, multidynamic, continuous process for establishing a base of information about clients. The focus of assessment needs to be on using the best and most appropriate information in the best and most appropriate ways to help clients. Therein lie both the basis and hope for truly socially responsive and socially responsible assessment.

Dedication

This chapter is respectfully dedicated to the memory of Dr. Nicholas A. Vacc, who authored the first version of it in the first edition of this book.

References

American Educational Research Association, American Psychological Association, & National Council of Measurement and Evaluation. (1999). *Standards for educational and psychological testing.* Washington, DC: Authors.

Anastasi, A. (1997). *Psychological testing* (9th ed.). Upper Saddle River, NJ: Prentice Hall.

American Psychiatric Association. (2000). *Diagnostic and statistical manual of mental disorders (4th ed., text rev.).* Washington, DC: Author.

Association for Assessment in Counseling. (1999). *Standards for multicultural assessment.* Retrieved December 10, 2004, from www.aac.ncat.edu/resources.html

Association for Assessment in Counseling. (2003a). *Responsibilities of users of standardized tests: RUST statement revised.* Retrieved December 10, 2004, from http://aac.ncat.edu/Resources/documents/RUST2003%20v11%20Final.pdf

Association for Assessment in Counseling. (2003b). *Standards for qualifications of test users.* Retrieved December 10, 2004, from aac.ncat.edu/documents/Standards%20for%20Qualifications%20of%20Test%20Users.doc

Association for Assessment in Counseling and Education. (1998). *Test takers rights and responsibilities.* Retrieved December 10, 2004, from aac.ncat.edu/documents/ttrr.html

Atkinson, D. R. (2004). *Counseling American minorities* (6th ed.). Boston: McGraw-Hill.

Barlow, D. H., Hayes, S. C., & Nelson, R. O. (1984). *The scientist practitioner: Research and accountability in clinical and educational settings.* New York: Pergamon Press.

Camara, W. J. (1988). *APA's role in fostering good testing practices.* Paper presented at the 96th Annual Convention of the American Psychological Association, Atlanta, GA.

Cohen, R. J., & Swerdlik, M. E. (2005). *Psychological testing and assessment* (6th ed.). Boston: McGraw-Hill.

Dana, R. H. (1993). *Multicultural assessment perspectives for professional psychology.* Boston: Allyn & Bacon.

Daniels, M. H., & Altekruse, M. (1982). Preparation of counselors for assessment. *Measurement and Evaluation in Guidance, 15,* 74–81.

Fair Access Coalition on Testing (FACT). (2000a). *The National Fair Access Coalition on Testing.* Retrieved December 10, 2004, from www.fairaccess.org

Fair Access Coalition on Testing (FACT). (2000b). *318 restricted tests recommended by Indiana Board of Psychologists.* (2004). Retrieved December 8, 2004, from www.fairaccess.org/states/in/restricted.htm

Fouad, N. A., & Chan, P. M. (1999). Gender and ethnicity: Influence on test interpretation and reception. In J. W. Lichtenberg & R. K. Goodyear (Eds.), *Scientist-practitioner perspectives on test interpretation* (pp. 31–58). Boston: Allyn & Bacon.

Garcia, J. G., & Marotta, S. (1997). Characterization of the Latino population. In J. G. Garcia and M. C. Zea (Eds.), *Psychological interventions and research with Latino populations.* Boston: Allyn and Bacon.

Goodwin, L. D., & Leech, N. L. (2003). The meaning of validity in the new Standards for Educational and Psychological Testing: Implications for measurement courses. *Measurement and Evaluation in Counseling and Development, 36*(3), 181–191.

Lee, C. C. (2001). Assessing diverse populations. In G. R. Walz & J. C. Bleuer (Eds.), *Assessment issues and challenges for the millennium* (pp. 115–120). Greensboro, NC: CAPS.

Linn, R. L., & Miller, M. D. (2005). *Measurement and assessment in teaching* (9th ed.). Upper Saddle River, NJ: Pearson Education.

Louisiana State Board of Examiners of Psychologists of the Department of Health and Human Services v. Boyd J. Atterberry 95.CA.0391. (LA. 1995).

Miller-Jones, D. (1989). Culture and testing. *American Psychologist, 44*, 360–366.

Moreland, K. L., Eyde, L. D., Robertson, G. J., Primoff, E. S., & Most, R. B. (1995). Assessment of test user qualifications: A data-based measurement procedure. *American Psychologist, 50*, 14–21.

Myers, J. E., & Sweeney, T. J. (2004). Advocacy for the counseling profession: Results of a national survey. *Journal of Counseling & Development, 82*, 466–471.

National Board for Certified Counselors. (1993). *A work behavior analysis of professional counselors*. Muncie, IN: Accelerated Development.

National Center for Fair and Open Testing. (2004). *FairTest home page*. Retrieved December 16, 2004, from www.fairtest.org

Paniagua, F. A. (1994). *Assessing and testing culturally diverse clients: A practical guide*. Newbury Park, CA: Sage.

Prediger, D. J. (1994). Multicultural assessment standards: A compilation for counselors. *Measurement and Evaluation in Counseling and Development, 27,* 68–73.

Rodriguez, R. (2002). *Brown: The last discovery of America*. New York: Penguin Putnam.

Rollock, D., & Terrell, D. M. (1996). Multicultural issues in assessment: Towards an inclusive model. In J. L. DeLucia-Waack (Ed.), *Multicultural counseling competencies: Implications for training and practice* (pp. 113–156). Alexandria, VA: Association for Counselor Education and Supervision.

Schmidley, D. (2001). *Profile of the foreign-born population in the United States: 2000* (Current Population Reports, Series P23–206). U.S. Census Bureau). Retrieved February 19, 2002, from www.census.gov/prod/2002pubs/p23–206.pdf

Thorndike, R. M. (2005). *Measurement and evaluation in education and psychology* (7th ed.). Upper Saddle River, NJ: Pearson Education.

Vacc, N. A. (1991). Changing times: Changing views about testing. *Journal of Humanistic Education and Development, 30,* 148–156.

Vacc, N. A., & Loesch, L. (2000). *Professional orientation to counseling* (3rd ed.). New York: Taylor & Francis.

Whiston, S. C. (2005). *Principles and applications of assessment in counseling* (2nd ed.). Belmont, CA: Brooks/Cole.

Chapter 12

Conducting Research That Makes a Difference

William E. Sedlacek

Can research make a difference in bringing about social change? My answer is, it depends on how well it is done. The purpose of this chapter is to offer suggestions as to what to do, and what not to do, to increase the chances of research making a difference, and to provide examples of success or failure. Doing good research has a particular meaning in this chapter. It is not necessarily a matter of the best design, most appropriate statistical analysis, or largest number of participants that is most important. Instead, issues such as understanding your audience, asking the right questions, and choosing methods of communication are critical.

Understand Your Audience

The first question the social action researcher should pose is, Who do I wish to influence with my study? Is it university faculty? Welfare recipients? State legislators? Children? One will likely perform different kinds of studies, yielding different results, and present them differently to each of these audiences.

Let us use the topic of reducing prejudice as an example and discuss ways research has influenced the preceding audiences. As part of understanding an audience, one should appeal to its self-interests and choose data that will move the group in what you regard as a positive direction. University faculty generally regard themselves as scholars and often are uncomfortable in the role of social workers; that is, helping without an intellectual component. I have had success influencing faculty with scholarly, published research that demonstrates their racial attitudes in a way that meets rigorous challenges as to method, statistics, and other factors (Sedlacek, 1994, 1995, 2004b). Publishing and presenting at meetings as one of them will increase the chances that most faculty will consider curricular change, better advising for students of color, or changes in campus activities.

Welfare recipients are not likely to be impressed with methodological issues but are more likely to be influenced by examples and case studies of people like them. Thus, training counselors to provide, during individual or group counseling, specific examples of other welfare recipients who followed certain paths can increase the chances that such clients will make the desired changes in their behavior. Changes such as following new welfare guidelines or securing employment are possible goals for the client. Such counseling could be seen as teaching welfare recipients to handle the prejudice that politicians, employers, and the general public have directed toward them. For groups who experience prejudice, learning to handle racism has been correlated with therapeutic success (Sedlacek, 1996, 2004a, 2004b).

State legislators are commonly influenced by what voters in their districts feel about an issue. They can be influenced by detailing popular support on an issue and by illustrating those positions with examples drawn from their constituents. If possible, arrange the situation so that politicians can take credit for being out in front on an issue or in initiating legislation. An example is the recent concerns about affirmative action. Surveying constituents about being fair to all citizens and helping those who deserve a chance, combined with examples of people who have benefited in a given district, may influence legislators. Here, direct contact with legislators and dramatic examples will likely work best.

Children are often influenced by their peers and by what they see rather than by what others tell them. To reach this audience, a community theater group and a research office in a school district collaborated in an innovative program that made a difference. The research office checked the literature and did surveys in the elementary schools about the types of prejudice that the students were most likely to see and feel. The theater group then developed skits and short plays around those themes. Students at various schools were recruited and included in the troupe. Students were also included at each school where performances took place. Surveys taken immediately afterward and some months later indicated a reduction in prejudice. This example also illustrates that needs assessment and follow-up evaluation are important parts of reducing prejudice in schools (Sedlacek, 2004a, 2004b; Sedlacek & Brooks, 1976).

Define Research Broadly

Research can be defined as any systematic inquiry into a topic. The methods can be quantitative or qualitative, statistical or impressionistic, and can involve paper-and-pencil techniques, computer technology, interviews, artistic perspectives, or naturalistic observations. I recommend using what works best given your audience and available resources. If you have access to certain resources (e.g., a college research office, computers, financial resources), by all means use them. If not, use what you have.

One technique I like to employ with research students is to ask them to pose a research question; then make observations for 1 week in the school, community, campus, or whatever place they are studying; and report back to the group on their conclusions. One student wanted to study community violence and its causes. For a week he chose to observe the events taking place in a part of the community where people often congregated. He made observations about the events preceding hostilities between groups and developed some preliminary answers to his question, which he used to devise additional studies on the topic. His method limited him to certain kinds of data and certain answers to questions, but he was engaging in research.

Focus Your Research Questions

Whereas we want to think broadly about our definitions of research, we want to be very specific about the question or questions we wish to answer. Generally, it is better to have only one or a few questions to answer, as opposed to trying to do too much in a single study. A clear answer to one question is better than vague answers to many questions. Other studies can be done to answer other questions. Concentrating on a few questions helps sharpen our goals and delineate what we want to learn.

Research questions can be categorized into one of three areas. Generally, results in one area do not answer questions well in the other areas, and confusion on this point often works against the social action researcher. The first research area is *information.* Anything factual, such as demographic information, frequency counts of events, or correct answers to test items, fits here. The change agent often needs information to identify the issues or to know which way to go. At one time, learned people believed that earth, wind, fire, and water were the four elements in nature. Without research, we would have no reason to think otherwise.

Sometimes information is compelling and results in immediate change. This is seldom true, however. The people and systems we are trying to change can often ignore or rationalize facts. Blacks prefer to live in certain neighborhoods, women cannot handle management responsibilities, welfare recipients are lazy, and so on. Sound familiar? Researchers have often assumed that the facts speak for themselves. Galileo assumed that once he presented his observations about the earth not being the center of the universe, the church would accept them. It did, but not until some 350 years later! Most of us prefer a quicker response.

The second area for research questions is *attitudes*. Here any affective data concerning feelings, opinions, or perspectives is the focus of research and change. The link between attitudes and information is complex. Presenting information generally does not change feelings, but as part of a larger strategy the two may be linked. For example, in the stages of eliminating racism, colleagues and I have shown that information on cultural and racial differences and racism, followed by attitude measurement, can lead to the desired reductions in racist or sexist behaviors (Sedlacek, 2004a; Sedlacek & Brooks, 1976). But if you are interested in changes in feelings, do not confuse that with information or behavior.

Trying to change attitudes among groups requires several conditions. First, all groups should view the negotiating conditions as favorable. Second, the groups should have equal power to affect the outcome; and finally, conditions for continued positive feelings should be developed (Dovidio & Gaertner, 1986). Doing assessments of feelings to determine the status of each of these conditions is important in any attitude-change process. There is a method of measuring prejudice (Situational Attitude Scale) that can be applied to a variety of situations, using experimental and control forms of a questionnaire, and that can be useful here (Sedlacek, 1996, 2004a, 2004b; Sedlacek, Troy, & Chapman, 1976).

The third area of focus for research is *behavior*. Here is where we often wish to concentrate, but it is an area in which it is difficult to get change, and information and feelings do not commonly lead to behavior change. I feel it is best to concentrate on reinforcing people for engaging in the desired behavior, without necessarily getting them to understand the information behind it or to feel good about it. If you want legislators to sponsor legislation that will help your cause, let them do it for their reasons, not yours. If a university can increase its population of students of color by using different admissions procedures, do not worry about school officials not understanding the issues. Concentrate on research that will achieve the desired behavioral outcomes.

Thus, in developing research questions, one should generally pick one of the three areas (information, attitudes, or behavior), focus the question or questions to be answered, and not look for change in other areas. It is very difficult to answer questions in more than one area in one study.

Control the Turf

One valuable function research can serve in achieving social change is to control the areas in which you wish to hold the argument or debate. Too often, counseling professionals react defensively to conditions set up by others. We are told that the situation is a certain way, and we feel that we have to counter what those in control of the system have set forth. By doing research, we can gain some power and put those in charge on the defensive by causing them to respond to our results. For instance, providing information on how early detection of HIV/AIDS can save governments and insurance companies money can increase the chances of better treatment for the individuals involved. An important part of social change is defining the issues one wishes to argue. Research can help do this.

The Long-Term View

One use of research is to provide an examination of issues over time in some relatively constant manner. Longitudinal studies involve following the same people or organizations over time to see how they change. This allows the change agent to avoid an emotional context or a quick fix that may not solve the problem. For example, I have done longitudinal studies of university students before and after matriculation. This has allowed me to observe the development of students of different races and groups and to provide others with some ideas on how developmental needs vary by race, culture, and gender. These studies have led to broader concepts and approaches to understanding student needs that are not apparent in an immediate crisis (Sedlacek, 1996, 2004a). I have also used this approach to study a university over time to see how it has reacted to issues (Sedlacek, 1995). Without a historical and a projected futuristic context, it is easier to overreact to immediate concerns. If we do not understand the past we are condemned to repeat it.

Here is a place where quantitative and qualitative methods are useful. We can track numbers of students, their attitudes, graduation rates, and so on, quantitatively, but we can also qualitatively explore the stories and issues behind the numbers. Public radio in the United States has used a qualitative approach to helping us understand the civil rights movement by presenting small, intimate stories of heretofore mostly unknown people who made contributions to civil rights. The program was called *Will the Circle Be Unbroken?* Most of the big stories and quantitative information are already available. The qualitative aspect should deepen our understanding of the issues and help those concerned with change in this area increase their chances of making deeper, more lasting changes in the future.

It is also possible to conduct a series of cross-sectional studies to observe change over time: for instance, doing studies of people in a given community every 5 years to track the information they have about recycling their used materials, their feelings about it, and their recycling behavior. Remember, there are many methods that can be used to answer the same question.

We developed a method of dealing with hate incidents on campus in a constructive manner using research information as an important step in the process (Schlosser & Sedlacek, 2001). We found a common pattern in examples of hate letters, e-mails, graffiti, speech, and so on, in that the incident caused a great deal of upset among some or many individuals for a relatively short period of time, but no constructive change emerged, and the next incident produced similar reactions. To break this pattern, we circulated accurate information about the incident from sources such as newspapers, police reports, and interviews. This reduced rumors and made use of the information function in research. As a next step, we conducted discussions of the incident around the campus in the context of research available from the campus and the larger literature. In this way we addressed the affective and behavioral aspects of research. Thus, we were able to provide a developmental context for helping people to process the incident, decide what actions needed to be taken, and reduce the chances that similar incidents would occur in future.

Become the Source

By providing research results over a period of time, one can become a reliable source of data. Part of being a reliable source is to provide data that are fair and honest and not always slanted in a certain direction. As you watch the evening news, whose results are you more apt to trust: those from a study done by a neutral party or one from a political party or a drug company? You should share your results regardless of the outcome. By asking the right questions and putting them in a context useful for the change you wish to bring about, you can maximize the chances of the data being used as you wish. However, preconceiving the outcomes of research means suppressing undesirable results, thus compromising your role as a source of reliable data.

The head of a state counseling association had done a study showing that 25% of elementary school students were interested in some form of counseling. He was trying to influence counseling legislation in the state. However, he considered not using the data because 75% of the students were not interested. His advisers suggested instead that he translate that 25% into actual numbers of students needing counseling, emphasizing the need for state legislators to trust the state counseling association to give them the truth. The strategy worked, and the state passed some favorable legislation.

It is probably most important to be perceived as a reliable source if one's goal is social change. However, it is possible to be both a reliable source and a change agent by providing data on a topic that has been useful to your audience over time.

An example of this is provided by research that I carried out at the University of Maryland for many years. When the university was faced with a lawsuit challenging its scholarship program for African American undergraduates (*Banneker Scholarship* case), the university administrators looked about for help in defending themselves against the lawsuit. My colleagues and I were the only viable source of long-term information on the racial climate at the school, so I became an expert witness.

The research provided four major types of evidence to document the university's racial climate. Most of the documentation was available from empirical articles in professional journals and internal campus research reports even before the lawsuit was initiated. The first type of research-generated evidence included numerous descriptive studies on the needs, problems, and interests of African American students on the campus. Many of these studies concluded that African Americans had unique problems and needs, including the need for more African American faculty and staff and help in dealing with a hostile campus climate. Much of the data here were informational.

A second type of research study focused on retention and identified a series of variables that correlated with the success of African American students. The variables identified were noncognitive and included being able to handle racism, developing a racial/cultural community on campus, and engaging in realistic self-appraisal despite the hostile environment. Many of the research articles were behavioral and suggested things that the school could do to reduce racism on campus (Sedlacek, 2004a).

A third type of study examined the attitudes of Whites toward African Americans on campus over a period of 25 years. These studies generally showed that despite increasing numbers of African American students and programs for them, Whites still had basically negative attitudes toward Blacks and that these were largely unchanged over the 25-year period (Balenger, Hoffman, & Sedlacek, 1992).

The fourth type of research evidence was a historical analysis of the campus newspaper, again over a 25-year period. Examples of negative incidents involving African Americans were counted and cataloged. The result of this effort showed a continuous stream of examples depicting a negative racial climate for African American students and faculty/staff. The examples provided informational, attitudinal, and behavioral data (Hill & Sedlacek, 1994).

So what happened in the case? The university eventually lost the case after two rounds in the circuit and appellate courts (Sedlacek, 1995). However, here is where an understanding of the audience was useful. Although I would have liked to have seen the university win the case, I was also trying to change the university. By getting the university to use the research on racial climate and acknowledge the issues affecting African American students, I had achieved a goal that I had been working on for many years. As one top administrator put it after the university had won a round in court: "I was glad we won but I wish we didn't have to admit we were racist to do it." Such thinking has led the university to assume more responsibility for programs in the scholarship and diversity areas that may not have been possible before the case.

Up the Conceptual Ladder

Research can help move conceptions of a problem to a higher level. An example in which a community solved a pollution problem might be illustrative. A town was struggling with the quality of its water supply; several years of trying different treatments had not resolved the problem. After some research, it became clear that the pollution was being caused by factors outside the community, including industrial waste disposal upriver, runoff of chemicals from farms, and soil leeching from timber-cutting policies. Armed with data from their studies, the researchers were able to influence some politicians from several states to adopt regional pollution-control programs. Without these broader concepts provided by data there was little hope of understanding what needed to be done to provide clean water in the town.

In the *Banneker Scholarship* case discussed previously, theories of racial identity (Helms, 1995) and eliminating racism (Sedlacek & Brooks, 1976) were used to organize the information to show how various types of data influenced one another. The arguments in the case included some concepts that were more likely to result in change as opposed to presenting the issue as a molecular series of unrelated incidents. The scientific principle of induction suggests that we integrate the information we have into the broadest concepts to explain the results.

Stick to Your Principles

It is easy to lose track of one's goals when engaging in social change research. I have a colleague whom more than one person has told that they are confused by her positions on certain issues. They said they "thought she was on their side." She usually explains that she tends to go where the data take her. Sometimes the data agree with the position of a given person, sometimes not. If we start supporting people or organizations, rather than issues, we are less likely to accomplish our social change goals.

In the *Banneker Scholarship* case, I worked out a set of principles to guide my activities and explained them to the lawyers and university officials involved. The first principle was to be helpful to the lawyers. Rather than to be self-righteous or guided solely by what any change agent with this unique opportunity might like to say, I attempted to put the research in a context that would be optimally useful to the lawyers. Sedlacek and Brooks (1976) noted that it is important for a social change agent to concentrate on what works, not on what one would like to see work.

A corollary of this principle was to concentrate work on the issues most salient for the case. It was tempting to comment on many issues not directly raised by the research, but an approach that focused on key research results seemed to have a better chance of being helpful to the lawyers and of making my contribution count. For instance, there was evidence indicating problems for students and faculty in racial/cultural groups other than African Americans or Latino/as (e.g., Arabs, international students, Jews, women, gays). Rather than to try to tie together issues affecting these groups into broader issues, I focused on the more narrow issues in the case.

The second principle was to use the opportunity to reduce racism against African Americans at the university. Racism was defined as policies or procedures (formal or informal) in an organization that result in negative outcomes for members of a certain group (e.g., African Americans) just because they are members of that group (Sedlacek, 2004a; Sedlacek & Brooks, 1976). Results, not intentions, are what mattered under this definition. The lawyers would have preferred a less forceful term to describe the problems faced by African Americans at the university, but adhering to this principle required defining racism and using the term in reports to the court.

Presenting the research in language the lawyers and a judge could interpret in legal terms while adhering to the second principle was a challenge. In reports to the court, I followed the second principle by concluding that there currently was racism against African Americans at the university and that there had been for some time. I also concluded that the scholarship program should be maintained exclusively for African Americans because it would take several if not many generations for African Americans to see the university as a comfortable place for them and their children to attend. Recruiting and retaining successful African American students was an important part of that process. The university needed to show its commitment to this goal by sticking with its programs, not by backing off under pressure.

The third principle was that racism against Latino/as be reduced at the university. Many Latino/as resented what they perceived as greater attention to the problems of African Americans than Latino/as on campus. Latino/as also struggled with racism and prejudice from non-Latino/as (White & Sedlacek, 1987). Many Latino/as watched with suspicion to see how the university would respond to the case.

I followed the third principle by calling for more university programs, including scholarships for Latino/as, in order to counter all forms of racism. Latino/as have unique needs and should not be lumped together with other groups or with students in general. Research on campus had shown that a major difficulty for Latino/a students was deciding when to seek out programs for Latino/as and when to use general programs (Fuertes, Sedlacek, & Westbrook, 1989). Helping students in that process could be an important counseling/advocacy service to offer.

As often happens in a lawsuit, both sides decided to focus on a more limited legal point. Consequently, the Latino/a issue was dropped from the case. The lawsuit concentrated on whether to continue offering the scholarships exclusively for African Americans or to open them to all students. Because it indirectly avoided the issue of Latino/as, this outcome could be interpreted as the university taking a racist position. For example, the university could be seen as concerned with African American issues only and as dismissing Latino/a issues as unimportant. This could have negative consequences for Latino/as seeking to reduce the racism directed against them by the university. Nevertheless, I did raise this issue in reports to the lawyers and the university, and the institution has initiated plans for several new programs for Latino/as.

The final guiding principle was maintaining personal integrity. The probability of my encountering serious role conflicts was very high. It was important to make decisions based on the best course, rather what than was politically correct or expedient. I implemented this principle by avoiding opportunistic behavior and by concentrating on doing what seemed best overall. The university was going through a series of budget reductions at the time and was anxious to improve its relationship with the citizens in its state. Departments within the university were vying for favor with the administration by suggesting that they were the diversity "experts" or that they had something special to offer African Americans, Latino/as, the university in general, or the case in particular. By putting the goal of social change first, I hoped that I would have the best chance of contributing to the reduction of racism at the school in the long run.

Patience and Persistence

Any social change activity requires time and persistence. If one thing does not work, try another. The research component in social change also requires time and many attempts. In many of the examples I have presented here, change took place slowly with help from many studies. Do not be discouraged by this. See each study as standing on its own and supporting key points you wish to make. However, also view that research as fitting into a mosaic—as one piece of a larger puzzle. Large gains can sometimes come from interconnected studies; however, smaller gains lead to bigger ones. Do not go for the big change too soon; be content with a small gain that moves your issue forward. Those who follow you can benefit from your work. Small victories attract allies and deter opponents (Weick, 1984).

Research that my students, my colleagues, and I had done for many years came together in the *Banneker Scholarship* case. A number of those earlier studies resulted in changes in student services and academic programs, including admissions policies, counseling programs, cultural activities, and multicultural course offerings (Roper & Sedlacek, 1988; Sedlacek, 2004a, 2004b; Sedlacek & Brooks, 1973). The culmination of the studies affected the university in a broader way and moved its leadership to see diversity as one of the school's strengths, with resulting program funding.

The Gates Millennium Scholars (GMS) program set out an ambitious and socially important series of goals for itself. It provides scholarships to financially needy African Americans, Native Americans, Latino/a Americans, or Asian Americans who are or will be studying mathematics, science, engineering, education, or library science. Applicants are required to be eligible for Pell Grants as a way of determining that they are in financial need, and awards cover all educational expenses at whatever institution the student is attending. It is a $1 billion program funded by the Bill and Melinda Gates Foundation and covering 20 years. Scholars are selected on their academic potential by demonstrating their abilities in ways other than the traditional standardized tests and prior grades. The noncognitive variables mentioned previously, which were developed in numerous studies conducted by me, students, and colleagues over more than 35 years are used as the primary method of selecting Gates Millennium Scholars (Sedlacek, 2004a). When one of my students asked me, "How did you get a gig like that?" I answered "Because we had completed and published the research on noncognitive variables that were fairer to students of color than traditional measures. Therefore, when the Gates Foundation was looking for some alternative measures that fit their program, they were available." Previously, that same student had expressed doubt that doing research ever seemed to make a difference in changing anything. At this writing, more than 7,000 GMS students are attending more than 900 different institutions in the United States and maintaining a grade point average of 3.25 on a 4-point scale (Sedlacek, 2004a, 2004b; Sedlacek & Sheu, in press a, in press b). That skeptical student has now finished school and is actively engaged in research. Patience and persistence.

Conclusion

I have attempted to discuss how research can play a vital role in social change. Research alone cannot bring about change, but dedicated professionals armed with good goals, good data, and some guiding principles can make a difference. We face many problems in our society, and there are many things that counseling professionals can do about them. Let us continue.

There are a number of references available in this publication and elsewhere on doing various types of research. References I recommend that I have not discussed previously include Denzin and Lincoln (1994); García, Hudgins, McTighe Musil, Nettles, Sedlacek, and Smith (2001); Isaac and Michael (1995); LaMahieu, Gitomer, and Eresch (1995); and Webb, Campbell, Schwartz, Sechrest, and Grove (1981).

References

Balenger, V. J., Hoffman, M. A., & Sedlacek, W. E. (1992). Racial attitudes among incoming White students: A study of 10-year trends. *Journal of College Student Development, 33,* 245–252.

Denzin, N. K., & Lincoln, Y. S. (1994). (Eds.), *Handbook of qualitative research.* Thousand Oaks, CA: Sage.

Dovidio, J. F., & Gaertner, S. L. (1986). *Prejudice, discrimination, and racism.* Orlando, FL: Academic Press.

Fuertes, J. N., Sedlacek, W. E., & Westbrook, F. D. (1989). *A needs assessment of Latino/a students at a predominantly White university* (Counseling Center Research Report No.21–89). College Park: University of Maryland.

García, M., Hudgins, C. A., McTighe Musil, C., Nettles, M. T., Sedlacek, W. E., & Smith, D. G. (2001). *Assessing campus diversity initiatives: A guide for practitioners.* Washington, DC: Association of American Colleges and Universities.

Helms, J. E. (1995). An update of Helms' White and people of color racial identity models. In J. G. Ponterotto, J. M. Casas, L. A. Suzuki, & C. M. Alexander (Eds.), *Handbook of multicultural counseling* (pp. 181–198). Thousand Oaks, CA: Sage.

Hill, M. D., & Sedlacek, W. E. (1994). *Using historical research methods in higher education.* (Counseling Center Research Report No. 8–94). College Park: University of Maryland.

Isaac, S., & Michael, W. B. (1995). *Handbook of research and evaluation* (3rd ed.). San Diego: EDITS.

LaMahieu, P. G., Gitomer, D. H., & Eresch, J. T. (1995). Portfolios in large scale assessment: Difficult but not impossible. *Educational Measurement: Issues and Practice, 14,* 11–28.

Roper, L. D., & Sedlacek, W. E. (1988). Student affairs professionals in academic roles: A course on racism. *National Association of Student Personnel Administrators Journal, 26*(1), 27–32.

Schlosser, L. Z., & Sedlacek, W. E. (2001). Hate on campus: A model for evaluating, understanding, and handling critical incidents. *About Campus, 6*(1), 25–27.

Sedlacek, W. E. (1994). Issues in advancing diversity through assessment. *Journal of Counseling & Development, 72,* 549–553.

Sedlacek, W. E. (1995). Using research to reduce racism at a university. *Journal of Humanistic Education and Development, 33,* 131–140.

Sedlacek, W. E. (1996). An empirical method of determining nontraditional group status. *Measurement and Evaluation in Counseling and Development, 28,* 200–210.

Sedlacek, W. E. (2004a). *Beyond the big test: Noncognitive assessment in higher education.* San Francisco: Jossey-Bass.

Sedlacek, W. E. (2004b). A multicultural research program. In F. W. Hale (Ed.), *What makes racial diversity work in higher education* (pp. 256–271). Sterling, VA: Stylus.

Sedlacek, W. E., & Brooks, C. C., Jr. (1973). Racism and research: Using data to initiate change. *Personnel and Guidance Journal, 52,* 184–188.

Sedlacek, W. E., & Brooks, C. C., Jr. (1976). *Racism in American education: A model for change.* Chicago: Nelson-Hall.

Sedlacek, W. E., & Sheu, H. B. (in press a). Academic success of Gates Millennium Scholars. *Readings on Equal Education.*

Sedlacek, W. E., & Sheu, H. B. (in press b). Correlates of leadership activities among Gates Millennium Scholars. *Readings on Equal Education.*

Sedlacek, W. E., Troy, W. G., & Chapman, T. H. (1976). An evaluation of three methods of racism-sexism training. *Personnel and Guidance Journal, 55,* 196–198.

Webb, E. J., Campbell, D. T., Schwartz, R. D., Sechrest, L., & Grove, J. B. (1981). *Nonreactive measures in the social sciences.* Boston: Houghton Mifflin.

Weick, K. E. (1984). Small wins: Redefining the scale of social problems. *American Psychologist, 39,* 40–49.

White, T. J., & Sedlacek, W. E. (1987). White student attitudes toward Blacks and Latino/as: Programming implications. *Journal of Multicultural Counseling and Development, 15,* 171–182.

Chapter 13

Training Counselors in Social Justice

Fred Bemak and Rita Chi-Ying Chung

Preceding chapters have discussed the relationship between social justice and the counseling profession, as well as the cultural, social, economic, historical, political, and ecological issues that influence social injustices. This information provides a strong rationale for why counselors must be actively and proactively involved in preventing and intervening in social justice issues that affect their clients, families, and communities. This chapter discusses how the George Mason University (GMU) counseling program prepares counselors to work in the social justice arena, and examines how the GMU program has infused social justice throughout its mission and training. The chapter also includes recommendations for designing other similar programs, as well as a discussion about the realities and challenges of changing a traditional, mainstream training program into a social-justice-focused program. To provide an understanding of why a program would undergo such an enormous and Herculean task, we begin with a brief description of our own personal social justice journeys and subsequent commitment that led to our vision, dedication, motivation, and determination to change a traditional counselor training program into one that prepares counselors to work with social justice issues.

Personal Social Justice Journeys

Fred Bemak

I grew up in a household that prized values of fairness, equity, and justice. Because of these values, as a child I was regularly placed in the role of being the objective, or fair, arbiter who judged if the ball was fair or foul, or if someone stepped out of bounds or not, even when I was on the opposing team. My peers always knew that I would be fair, and my judgment stood as the deciding factor in numerous conflicts. I was also the person who tried, though not always successfully, to intervene in situations in which people were bullied or discriminated against. Subsequently, when I entered university in the late 1960s, I was active in civil rights and also took a summer job at Upward Bound (John F. Kennedy's response to poverty in the United States), working primarily with African American and Latina/o youth and families. Many years later, I went on to direct that Upward Bound program. During my years there I learned deep lessons about poverty, inequities, discrimination, and racism, as well as about differences in opportunity and access. I have treasured these lessons and values and carried them with me in all the counseling and administrative work that I have done over the years and still do today. Although in 1990 I had six different opportunities for faculty positions around the United States, I came to George Mason because it offered me full support to develop a graduate program with an emphasis on social justice and multiculturalism, a long-standing dream.

Rita Chi-Ying Chung

A friend and colleague once told me that as a child of refugee and immigrant parents growing up in British colonies, I experienced triple oppression: one, for being a women, two, for being Chinese, and three, for living in British colonies. My first memories are of social injustices, the experiences of racism and classism. Although at that time I was just learning to walk and talk, and I did not fully understand the situations, the pain and anguish on the faces of my family are forever branded in my memory (when I talk about family I'm referring to extended family, because I grew up in a multigenerational household with extended family members). Compounding the refugee experience, my parents migrated to a country that had signs stating "No Dogs or Chinese." Through their experiences, they vowed that their children would stand up for themselves and others, and not be treated as second-class citizens. My parents in their humble way worked toward creating a better, fairer, and more equal life and opportunities for our family and community. They instilled social justice values in their children, and it became second nature for us to help, stand with, and fight with and for those who were subjected to social injustices and potential human rights violations. As long as I can remember all my family has been—and still is—involved in some form of social justice work. Therefore, social justice issues became a natural extension of my professional work. I made my decision to work at George Mason University because of the opportunity and support provided to develop a program of my dreams—that of social justice and multiculturalism.

George Mason University's Counseling and Development Social Justice Training Program

GMU is the largest publicly funded university in the Commonwealth of Virginia, with 29,000 students and more than 100 degree programs. The university is located just outside Washington, DC, and was identified in 2004 by the *Princeton Review* as the most diverse campus in the United States. The Counseling and Development (C&D) Program is housed in the College of Education and Human Development, a college which has 100 full-time faculty. The C&D Program offers a doctoral degree through the Graduate School of Education, a master's degree with specializations in community agency counseling and school counseling, two postmaster's certificate licensure programs, and a certificate in international school counseling.

Counseling and Development Program Transitions

To provide an understanding of the intricacies in changing the counseling program to prepare counselors for social justice work, we begin with a brief description of the GMU C&D Program transition during the past 6 years. In 1999, the counselor training program at GMU was in a state of transition, following the departure of all three full-time faculty members. This left the College of Education and Human Development (CEHD) with serious decisions about what to do with the existing program. During the year of transition (1999–2000) CEHD hired two interim visiting faculty to hold up the program while the CEHD administration decided its future. The administration made a decision in 2000 to continue the program by recruiting two faculty members (the two authors) to take a leadership role in revitalizing the program. In discussions about coming to GMU, the two authors presented to CEHD administration their vision of social justice and multiculturalism and their interest in revamping the C&D graduate program to be consistent with this vision. The administrators fully agreed, and with concurrence about the direction for a new program, we assumed positions as senior faculty with the C&D Program in September 2000.

Simultaneously the two visiting faculty who had been holding up the program during the transition year had applied for faculty positions. Each of them had substantial experience in the field but was new to academe. They were both very receptive to moving toward a social justice and multicultural agenda and were subsequently both hired. Thus, at a key transition point in the program in 2000, the full-time faculty changed from two 1-year temporary positions to four full-time faculty. The infusion of four new faculty and full administrative support within the university created an ideal situation to develop a new program cocreated as a full group of faculty. One year later, in 2001, a fifth full-time faculty member was added to the program. This hiring took place following national advertisements for a faculty member who was committed to social justice, and the hiring process emphasized social justice in prescreening and final interviews. Based on an extensive national search, another faculty member who was in full agreement with the social justice and multiculturalism program mission was hired in 2005.

Mainstream to Social Justice: A Process of Transformation

In this section we present the steps we have taken to transform the GMU C&D Program, including a discussion on the development of our new social justice mission statement; new recruitment initiatives; curriculum revisions; program development; research; and local, national, and international partnerships.

Our philosophical belief coming into the C&D Program was that a significant program change would be far more effective if *all* faculty were on board and in agreement about the direction of the program. The two new junior faculty members agreed. Therefore, during the first year, the four new faculty held three retreats, two of them overnight, to discuss (a) their beliefs, concept, and definition of social justice; and (b) a new program mission and direction that reflected a shared consensus of all faculty. In addition there were bimonthly 2- to 3-hour C&D faculty meetings to maintain ongoing discussions about the development and implementation of the new program.

The discussion regarding the concept of social justice was critical. Although the two senior faculty shared a vision of a training program to prepare graduate trainees to work on social justice issues as counselors, it was unclear whether the two junior faculty had the same vision and perspectives about the relationship between social justice and the counseling profession. The two of us believed that without full faculty consensus, it would not be possible to develop a program that truly focused on social justice issues. To achieve a consensus required significant time for critical dialogue and reflection regarding social justice, so that everyone had a chance to articulate and share their values, beliefs, opinions, and ideas, and to be heard. Thus, we needed to commit to a process of engagement for which there were no shortcuts or ways to circumvent the time and energy required to make such a significant shift in training and curriculum.

After a month of extensive conversation and meetings, the faculty came to consensus about the meaning and definition of social justice. The essence of our agreement was captured in the following statement: Social justice is

> a basic value and desired goal in democratic societies and includes equitable and fair access to societal institutions, laws, resources, and opportunities, without arbitrary limitations based on observed, or interpretation of, differences in age, color, culture, physical or mental disability, education, gender, income, language, national origin, race, religion, or sexual orientation. (King, 1996, p. 1)

Developing a Mission Statement

Once all faculty members agreed on a general concept of social justice, the next step was to develop a mission statement for the C&D Program. The development of this mission statement drew on multiple sources, including the multicultural counseling competencies (e.g., Arredondo et al., 1996; Sue, Arredondo, & McDavis, 1992); social justice literature (e.g., D'Andrea & Daniels, 1999; Helms, 2003; Helms & Cook, 1999; Ivey & Collins, 2003; Lee & Walz, 1998; Parham & McDavis, 1987; Vera & Speight, 2003); counselor efficacy in a rapidly changing technological, ecological, and global world (Bemak & Conyne, 2004); counselor roles that work toward social justice (Bemak, 2000; Bemak & Chung, 2005), our work with marginalized populations, and our personal experiences. In addition we examined mission statements from other counseling and psychology programs as well as from other disciplines.

The aim of the mission statement was to provide a foundation and a philosophy that would offer direction for a training program that would teach counselors to embrace social justice from an ecological framework. This approach extended beyond traditional counselor training and required that counselor trainees acquire an awareness, acceptance, acknowledgement, and understanding of sociopolitical, historical, psychosocial, economic, cultural, physical, and spiritual health of individuals, families, communities, organizations, and systems. We believed that acquiring this new awareness and knowledge would contribute to the advancement of a global well-being and the prevention of and intervention in social injustices and potential human rights violations. We realized we were paving new ground in the counseling field, but were all excited and eager as we engaged in the process of transformation.

After much deliberation and discussion, the faculty developed the following mission statement:

> The program strives for national and international excellence in implementing a counseling perspective that provides a foundation in basic counseling skills and focuses on multiculturalism, social justice, leadership, and advocacy. It is our belief that a global perspective on development across the life span, and an understanding and appreciation of multiculturalism, diversity, and social justice are integral to the preparation of professional counselors, requiring that they are prepared to assume leadership roles, be proactive change agents, and become advocates for social, economic, and political justice.

This mission statement set the stage and direction for students in the C&D Program to focus on social justice and multicultural issues and gain skills as leaders and advocates working toward social justice. We must mention that in creating a climate and commitment to do social justice work, it was critical to develop a diverse and responsive learning community that embraced cultural and socioeconomic differences and international and global perspectives with support for a critical discourse by both students and faculty. One way of creating a culturally diverse training program was to increase efforts to recruit and retain faculty and students of color in order to provide diversity at all levels of the program. Concurrently, the program emphasized the importance of and respect for differences in values, worldviews, attitudes, backgrounds, ethnicity, race, religion, gender, and sexual orientation. The program clearly moved away from a traditional counseling value of unconditional positive regard to a value-filled program that promoted social justice; tolerance; respect for racial, cultural, social, economic, and political equity; fairness; and equal access to opportunities and resources. In one sense it could be said that the C&D Program adopted a zero tolerance policy with regard to discrimination, racism, sexism, classism, ageism, homoprejudice, unfair treatment with regard to disabilities, religious prejudice, and so on.

Essential in developing a value-filled program was the facilitation of a deep awareness and acknowledgement of one's worldview and the impact of one's personal values, beliefs, attitudes, biases, prejudices, privileges, and subsequent behaviors on individuals, groups, communities, and society at large. In our opinion, when counselors promote social justice and advocacy without self-awareness and the skills necessary to effect change, they run a great danger of being misdirected, misguided, and ineffectual. Subsequently there is a vital need for a worldview. Multiple methods for educating individuals regarding their worldviews have been identified, such as field-based experiences and intensive personal exploration through structured exercises (Helms & Cook, 1999; Pedersen & Hernandez, 1997).

Infusing Social Justice Throughout the Curriculum

It is not enough simply to add social justice as a training mission for a counseling program. Furthermore, simply adding one class in social justice would fall short of fulfilling the mission. Subsequently, the faculty took definitive steps to explore how social justice could be infused throughout the program curriculum. As we investigated this, we came to agreement that in order to have a truly social-justice-focused program we would need to infuse social justice activities and lessons throughout the courses.

Consequently, the C&D Program is founded not only on a mission of social justice, but also on the embedding of social justice throughout the program. As a result social justice is a cornerstone of the program and drives every aspect of it, including research and scholarship, admissions, hiring of adjunct faculty, course content, student dispositions, invited speakers, and evaluations of student performance. This focus has led us to diversify the faculty and student body, add courses and internships in social justice and social change, and create admissions criteria that emphasize human rights and social justice. Furthermore, the program has developed an emphasis on interdisciplinary training that includes public policy, public health, political science, sociology, social work, anthropology, law, history, and education as important components of social justice work (Bemak, 1998). For example, potential internship sites include the Peace Corps, the American Counseling Association, the Center for Multicultural Human Services, the U.S. Committee for Refugees, and the American School Counselors Association. In the GMU Counseling and Development Program, social justice is in the foreground as a core issue in training. This is unique in the counseling field, and to our knowledge, similar efforts are being made in only a handful of counseling graduate training programs. The next sections discuss in more detail various aspects of the program.

Faculty and Student Recruitment and Retention

The development of the social justice program not only revitalized the C&D Program, but also brought excitement to the faculty. The enthusiasm and excitement was shared by administrators and students. After the first year, with significantly more student applications and increased national visibility for the program, it was decided to hire an additional faculty member. The position advertisement emphasized the need for a candidate with a commitment to and experience with social justice and multiculturalism. Interviews were consistent with the social justice and multiculturalism emphasis and explored applicants' beliefs about these issues and commitment to join a faculty team that was in the midst of establishing a new and innovative program along these lines. The result of this search was the hiring of an additional faculty member who demonstrated an established commitment to multiculturalism and social justice issues, a process we repeated in the academic year 2004–2005. As of 2005, 50% of the full-time C&D Program faculty are people of color, with one third being from outside the United States. Simultaneously, the adjunct faculty pool has changed dramatically, from being predominantly European American (95%) to being approximately 40% faculty of color.

The student body reflects the changes in faculty with regards to diversity. Four years ago the program had predominantly European American students with very few students of color. A major goal of the faculty was to facilitate a culturally diverse learning environment by significantly increasing the representation of students of color in our master's- and doctoral-level programs. In the past 4 years the ethnicity of the student body has changed dramatically from approximately 95% European Americans to approximately 30% students of color and 70% European Americans. These changes in faculty and student racial and ethnic composition are closely linked and reflect changes in the program's mission. Part of this transformation has been the growing recognition of the program and its mission regionally and nationally, which in turn has substantially increased applications by students of color to the program.

Admissions Procedures

The move toward a social justice agenda also required shifts in all aspects of the program. One area of major change was admissions procedures. Prior to its transformation the C&D Program had used traditional admissions criteria that emphasized standardized test scores. Recognizing inherent biases in traditional admissions procedures (e.g., standardized scores and an emphasis on grades at the expense of other qualifications), and in light of Helms' (1992) research on test bias, the faculty reexamined the admissions process and decided to incorporate alternative admissions criteria while maintaining the quality of students admitted to the program. A more holistic approach was adopted that included an initial evaluation of personal, social, educational, and work values and experiences; a thorough review of letters of reference; and a final essay. Test scores remained a part of the evaluation process but were no longer the main factor determining acceptance to the program. This approach allowed faculty to review the broader personal, social, and educational values of applicants and ascertain their concurrence with the social justice mission of the program.

Faculty review of these items leads to decisions about which students to invite for admissions interviews. Approximately, 80% of applicants are eventually invited for a program interview, which occurs in a group format. The group interview is intentional, allowing faculty to observe interpersonal skills and interactions. During the interview applicants are asked about their experience as advocates, their commitment to social justice, and their views about the program's mission statement. A writing sample is also obtained during the interview by having applicants respond to the program's mission statement.

Curriculum and Training

As we have mentioned, in 2000, in the early stages of developing the new program, the faculty redefined the mission statement to focus on social justice, multiculturalism, leadership, and advocacy. The next step was to align the program curriculum with the new mission so that the mission would actually be accomplished. Thus, faculty began a serious discussion about how to infuse the mission into all the courses of the program. As with any group, it was quite a task to blend five individuals' ideas into a consensual curriculum, while at the same time allowing for academic freedom. Faculty agreed to undertake this difficult task, keeping in mind the ultimate goal of meeting the mission to prepare future social justice counselors. The process of finding consensus involved difficult discussions, differing opinions, self-awareness activities, and at times strong feelings. After arriving at consensus about which classes would be kept, which would be changed, and which would be eliminated, the faculty took on the daunting task of reviewing each syllabus to see where and how to incorporate social justice, multiculturalism, leadership, and advocacy, as well as how to change teaching styles, course objectives, textbook choices, and assignments.

Thus, social justice issues were introduced and incorporated right from the introductory classes through to practicum and internship experiences. For example, "Foundations in Counseling" was added as the first class in the program. In this course, considerable time is spent introducing the program's mission statement and having students reflect upon and engage in critical dialogue on social justice issues. This process can be challenging and quite different from the standard foundations course, in which social justice is barely mentioned if it is at all. Other classes explored issues such as poverty, racism, sexism, discrimination, violence, public policy, or funding in relationship to counseling and mental health. Practicum and internship classes incorporated assignments to develop prevention programs targeted at issues of social justice.

Even though social justice and human rights issues were included in all the courses, we also felt there needed to be a course specifically focusing on counseling and social justice. Thus, a new required core class was developed entitled "Counseling and Social Justice." In addition to the "Multicultural Counseling" class, this class challenges students with direct, hands-on experience in the field as well as critical reflection and discussion. Field experiences in this class involve social justice work with public, private, federal, state, regional, and professional organizations.

The "Counseling and Social Justice" course provides students with opportunities to contribute to the C&D Program, the college, the university (GMU), professional organizations, and the broader profession. As an example, the C&D students had an opportunity to contribute to the counseling program by developing social justice assignments for every course in the program. Faculty discussed their ideas, suggestions, and recommendations and then incorporated them into course syllabi. On a larger scale the C&D students developed and created learning scenarios about child abuse for the GMU Office of Diversity Programs to use in its annual Tunnel of Oppression Exhibition. The Tunnel of Oppression is a university-wide exhibition to educate the 29,000 students at the university.

The students have also contributed to professional associations. They developed a school- and community-wide gang prevention program for a social justice project in cooperation with the American School Counselors Association (ASCA). Students field-tested the project during their practicum and internship courses. Based on the quality of their work and the results from the field testing, the program has been made available to school counselors nationally via the ASCA Web site. ASCA is also in discussion with the Counselors for Social

Justice Division of the American Counseling Association to copublish the gang prevention program. Experiences such as these provide students a chance to experience firsthand the outcome and impact of their social justice work.

The social justice fieldwork is an important component in developing skills and competencies. Students face challenges on both institutional and personal levels and must learn how to change and work more effectively with these challenges. In doing field experiences they have opportunities to experiment with the practical application of skills needed to facilitate change on local, regional, and national levels.

To further promote training in social justice, the practicum and internship classes were expanded beyond the traditional counseling experience activities to include social justice fieldwork. The courses require the development of prevention programs that target social justice issues and the evaluation of existing programs in community agencies and schools within the framework of social justice and human rights. This work required close collaboration with field sites that were not focused on social justice concepts and whose expectations for graduate students were for traditional on-site placements that required only direct counseling work. This required C&D faculty to educate potential placements regarding the program mission and rationale for incorporating social justice activities.

New Doctoral Courses

Given the mission of social justice, new courses were developed at all levels of the program. Four new courses specifically aligned with the program's mission statement were developed and added to the doctoral program. The courses were "Advanced Internship in Social Justice," "Advanced Internship in Leadership," "Advanced Group Counseling," and "Advanced Internship in Multiculturalism." These classes provide students with skills, theoretical understandings, and advanced field experiences that allow them to integrate their counseling skills with social justice in the field.

In conclusion, the C&D Program faculty collaboratively redesigned the entire mission of the program to focus on social justice, multiculturalism, leadership, and advocacy. Every course was revised to align with the mission. Courses that did not fit with the mission were eliminated, and new courses were added at both the master's and doctoral levels. The aim of the training was to incorporate social justice through systemic and interdisciplinary perspectives that fostered social change and social justice, while developing an understanding of organizational dynamics and acquiring assessment and research skills (Kiselica & Robinson, 2001).

Research and Professional Development Activities

A commitment to social justice requires that faculty become role models for students on multiple levels, not only teaching about social justice, but also exemplifying these concepts in terms of research, scholarship, and service. To this end faculty are highly involved as leaders in state, national, and international professional organizations as well as federal projects. These positions range from president or leaders of state professional organizations to executive and advisory board members and committee chairs for national and international professional organizations and agencies. In each of these positions, faculty carry forward the mission of social justice and model what they are teaching in the classroom.

Concurrently, faculty members are involved in scholarship consistent with the C&D Program mission of social justice, multiculturalism, leadership, and advocacy. Faculty regularly present at state, national, and international meetings and publish in major journals and books. Many of the publications emphasize social justice and multiculturalism and reflect the program mission. In fact, we are currently completing a book on social justice and counseling (Chung & Bemak, in press). These types of scholarship and service provide a model and basis for encouraging and supporting student involvement, with the result that in the past 2 years students have increasingly presented to, attended, and served on committees in state and national professional associations.

It may help to share a few projects that we are each engaged in. One example of social justice work is work that the first author did when he came to Virginia in 2000. At that time the state had no coordination or central-level administrator for school counseling at the Virginia Department of Education, and each school district was working independent of any formal structure. The possibility of creating any statewide change in school counseling practices that would foster greater fairness, equity, and benefits for all students was essentially nonexistent. With the cooperation of colleagues, he organized a group in northern Virginia composed of other university faculty and district directors for school counseling to promote coordination and work toward providing services for all students. An outcome of this group was that the Virginia Superintendent of Education facilitated the appointment of an assistant superintendent from the Virginia Department of Education as a liaison for school counselors and a subsequent liaison to the northern Virginia group, which identified itself as the School Counseling Leadership Team (SCLT). Further action by SCLT led to a meeting with the president of the State Board of Education, resulting in a highly visible voice in the state for school counselors and the creation of a position in the Virginia Department of Education for a school counseling coordinator. Four years later this team is still active and a leader in Virginia, is consulting with other regions, and is working on changing laws and practices throughout the state.

Another example is a current project of the second author, who is working with nongovernmental organizations, universities, and United Nations organizations in six Asian countries to develop an Asia-based conference in Singapore to address the growing and alarming issue of trafficking in Asian girls and violence against children. The aim of the interdisciplinary conference is to educate service providers about how to recognize and deal with survivors and potential victims of trafficking and violence from country-specific and international viewpoints. An outcome of the conference will be to write a series of working papers designed to influence national and international policy and law. A third example is that the first author is working in Northern Ireland to address youth suicide within the context of the sectarian conflict, or "the troubles." Domestically, both authors continue to work in schools and communities as consultants and are developing projects to address issues of social injustice. Similar activities focusing on social justice are also being undertaken by the other faculty in the C&D Program, who are working in schools and communities to research racial and ethnic disparities in health and counseling; gaps in academic achievement related to race, ethnicity, and socioeconomic status; and issues of racial identity and equity. All of these examples point toward consistency with service and scholarship that is based on working toward social justice.

Transformation: The Long Journey

Taking steps to change a traditional counselor education program into one that endorses social justice, multiculturalism, leadership, and advocacy is fraught with challenges. A critical issue is how to make the training relevant to the surrounding world and incorporate values and ideals that are consistent with the program mission.

Transforming the program challenges students to change how they think, feel, and act in the world. One ongoing challenge for students is the issue of White privilege. To reflect on, reconsider, and reevaluate White privilege means, particularly for White students, reexamining one's outlook and sense of entitlement, privilege, and power. A second, related challenge is having faculty members who are women or people of color teach courses that challenge preconceived notions about race, ethnicity, or identity, which raises issues for both students of color and White students alike. The very dynamic of having a woman or faculty member of color teaching courses that question students' position, identity, and worldview has caused strong feelings. This dynamic has also promoted interracial tension, when some students from one racial group initially feel antagonism about a faculty member from another racial group teaching them about multiculturalism.

The C&D Program also finds itself in an unusual situation when students who initially endorse the mission statement later find themselves confronted with becoming leaders and advocates for multiculturalism and social justice. This can result in frustration and resistance to the mission. This dynamic recently occurred with a deeply religious student who had done outstanding work throughout the earlier part of her program. The social justice class involved confronting students to further challenge their belief systems; she shared that her religion forbids homosexual relationships. Although she had already changed dramatically and was a proponent of the mission statement, the issues raised in the social justice class brought her dissonance to a new level.

A fourth challenge is finding practicum and internship sites and supervisors that share the C&D Program values. Three students were recently placed in an agency that is renowned for its work in multiculturalism and social justice; this placement resulted in a meeting with three supervisors who asked about the relevance of social justice projects. Ongoing situations like this require the C&D Program faculty to meet with agency and school field supervisors and carefully educate them about the program mission and expectations for field placements.

The final challenge is ensuring that part-time, adjunct faculty are committed to the mission statement and enthusiastic about incorporating these principles and values into their teaching strategies and coursework. To address this issue, meetings were held to discuss our mission statement with adjunct faculty and to create formal paired relationships between full-time faculty and part-time faculty that open communication about how to incorporate the mission into the coursework.

Recommendations for Graduate-Level Training in Social Justice

As we reflect on our journey over the past 4 years, we can identify a number of lessons we have learned. Based on those lessons, we make the following eight recommendations for counseling programs that are implementing a social justice agenda:

1. *Ensure significant faculty communication and dialogue.* Open faculty communication and discussion regarding social justice is imperative. Our faculty spent significant time exploring what social justice meant to us, how it related to a counseling program, what our own personal values were, what students should look like at the completion of a master's or doctoral program, and how all of these components came together in a mission statement. To facilitate this level of communication and open dialogue, the faculty went on several overnight and daylong retreats to discuss our different ideas, perspectives, views, and thoughts about operationalizing social justice in our teaching, practice, and research. Consensus rather than majority ruled.

2. *Educate adjunct faculty and field supervisors.* As previously mentioned, adjunct faculty and field supervisors are frequently less aware of, untrained in, and less committed to social justice than the program faculty. There is the potential for adjunct faculty to feel alienated from the larger program or disconnected from the mission. Field supervisors who have not been educated about social justice may be confused and question how social justice assignments fit into counseling. To address some of these issues, adjunct faculty are told when they are hired about the mission and the need to infuse it into their teaching. All adjunct faculty maintain periodic contact with a full-time faculty point person on an as-needed basis and meet together once each semester. Simultaneously, the field supervisors are in close contact with the C&D Program clinical coordinator for practicum and internship placements and have regular and ongoing contact with the university faculty course instructor. Expectations for assignments, including social justice assignments, are clearly defined at the beginning of the semester and reviewed at on-site faculty visits with the field supervisor.

3. *Clearly articulate a value-filled program mission.* Social justice, openness, tolerance, diversity, and respect for differences—all of these concepts are based on a philosophy and clearly defined worldview. It is critical that a program be clear with students regarding its values and belief system. The GMU C&D Program informs applicants about the program values and expectations for

students. This is important for programs emphasizing social justice training.

4. *Create a culture of empowerment.* To effectively teach about social justice, one must model the values inherent in social justice. Therefore, students are encouraged to participate and be highly active in the program. Feedback about the program, courses, and instructors is encouraged; program activities are generated; input about elective courses is welcomed; and regular contact with faculty is encouraged. Chi Sigma Iota (CSI—the international honor society for counseling), is another vehicle for open communication between faculty and students. Underlying these activities is the formation of collaborative relationships with students that empower them to gain a voice regarding the program and their education.

5. *Collaborate with university administrators.* Essential in developing a program focusing on social justice is the support of administration. The C&D Program faculty maintained a clear and open dialogue with the dean's office regarding the program changes. Any questions about the program were answered willingly. As a result university administrators gave their full support for the program to develop its current mission and for the process of changing the courses and curriculum to align with it. It is critical to discuss proposed changes with the dean's office so that both the process and the outcome are clearly understood and sanctioned in advance.

6. *Build multilevel partnerships for social change.* Social change should not apply only to counselors in training, but also should direct other aspects of faculty work and research. We recommend that partnerships be developed to address social justice reform at local, state, national, and international levels and that faculty become role models for students. Examples of this in the C&D Program are formation of and partnerships with SCLT, a leader in school counseling reform in northern Virginia that was begun by the C&D Program faculty. In addition, faculty serve in leadership roles in state, national, and international organizations, as well as sit on advisory boards and boards of directors of national organizations, all with an aim of promoting social change and social justice.

7. *Evaluate program activities.* Program assessment is essential. Is the program accomplishing what it set out to do? Where are the areas for improvement? What needs to be changed? And so on. These are key questions for evaluating the impact and quality of any program. Furthermore, it is helpful to report this information to the dean's office, other administrators, and field sites.

8. *Support social justice with research and scholarship.* The faculty in the GMU C&D Program are all interested in social justice and multiculturalism and pursue these areas as a line of research, publications, and presentations. This is particularly helpful in developing a comprehensive graduate program in social justice. It also promotes collaboration with students, who now regularly present and increasingly publish with C&D Program faculty.

Conclusion

Attention to social justice has increased in the counseling profession through the auspices of both the American Counseling Association and the American Psychological Association. Even so, only a handful of programs have incorporated social justice into their mission statements, and even fewer have translated the commitment to social justice into their graduate-level training programs. At GMU we have been actively involved for almost 5 years in developing a program that trains students to become social justice counselors. In our work we have drawn from the multicultural competencies, social justice literature, internationalism, multiculturalism, technological advances, and our own personal experiences to develop a training model that addresses oppression, violence, poverty, discrimination, racism, sexism, privilege, social inequities, and social justice. We attempt to "walk the walk" by empowering our students and educating those individuals who have an association with the program, such as adjunct faculty, field supervisors, university administrators, and colleagues within and outside GMU. We attempt to be living models for our students by working on social justice issues ourselves.

The transformation of our program has had some tangible results, such as a significant increase in the number of students of color applying to the program, a critical discourse within the program itself about issues of social justice and multiculturalism, and a change in demographics among the full-time faculty, which is now 50% people of color and

33% international. Our hope and intent is to train students not only to become highly skilled counselors in communities and schools, but also to become committed to being leaders and advocates in promoting social change, equity, fairness, and justice through their work in the counseling profession.

References

Arredondo, P., Toporek, R., Brown, S. P., Jones, J., Locke, D., & Sanchez, J. (1996). Operationalization of the multicultural counseling competencies. *Journal of Multicultural Counseling and Development, 24,* 42–78.

Bemak, F. (1998). Interdisciplinary collaboration for social change: Redefining the counseling profession. In C. C. Lee & G. R. Walz (Eds.), *Social action: A mandate for counselors* (pp. 279–292). Alexandria, VA: American Counseling Association.

Bemak, F. (2000). Transforming the role of the counselor to provide leadership in educational reform through collaboration. *Professional School Counseling, 3,* 323–331.

Bemak, F., & Chung, R. C-Y. (2005). Advocacy as a critical role for urban school counselors: Working toward equity and social justice. *Professional School Counseling, 83,* 196–202.

Bemak, F., & Conyne, R. C. (2004). Ecological group work. In R. K. Conyne & E. P. Cook (Eds.), *Ecological counseling: An innovative approach to conceptualizing person-environment interaction.* Alexandria, VA: American Counseling Association.

Chung, R. C-Y., & Bemak, F. (in press). *Social justice and multiculturalism: Application, theory, and practice in counseling and psychotherapy.* Columbus, OH: Prentice Hall.

D'Andrea, M., & Daniels, J. (1999). Exploring the psychology of White racism through naturalistic inquiry. *Journal of Counseling & Development, 77,* 93–101.

Helms, J. E. (1992). Why is there no study of cultural equivalence in standardized cognitive ability testing? *American Psychologist, 47,* 1083–1101.

Helms, J. E. (2003). A pragmatic view of social justice. *The Counseling Psychologist, 31,* 305–313.

Helms, J. E., & Cook, D. A. (1999). *Using race and culture in counseling and psychotherapy: Theory and practice.* Boston: Allyn & Bacon.

Ivey, A. E., & Collins, N. M. (2003). A long-term challenge for counseling psychology. *The Counseling Psychologist, 31,* 290–298, 305–313.

King, D. (1996). What is social justice? *Perspectives on Multicultural and Cultural Diversity, 6,* 1–3.

Kiselica, M. S., & Robinson, M. (2001). Bringing advocacy counseling to life: The history, issues, and human dramas of social justice work in counseling. *Journal of Counseling & Development, 79,* 387–397.

Lee, C. C., & Walz, G. R. (Eds.). (1998). *Social action: A mandate for counselors.* Alexandria, VA: American Counseling Association.

Parham, T. A., & McDavis, R. J. (1987). Black men, an endangered species: Who's really pulling the trigger? *Journal of Counseling & Development, 66,* 24–27.

Pedersen, P. B., & Hernandez, D. (1997). *Decisional dialogues in a cultural context: Structured exercises.* Thousand Oaks, CA: Sage.

Sue, D. W., Arredondo, P., & McDavis, S. (1992). Multicultural counseling competencies and standards: A call to the profession. *Journal of Counseling & Development, 70,* 477–486.

Vera, E. M., & Speight, S. L. (2003). Multicultural competence, social justice, and counseling psychology: Expanding our roles. *The Counseling Psychologist, 31,* 253–272.

Conclusion:
A Counselor's Call to Action

Courtland C. Lee

For to be free is not merely to cast off one's chains, but to live in a way that respects and enhances the freedom of others.
—Nelson Mandela

Counseling for Social Justice has challenged professional counselors to intervene not only in the lives of clients or students, to help with problem resolution or decision making, but also in the world that affects those lives. This is critical when that world is characterized by social inequities or lack of access to full participation for any group of people. Implicit in all of the chapters is the important notion that promoting psychosocial development must be considered from a social justice perspective.

Counseling for social justice requires a paradigm shift. Counselors need to consider roles that heretofore have not been particularly associated with their profession. A goal of this book has been to provide a context for social justice and, hence, to promote social action on the part of professional counselors. A close reading of the book suggests that part of the paradigm shift required if counselors are to become agents of social justice involves new ways of conceptualizing the theory and practice of counseling. These new ways of viewing the profession are predicated on recognizing that the inherent dignity and the equal and inalienable rights of all people are the foundation of freedom, justice, and peace in any society.

The call to action, however, begins at the personal level with self-exploration. Within the context of all that has gone before, I focus now on the counselor as an individual and what personal action he or she must take in order to become an effective force for social justice. Counseling for social justice is more than a professional obligation; it is about living one's life in a manner that is dedicated to promoting access and equity. What follows are specific steps that will help counselors live a life that is committed to social justice. Counseling for social justice must be about not only "talking the talk" but also about "walking the talk."

Personal Action Steps

1. *Explore your life's meaning and your commitment.* Begin by asking yourself some existential questions: What do I do and why do I do it? How do I do it? Who do I do it for? What do I believe about my students/clients? What do I believe about myself? What are the results of my efforts? Am I committed to fostering and supporting a society that is more enlightened, just, and humane through my life and work?

2. *Explore personal privilege.* Explore the nature of your personal cultural privilege. In other words, evaluate the unearned privileges you enjoy in society by virtue of your skin color, gender, socioeconomic status, or any other demographic or cultural characteristic. This exploration must begin with a personal acknowledgement of such privilege and the how it contributes to societal inequities. Challenge yourself to find ways to exploit your cultural privilege in any venue that will promote equity, human rights, and a fair allocation of societal resources.

3. *Explore the nature of oppression.* Counseling for social justice must be based on an understanding of the nature of oppression. Oppression occurs whenever power or authority are used in an unjust fashion. From a social justice perspective, whenever people are denied access to full and equitable participation in the life of a society, they experience oppression. It is important, therefore, to consider the impact of oppression on your life and work. Ask yourself, How have I been a victim of oppression? How have I contributed to the perpetuation of oppression? Have I used personal or professional authority or power in unjust ways?

4. *Work to become multiculturally literate.* Become committed to living cultural diversity as a reality rather than experiencing it as an abstraction. Embrace a lifestyle that will help you to become multiculturally literate. To be multiculturally literate is to possess basic information needed to negotiate the diverse, interconnected global society of the 21st century. Multicultural literacy goes

beyond mere competency to embracing a way of life that encourages maximum exposure to and understanding of the many-faceted realities of multiculturalism. Ways to promote your multicultural literacy include gaining knowledge of ethnic variations in history, traveling (both nationally and internationally), reading a variety of newspapers and other periodicals from diverse cultural groups, being open to new cultural experiences, reading literature from diverse cultures, working toward religious/ spiritual tolerance, and possibly learning a new language.

5. *Establish a personal social justice compass.* Develop a set of personal principles and ideals to direct your commitment to social justice. These principles and ideals should provide a moral compass to guide both your life and work. I suggest reading several important documents that may influence your thinking about such a compass.

- The first of these documents is the *Universal Declaration of Human Rights* adopted by the United Nations (1948). This historic and landmark document, in its preamble and 30 articles, establishes a set of universal principles that were conceived as the foundation of global freedom, justice, and peace. Any counselor committed to social justice should be familiar with this document and its enlightened ideas about the possibility of a better world.
- The second major document is the *ACA Code of Ethics* (2005). All counseling should be predicated on ethical practice. A social justice perspective on counseling, in particular, rests on understanding and adhering to those recently added sections of the code which state that counselors have an ethical responsibility to engage in advocacy initiatives, both with and on behalf of their clients, in order to challenge systemic barriers to psychosocial development.
- The *Advocacy Competencies* developed by Counselors for Social Justice of ACA (Lewis, Arnold, House, & Toporek, 2003) represent the third significant source of information to consider in establishing a personal compass. From the student or client level to the public

arena, these competencies prescribe best practice in advancing advocacy on behalf of those individuals with whom counselors work. Social justice in counseling is predicated on advocacy, so this document is a manifesto for social action.

- The last document I suggest is the *Multicultural Counseling Competencies and Standards* developed by the Association for Multicultural Counseling and Development of ACA (Sue, Arredondo, & McDavis, 1992). This document provides the competencies to guide cross-cultural counseling interactions. It lays out important competencies with respect to awareness, knowledge, and skills for culturally responsive counseling.

Although this list of documents is not intended to be exhaustive, it represents key work that has contributed to the growing emphasis on issues of social justice in counseling. Taken together, these documents embody the essence of social justice ideals and principles. They provide both the ethical and philosophical frameworks for developing a personal perspective to advance social justice in one's work as a professional counselor.

Conclusion

The five steps I have discussed are about realizing the important view of freedom reflected in the quotation from Nelson Mandela that begins this chapter. An implicit goal in these steps is to free oneself from the shackles of oppression, privilege, and ignorance in order to live a life that is meaningful and committed to enhancing freedom for all. The social justice call to action, therefore, is for counselors to assess themselves and to make decisions about their roles as both professionals and citizens of the planet. Both of those roles must entail freeing ourselves to be instruments of change that promotes access and equity, and, thereby I hope, ensures freedom for all.

Although at times social justice may be a difficult concept to define operationally, the contributors to this book have presented ideas on the nature of this crucial construct and its relevance for counseling. What I hope is clear from a reading of the chapters in this book is that counselors have a professional, ethical, and moral responsibility to take an active part in building a world that is more enlightened, just, and humane.

References

American Counseling Association. (2005). *ACA code of ethics.* Alexandria, VA: Author.

Lewis, J., Arnold, M. S., House, R., & Toporek, R. (2003). *Advocacy competencies.* Retrieved February 19, 2005, from http://www.counselorsforsocialjustice.org/advocacycompetencies.html

Sue, D., Arredondo, P., & McDavis, R. (1992). Multicultural counseling competencies and standards: A call to the profession. *Journal of Multicultural Counseling and Development, 20,* 64–88.

United Nations. (1948). *Universal declaration of human rights.* San Francisco: Author. Available online at http://www.un.org/Overview/rights.html

Contributors

Courtland C. Lee received his PhD in counseling from Michigan State University. He is professor and director of the Counselor Education Program at the University of Maryland, College Park. His areas of research specialization include multicultural counseling and men's issues in counseling. He has written, edited, or coedited four books on multicultural counseling and written three books on counseling African American male youth. In addition, he has written numerous articles and book chapters on counseling across cultures. The former editor of the *Journal of Multicultural Counseling and Development,* Dr. Lee serves on the advisory board of the *International Journal for the Advancement of Counselling.* Dr. Lee is a past president of the American Counseling Association and the Association for Multicultural Counseling and Development.

Kathleen L. Armstrong received her PhD in counselor education from the University of Virginia. She is an assistant professor at Monmouth University in West Long Branch, New Jersey. She has extensive clinical experience in the areas of addictions, dual diagnosis, crisis intervention, family counseling, and generalist counseling. Her research interests include multicultural counseling and identity development. Currently, she is investigating the application of multicultural frameworks to issues of gender, ethnicity, and sexuality.

Bob Barret received his PhD in counseling psychology from Georgia State University and is professor emeritus in the counseling program at the University of North Carolina at Charlotte. He also maintains a clinical practice. He has written extensively in the areas of sexual minority counseling, grief, and loss, and has been associated with the American Psychological Association's Office on AIDS since 1988. In addition to serving as president of the Association for Gay, Lesbian and Bisexual Issues in Counseling (AGLBIC), Dr. Barret completed terms on the boards of AGLBIC and ASERVIC. He has coauthored or coedited five books and many articles and book chapters.

Fred Bemak, EdD, is currently a professor and the program coordinator for the Counseling and Development Program in the College of Education and Human Development and the Graduate School of Education at George Mason University. He has done extensive work in the areas of social justice and mental health, working in 30 countries and throughout the United States. Dr. Bemak is a former Fulbright

Scholar, a Kellogg International Fellow, and a recipient of the International Exchange of Experts and Research Fellowship through the World Rehabilitation Fund. At George Mason University, Dr. Bemak has facilitated the development of master's and doctoral training programs that emphasize multiculturalism, social justice, leadership, and advocacy, having worked with these issues for more than 30 years. He is a former director of an Upward Bound program, the Massachusetts Department of Mental Health Region I Adolescent Treatment Program, and a NIMH-funded program that provided national consultation and training to community-based mental health programs. Dr. Bemak continues to provide consultation, training, and workshops for many community and school-based programs and has published numerous professional journal articles, book chapters, and four books that emphasize cross-cultural counseling, equity, and social justice.

William A. Borgen, PhD, is a professor of counseling psychology at University of British Columbia (UBC) in Vancouver, Canada. He is the coordinator of the counseling psychology program at UBC and the director of the CNPS doctoral program. He has studied and published for several years in the area of life transitions, specifically focusing on career and employment issues. Dr. Borgen has worked extensively in the development of the counseling profession both in Canada and internationally. He is a past president of the Canadian Counselling Association and has recently co-authored standards for the accreditation of counselor education programs in Canada. Employment counselor training programs based on his research have been implemented in Canada, Sweden, Denmark, Finland, and Hungary. Dr. Borgen is the president of the International Association for Counselling, which facilitates the development of counseling research and practice worldwide.

Rita Chi-Ying Chung, PhD, is an associate professor in the Counseling and Development Program, College of Education and Human Development and Graduate School of Education, George Mason University. Her research focuses on social justice and multiculturalism through the psychosocial adjustment of refugees and immigrants, interethnic group relations and racial stereotypes, trafficking of Asian girls, strategies for coping with racism and its impact on psychological well-being, cross-cultural and multicultural issues in mental health, and cross-cultural achievement motivation and aspirations. Dr. Chung has lived and worked in the Pacific Rim, Asia, and Latin America. She is currently coauthoring a book with Dr. Fred Bemak on social justice and multiculturalism.

Allison A. Cox received both her BS in elementary education and her MEd in school counseling from the University of Maryland, College Park. She is currently a third-grade teacher in Prince George's County, Maryland. This is her first publication. An active member of the American Counseling Association, the American School Counseling Association, and Chi Sigma Iota, she has an emerging interest in the achievement gap and multicultural counseling.

Ellen S. Fabian received her PhD in counseling from the University of Maryland. She is an associate professor and director of the Rehabilitation Counseling Program at the University of Maryland, College Park. Her areas of research specialization include disability and youth transitions. She has written two books on rehabilitation issues, in addition to numerous articles and book chapters on these topics. Dr. Fabian is editor of the *Journal of Applied Rehabilitation Counseling*, and is a past president of the American Rehabilitation Counseling Association.

Barbara Richter Herlihy received her PhD in counseling psychology from Northwestern University. She is a professor in the Counselor Education Program at the University of New Orleans. Her primary area of research specialization is ethics, which she combines with her other interests in multicultural counseling, clinical supervision, and feminist therapy. She has published numerous articles and book chapters on these topics, and is the coauthor of five books on counselor ethics. She is a past chair of the ACA Ethics Committee and has contributed to revising the ACA *Code of Ethics* in 1988, 1995, and 2005.

Carlos P. Hipolito-Delgado is a doctoral student in counselor education at the University of Maryland. He holds an MEd in counseling in student affairs from the University of California at Los Angeles. His research concentrates on ethnic identity development and on the effects of internalized racism on Chicana/o and Latina/o students. Further, he is interested in the use of empowerment theory in working with clients of marginalized communities and in the infusion of a social justice curriculum into counselor education. Mr. Hipolito-Delgado serves as an ad hoc reviewer for the *Journal of Counseling & Development*.

Cheryl Holcomb-McCoy received her PhD in counseling and educational development from the University of North Carolina at Greensboro. She is an associate professor in the Department of Counseling and Personnel Services at the University of Maryland, College Park. Her areas of research specialization include multicultural school counseling, school counselor multicultural self-efficacy, and urban school counselor preparation. She has written numerous book chapters and refereed articles on issues pertaining to diversity in counselor education. Dr. Holcomb-McCoy is a former national secretary of Chi Sigma Iota International and has served on the editorial boards of the *Professional School Counseling* journal and the *Journal of Counseling & Development.* Dr. Holcomb-McCoy is the American School Counselor Association (ASCA) diversity professional network chairperson.

Mark S. Kiselica, PhD, is professor and chairperson of the Department of Counselor Education at the College of New Jersey. He has completed more than 90 publications, including four books. He was named researcher of the year by two different organizations—the American Mental Health Counselors Association and the Society for the Psychological Study of Men and Masculinity—in recognition of his coedited book, *The Handbook of Counseling Boys and Adolescent Males,* which was published by Sage in 1999. In honor of his widespread influence on the provision of mental health services to boys, especially his extensive work on counseling teenage fathers, he was named a consulting scholar to the Federal Fatherhood Initiative of the Clinton Administration for 1996–1997 and to the National Institute of Mental Health for 1999. Dr. Kiselica was also elected president of the Society for the Psychological Study of Men and Masculinity for 1999. He provides workshops on counseling boys to schools and mental health agencies throughout the United States and Canada and has served as a guest commentator on the subject of boys for every major television network and National Public Radio. He is featured in the video *Parenting Boys,* which is distributed by Allyn & Bacon. Dr. Kiselica has given keynote addresses at numerous conferences and invited lectures at Columbia University, McGill University, University of Wisconsin–Madison, William Paterson University, and Johns Hopkins University. In 2005, the American Counseling Association named him the recipient of the Gilbert and Kathleen Wrenn Award for a Humanitarian and Caring Person in recognition of his extensive work to combat racism and teenage pregnancy.

Pamela S. Lassiter received her PhD in counseling from Georgia State University. She is an assistant professor and coordinator of the Substance Abuse Certificate Program at the University of North Carolina at Charlotte. Her areas of research include multicultural counseling, gay and lesbian issues in counseling, GLBT parenting issues, substance abuse counseling, and women's issues in counseling. She has written several articles and book chapters on these multicultural counseling topics. Dr. Lassiter is a current member of the Association of Gay, Lesbian, Bisexual, and Transgender Issues in Counseling and president-elect of the International Association of Addictions and Offender Counseling.

Judy A. Lewis, PhD, is a past president of the American Counseling Association and the International Association of Marriage and Family Counselors. In addition, she is former communications officer of Counselors for Social Justice, of which she is a founding member. She chaired the American Counseling Association task force that developed ACA's advocacy competencies. She has published a number of books related to counseling, advocacy, and program management. Dr. Lewis is currently chair of the behavioral health department at Governors State University.

Larry C. Loesch received his PhD in counselor education from Kent State University in 1973. He is a professor in the Department of Counselor Education at the University of Florida. His areas of professional specialization include assessment and research. In addition to writing numerous journal articles, book chapters, and monographs on assessment, he has served as an evaluation consultant for the National Board for Certified Counselors since its inception. He is a former editor of *Measurement and Evaluation in Guidance.* Dr. Loesch is a past president of both the Florida and the national Association for Measurement and Evaluation in Guidance. He was a Fulbright Scholar, lecturing in assessment, in Slovakia. Dr. Loesch is a fellow of the American Counseling Association.

Natasha A. Mitchell received her PhD in counseling and counselor education from the University of North Carolina at Greensboro. She is currently an assistant professor in the Counselor Education Program at the University of Maryland, College Park. Her areas of research specialization include acculturation and psychosocial factors that affect achievement. She has written several articles and conducted presentations on promoting student achievement through urban school counseling programs. Dr. Mitchell serves on the editorial board of the *Journal of Counseling & Development* and on the National Membership Committee for the Association of Counselor Education and Supervision.

Jane E. Myers, PhD, a professor of counselor education at the University of North Carolina at Greensboro, is a National Certified Counselor, a National Certified Gerontological Counselor, and a Licensed Professional Counselor. She is a fellow of the Gerontological Society of America, the Association for Gerontology in Higher Education, and the National Rehabilitation Counseling Association, and a charter fellow of the Chi Sigma Iota Academy of Leaders for Excellence. A past-president of the American Counseling Association and two of its divisions, the Association for Assessment in Counseling and the Association for Adult Development and Aging, of which she was founding president, Dr. Myers also served as chair of the Council for Accreditation of Counseling and Related Educational Programs (CACREP). Dr. Myers developed a model and curriculum resources for infusion of gerontological counseling into counselor education, coauthored (with Dr. Tom Sweeney) the national competencies for training gerontological counselors, and coproduced eight training videotapes in gerontological counseling.

William E. Sedlacek, PhD, is a professor of education and assistant director of the Counseling Center at the University of Maryland. He has served as editor of *Measurement and Evaluation in Counseling and Development*. In addition, he has consulted with more than 300 different organizations, colleges, and universities on interracial and intercultural issues, and has served as an expert witness in race and sex discrimination cases. He received the Ralph M. Berdie and annual research awards from the American Counseling Association and the Contribution to Knowledge Award and Senior Scholar designation from the American College Personnel Association. His latest book is *Beyond the Big Test: Noncognitive Assessment in Higher Education*.

Zarus E. P. Watson received his BA from Tulane University and MA and PhD degrees in counselor education and research methods from the University of New Orleans. He is associate professor within the Counselor Education Program at the University of New Orleans and is director of the Research Center for Multiculturalism and Counseling. His areas of research include social systems theory, systemic conditioning, and multicultural issues in organizations and peripheral social groups. He has written articles and book chapters on counseling across socioracial groups, gender role conditioning, and communities. Dr. Watson serves on several community and organizational boards, and has consulted within business and industry in the areas of contextual program evaluation using an overall system-as-client approach to organizational development, research, and analysis. In addition, he has made more than 60 presentations covering the salient issues of culture and socialization across multiple settings, groups, and contexts. Dr. Watson is the past president of the Louisiana Association of Multicultural Counseling and Development.

Mark S. Woodford is an assistant professor and coordinator of the Community Counseling Program in the Department of Counselor Education at the College of New Jersey in Ewing, New Jersey. He is a graduate of the College of William and Mary (BA, MEd) and received his PhD in counselor education from the University of Virginia. His research interests are in the fields of substance abuse and family counseling. He has worked as a home-based family counselor in tidewater Virginia and as an addictions counselor in East Boston, Massachusetts. Dr. Woodford was also the clinical supervisor and counseling services coordinator for the University of Virginia Women's Center during his doctoral studies.

Index

A

A Mind That Found Itself (Beers), 162

Abortion Non-Discrimination Act, 106-7

achievement gap
extent of, 3-4
psychosocial and economic impact of, 5-6
reasons behind, 4-5

Administration on Aging, U.S., 53-54

administrative advocacy, 149

Adult Development, Aging, and Counseling Interest Network, 55

advocacy
advocacy counseling, 112
advocacy-focused counseling interventions, 147-51
defined, 147
male advocacy groups, 121, 122-25
older persons and initiatives for, 64-67
social and political, 105-8
women's issues and advocacy-oriented counselors, 101-2

African Americans
Banneker Scholarship case, 229-33
Black racial identity development models, 188
disability among, 76, 80
feelings about upward mobility, 21
financial resources and access to counseling, 22

impact of racism on, 102
older, 53
oppression against, 140, 143, 146
racism in university setting, 229-33
See also poverty

ageism, 51, 68-69
action strategies for counselors, 63-68
changing our ageist language, 74
consequences of professional neglect, 55-57
counselors' responses to population aging, 53-55
1961 White House Conference on Aging, 72-73
older adults in poverty, 20
personal impact of, 62-63
problem of, 52-53
Rights and Obligations of Older Americans, 72-73
what, where, when, how, and why?, 57-62

aggression, masculinity and, 126

AGLBIC (Association for Gay, Lesbian, and Bisexual Issues in Counseling), 43-44

Aid to Families With Dependent Children, 25

Akbar, M., 22

Allen, J. A., 118, 119

Altekruse, M., 214

American Academy of Pediatrics, 39